Discipline and liberty

D1100450

MANCHESTER
UNIVERSITY PRESS

Discipline and liberty

Television and governance

GARETH PALMER

MANCHESTER UNIVERSITY PRESS

Manchester and New York

distributed exclusively in the USA by Palgrave

The right of Gareth Palmer to be identified as the author of this work has been asserted by him in accordance with the Copyright, Designs and Patents Act 1988.

Published by Manchester University Press
Oxford Road, Manchester M13 9NR, UK
and Room 400, 175 Fifth Avenue, New York, NY 10010, USA
www.manchesteruniversitypress.co.uk

Distributed exclusively in the USA by
Palgrave, 175 Fifth Avenue, New York,
NY 10010, USA

Distributed exclusively in Canada by
UBC Press, University of British Columbia, 2029 West Mall,
Vancouver, BC, Canada V6T 1Z2

British Library Cataloguing-in-Publication Data
A catalogue record for this book is available from the British Library

Library of Congress Cataloging-in-Publication Data applied for

ISBN 0 7190 6693 X *hardback*
     0 7190 6692 1 *paperback*

First published 2003

11 10 09 08 07 06 05 04 03   10 9 8 7 6 5 4 3 2 1

Typeset in Palatino
by Servis Filmsetting Ltd, Manchester, UK
Printed in Great Britain
by Bell & Bain Ltd, Glasgow

To the memory of my mother
Joan Palmer (née Rattenbury)

Contents

Acknowledgements

This book attempts to use Foucault-inspired work on 'governance' to understand the ways in which television works to monitor and offer directions for our behaviour. I hope that it will open up the subject for further discussion.

I wish to express my thanks to colleagues at the School of Media, Music and Performance, Salford University, for providing a supportive climate, and to Ian Calloway of the Contemporary Document Archive for his considerable assistance. I thank also my co-members of the ESRC Surveillance seminar for the careful attention they gave to the issues here discussed. Clive Norris was especially supportive.

To the international documentary scholars who – over the ten years of its existence – comprised Visual Evidence: thank you for laughing at my papers in all the right places. Particular thanks to John Corner, Jon Dovey, Annette Hill, Derek Paget, Brian Winston, Chuck, Julia and John, and Jane Roscoe.

Some of the chapters contain material which has featured in other publications. Elements of chapters 2 and 3 appeared in Douglas Thomas and Brian Loader (eds) *Cybercrime* (Routledge, 2000). Parts of chapter 4 appeared as 'Governing through crime: surveillance, the community and local crime programming' in *Policing and Society*, 10 (2000), and 'Keeping track of the locals' in John Izod, Richard Kilborn and Matthew Hibberd (eds) *From Grierson to the Docu-Soaps* (Luton University, 2000). A version of chapter 5 appeared as '*Neighbours From Hell*: productive incivilities' in Jim Friedman (ed.) *Images of Reality* (University of Illinois Press, 2000). Parts of chapter 6 were included in a paper on *Judge Judy* in *New Television Formats*, 100 (2001). A version of chapter 7 appeared as 'Light entertainment and spectacles of shame' in *Salford Working Papers in Sociology* (Salford University, 1999). The Conclusion featured in a collection of articles on *Big Brother* published as an issue of *Television and New Media* (Sage, 2002) which I co-edited with Annette Hill.

But, of course, my most profuse thanks are offered to my wife Sheena and to my children, Amy and Joe.

Introduction: governance and documentary

On a Saturday night in December 2001 Britain's channel Five screened a programme entitled *Stupid Behaviour Caught On Tape*. This extraordinary title was clearly not the product of mass audience research or the carefully honed deliberation of a focus group. Indeed, so plain, even blunt, is this title that it sounds like the exasperated cry of a channel controller much vexed at the inability of his or her minions to come up with anything witty or clever.

But in many ways *Stupid Behaviour Caught On Tape* is a wonderful title, for it perfectly encapsulates the perspective of so much factual television in the late twentieth and early twenty-first centuries. The programme is typical of how the focus of documentary projects has shifted from informing citizens about issues in particular contexts to a wider field in which the subject is human behaviour itself.

My focus is on behaviour and the ways in which television recommends that we conduct ourselves in the diverse spheres of our lives. I attempt to describe television's place in the processes of governance – the conduct of conduct – and to understand the role it has in the development of certain regimes of practice. To that end, I discuss a variety of 'factual' television programmes linked only by their focus on human behaviour.

The book looks at a range of factual forms as texts intertwined in the work of governing. I discuss how the old, relatively stable, documentary production base addressing a citizen who had few other channel options has been transformed into a new and unstable production climate with a viewer–citizen–consumer who is confronted with a considerable range of choices. Documentary used to be one of the constants of television, with its community of practitioners, a much-discussed and revered canon and a set of established practices. The contemporary scene is better described as a 'field of documentary practice' in which the codes and stylistic characteristics of the old genre are taken up and used by the new. Factual forms are now adopted by a wide variety of groups and individuals, and with myriad intentions. Some of these hope to inform the public with issue-based programmes, while others have unashamedly lightweight and commercial aspirations. This new instability within factual programming is disorientating, exciting, liberating and frightening, depending on one's point of view. The changes have produced a rash of critiques from right to left. My aim here, however, is not to join this chorus but to re-examine factual forms as both speaking for themselves as 'television productions' as well as being conduits for the work of governance.

This Introduction explores the complex new position in which documentary finds itself. This will involve discussing its history, the changes it faced in the 1980s and 1990s, and how it has been informed by agencies that seek, in varying ways, to claim authority through the form. I begin with an explanation of the terms *government* and *governance*.

Government and governance

The terms 'government' and 'governance' are used here in ways other than those of their traditional definitions, which link them to political party or state. My use of 'government' derives from Foucault's later writings on the problems of rule. Writers such as Mitchell Dean (1995, 1999), Nikolas Rose (1995, 1996) and Graham Burchell (1991) have built on Foucault's work to suggest that 'government' concerns the shaping of behaviour to desired ends – 'how we govern, how we are governed, and . . . the relation between the government of ourselves, the government of others and the government of the state' (Dean 1999:2).

For Foucault, successful government operates through the capacity of both those who govern and those who are governed to regulate their own behaviour. The term has since been taken up and used by writers exploring fields as far apart as medicine and agriculture. What characterises this use is not so much its theory as its use as a problem-solving rationale.

> Government has as its purpose not the act of government itself, but the welfare of the population, the improvement of its condition, the increase of its wealth, logevity, health etc; and the means that the

government uses to attain those ends are themselves all in some
sense immanent to the population. (Foucault 1991: 95)

The term 'governance' has gained currency recently as a description of new strategic efforts to change the operation of power and management by the authorities. Some writers claim that governance, at the
start of the new century, is becoming a defining narrative of British
government. Janet Newman (2001: 11) elaborates on this: 'Governance
is an analytical concept giving rise to questions about what forms of
power and authority, patterns of relationships and rights and obliga-
tions might typify a particular approach to governing.'

Government is concerned with the conduct of conduct or, more
specifically, with the calculated direction of conduct to shape behaviour to certain ends. Crucially, government is not an explicit expression or obvious direction of power. The individual is not told or
ordered to behave in a certain way. Government works, rather, by
seeming to give the individual a sense of autonomy. His or her
freedom lies in what appear to be choices. The governed are capable
of thinking otherwise. Indeed, the active agency of those who are thus
governed is crucial to their role: 'In modern society, the behaviour of
individuals is regulated not through overt repression but through a
set of standards and values associated with normality which are set
into play by a network of ostensibly beneficent and scientific forms of
knowledge' (McNay 1996: 95).

In this model power is envisioned in a capillary form – that is to
say, as exercised within the social formation rather than imposed from
above. Government is achieved through various authorities, actors
and agencies rather than via a central state apparatus. Indeed, as will
be seen, the old conception of the state as a monolithic enterprise is
replaced by one which envisages it as 'no more than a composite
reality and a mythicised abstraction'. Governance is achieved through
a regime of practices in which the governed and the governors have
parts to play: 'the population . . . is the subject of needs, of aspirations,
but it is also the object in the hands of government, aware, vis-à-vis
the government, of what it wants but ignorant of what is being done
to it' (Foucault 1991: 103).

It has always been the aim of 'the authorities' to make individuals politically useful: populations have to be controlled and made efficient. My concern is with the role that television plays in this process.
How are the processes of government set in train through television?

To a degree, it is a question of identification: 'How is someone who buys goods at a a supermarket made to identify as a consumer . . . How are we all to become good citizens? All these imply a work of government, a way of acting on conduct to elicit various identifications for various reasons' (Dean 1999: 33).

This is not to argue that some ideological force is at work behind the text, the analysis of which reveals 'the truth'. Foucault rejected ideology because 'it always stands in virtual opposition to something else which is supposed to count as truth' (Foucault 1980: 118). Thus my aim is not to uncover some ideological project but to discuss the truth-effects produced by the text. In place of ideology, I consider *discourse*. Discourses are highly regulated sets of statements which delimit a field and constitute objects for us. Discourses allow people to speak 'in the true': 'a discourse is a set of sanctioned statements which have some institutional force, which means that they have a profound influence on the way that individuals think and act' (Mills 1997: 62).

We establish and experience our individuality by inhabiting a range of discursive subjectivities. There is a degree of fluidity to discourses as they seek to win recognition. What I examine here is how documentary is both inhabited by and contributes to discursive formations which help us to make sense of experience. This is an eminently practical task which points us towards those discourses whose institutional force invites us to think through the way we are to how we should be. How does documentary organise discourses which form the citizen–subject? How does it help that agent to construct himself or herself as an individual with particular capacities and possibilities for action?

Such an inquiry is stimulating because the traditional identification between citizen–viewer and documentary–text within Britain's four-channel set-up has become slowly destabilised by the wider changes wrought by neo-liberalism. The past twenty years have seen an assault on the social in which documentary is rooted. While the death of the welfare state may have been exaggerated, our understanding of *the social* is certainly going through a mutation. Yet the project of governance in guiding the choices of subjects towards that of the authorities still goes on. In what follows, I consider the extent to which new documentary forms offer platforms for identities as part of the ongoing work of governance. How might the new broadcast environment change the relationship between authorities and subjects? Which voices have emerged? Who speaks and how? Before we can answer these questions we must ask how documentary can be connected to the processes of governance. This is necessary, given documentary's self-identity as a form of principled opposition to the status quo.

Roots

Documentary has always been wedded to this notion of the citizen. John Grierson is the oft-cited founder of the British documentary tradition, both in terms of its craft and as its principal theorist. As a publiciser of the idea of documentary, he has no equal. It was Grierson who held to the notion that documentary could expand and enlarge citizenship. Indeed documentary could, though its corps of educated and enlightened middle-class experts, help us all to celebrate the working man (Hardy 1979).

Documentary in Britain was sponsored by the Empire Marketing Board, the General Post Office and, later, by large industrial concerns, such as the Gas, Light and Coke Company. Much is made of the fact that the movement was a left of centre grouping which was creating radical documents of working life, and in so doing was constructing a language for the production of the social. The social, as defined by Dean (1999: 212), has a high degree of fit with this work 'as an attempt to install a form of social citizenship compatible with a liberal–democratic–capitalistic form of government, i.e. one that can address the questions of poverty and inequality in a society of equals'.

Although these pioneers represented a grouping more often aligned with artists and writers of the period, their socially inspired work can be connected to that of the Next Five Years Group and to political and economic planning, whose membership consisted of policymakers, writers and MPs positioned to the left of the Conservatives and to the right of Labour. They espoused a scientific doctrine which held that the solution to social problems could be created by a corps of experts. In their reports they offered logical solutions for the control of the various new populations. A series of documents on health, housing and poverty was part of a redesign of the human subject:

> [G]overnment has as its purpose not the act of government itself, but the welfare of the population, the improvement of its condition, the increase of its wealth, longevity, health etc; and the means that the government uses to attain these ends are themselves all in some sense immanent to the population. (Foucault 1991: 100)

In the 1930s an increasing number of sites were opened up to the scrutiny of the psy-disciplines and the evolving project of managing behaviour. The growing panoptic mechanism finds its way into many different sectors of society and seeks to order those within institutions such as the school, the hospital and the barracks. Such mechanisms ensure the docility of the body as more and more aspects of life are made open to examination. Such examinations in turn form new kinds of knowledge with which the problem of population can be managed. 'Man' becomes increasingly knowable, so that the focus can slowly shift from the body to the soul.

The experts of bio-politics created a range of documents which were to find expression in works like the 'Beveridge Report' of 1942 and the implementation of the welfare state under Labour in 1945–50.

> 'The welfare state' was one formula for reconciling, along a number of different dimensions, the relations between the political field and the management of economic and social affairs, in which the authority of truth and of experts as those who can speak and enact truth, was to be accorded a new role. (Rose 1993a: 293)

In its objective scientific perspective, its immersion in social rather than political issues and its desire to offer up expert solutions, the documentary movement was an ally of the new disciplines. Although physically and culturally remote from these technicists of population, documentary can usefully be read as bound up with the production of the social through its own corps of experts. In its explorations of the 'jungles of the Clyde' and other hidden urban zones it produced documents which rendered up the hidden and obscure working folk for administrative treatment.

Despite Grierson's considerable efforts, the audiences for these films were modest. For the most part they consisted of school children and visitors to cinema clubs and museums. Other audiences included civil servants and policy designers – a very middle-class grouping and one which was to be responsible for the administration of the working classes (Swann 1989).

These early documentaries evolved and were consumed in a climate in which the working man as an object of scientific study was being reconsidered as a challenge for progressive social engineers. The public was presented with an image of itself as noble, capable and integrated, while also being amenable to treatment. In many ways the public was represented as comprised of ideal citizens. The language formulated by the documentary-makers for capturing this object is, to a large extent, still with us today. Its principal features are: the use of narration which is objective and anxious to stress both sides of the story; the received pronunciation of the narrator, which is heard prior to the voices and – perhaps – regional speech of the subjects; and the whole mastered by the proliferation of experts both behind and in front of the scene who can be trusted to adhere to balance and objectivity.

In short these early documentaries assembled individuals in formats which made reasoned cases for change in the social sphere that they were simultaneously helping to create. Documentary gave us ways of thinking: 'societies like our own are characterised by particular ways of thinking about the kinds of problems that can and should be addressed by various authorities' (Miller and Rose 1990: 2).

The documentary form and ideal soon found a place in the public service ethos of the BBC. In the 1950s, under Paul Rotha, the first head of documentaries and critic–fellow-traveller of the British Dcoumentary Movement, documentary soon found the audience it had always wanted to reach – the workers (Bell 1986). Here the citizenship project espoused by Grierson could be continued. Rose (1993b: 158) has argued that in the early twentieth century the image of the citizen as a human being 'opened a contract between government and citizens, articulated in the language of social responsibility and social welfare . . . Pedagogic techniques from universal education to the BBC were construed as devices for forging responsible citizens.'

The documentary tradition found expression through a variety of formats like current affairs and the magazine programme. By the end of the 1950s documentary had become an accepted and much-respected part of British television. When, in 1955, ITV began it, too, looked to current-affairs' formats, and it was soon designing new factual formats for dealing with social issues which won critical plaudits for the sponsoring institution and helped implant the documentary idea more deeply in the public mind (Corner 1986).

Throughout the development of new documentary forms the notion of balance remained important. The citizen–subject was to be informed on problems within the social fabric by a dedicated corps who held balance and objectivity to be important principles. A history of the documentary might be written which celebrates how the form has helped bring to light certain injustices, as well as to publicise a variety of worthy institutions. Indeed the state of the documentary industry is sometimes used by critics as a measure of the health of the nation when it asks to what extent a critique can be sustained by the authorities. Yet it is important to be clear that such dissent always occurs within the consensus:

> Television in its Public Service guise is an extension and expression of the welfarist schemes of the past and documentary as its prime exemplar. Its leftist history, its relatively protected status, its intellectualism, its sympathy with those masses out of which the recognisable groups of worthy citizens would emerge. It argued against problems within the system and was decidedly reformist and nonpartisan. (Boyne 2000: 321)

Documentary workers were licensed to criticise the operations of the State while still deriving their income from publicly funded bodies such as the BBC or in the relative security (in today's terms) of independent television. Although the language of the documentary evolved, it was always informed by the same dependence on expertise and the need for objectivity and balance. The critiques they produced helped to fashion the consensus around certain social issues. As is inevitable in the large institutions in which they worked, documentary-makers developed their own practices, codes and working arrangements. Gradually a documentary lexicon arose, and certain ways of telling stories became dominant as traditions developed. The public became used to this language, this way of seeing: 'All government depends on a particular mode of representation: the elaboration of a language for depicting the domain in question that claims both to grasp the nature of the reality represented and literally to represent the form in a way amenable to political argument and scheming' (Miller and Rose 1990: 6).

All change

But what began in 1979, with the arrival of the new Tory Government, was a series of changes which would disturb documentary's production base and its relationship with the citizen. Those changes are rooted in policies which shook the consensus on other issues, such as crime and punishment, the role of 'the state' and monetary policy. It is no overstatement to say that this consensus involved questioning the certainties of the welfare state and the citizenship contract which underpinned it.

In practical terms the institutional foundations of television were shaken by the Tory Party's avowed intention of doing away with the broadcast unions, which Mrs Thatcher described as 'the last bastion of restrictive practices'. The unions were the 'British curse' and defeating them empowered other businessmen such as Eddie Shah and his Messenger Group, and Rupert Murdoch and his News Corporation.

This attack on union power was coupled with a critical assault on television undertaken by figures such as Norman Tebbit, who was quick to accuse the BBC of bias. Perhaps the first significant attack came with the accusation that the BBC, in giving time and space to consider the plight of the 'enemy', was not fully supportive of the Falklands War. There is, of course, a tradition of the incumbent administration finding anti-government bias in the BBC, but what distinguished this critique was that the Tories were preparing broadcasting legislation which would threaten the BBC's funding source – the licence fee. In the prevailing climate, it was made clear that documentaries represented a dangerous and potentially subversive element in the television landscape (O'Malley 1994). Programmes such as *Death On The Rock* and several editions of *Panorama* were admonished for criticising the work of the Government. Any suggestions made by the broadcasters that the Government was at fault – over, say, the Zircon satellite affair – were quickly highlighted as examples of opposition from within the BBC. Documentary's ability to forge a consensus was destabilised by these threats.

One acknowledgement of the power of the media was the centralising of information in Downing Street and the increased roles and responsibilities given to press officers. News management became so prioritised that civil servants were complaining about having to write press releases for the Tory Party rather than objective reports. The appointment of a high-profile and aggressive press officer in Bernard Ingham was another indicator of the new Government's view that the media was a significant battleground which it was determined to conquer (Franklin 1997). During the administration's period of office it was noteworthy that the only opposition to Tory policies came from just a few newspapers. What occurred during this time was the rise of a conflict paradigm. The news media began to make less subtle distinctions in industrial and other disputes between workers and bosses, thus establishing a cruder set of rules for understanding the social world, rules which had implications for factual programming. The closure of now-unfashionable and unprofitable concerns like nationalised industries could be presented as a triumph for the plucky entrepreneurs who managed to brush themselves down and build up their own businesses (Wykes 2000). In celebrating the individual while neglecting or criticising those institutions that had depended on the collective, the news media were forging a consensus which made documentary-makers' interest in such concerns appear unfashionable and out of touch. Documentary was now having to consider the fashionable in place of the socially significant (Dovey 2000).

A more direct threat to documentary came from the marketplace. Indeed, the market was to work here as it did in other segments of public life, as the commercially attractive alternative to publicly funded institutions. The market was the natural device for providing citizens with what they wanted. This view was given legislative expression with the Broadcasting Act of 1990, which freed-up the system so that the lucrative ITV franchises could be subject to bidding by those with the most money. After a small struggle, a clause concerning quality was inserted, although of course what was signified by 'quality' remained open to definition. Another change was the replacement of the Independent Broadcasting Authority (IBA) with the lighter-handed Independent Television Commission (ITC), a licensing, not a broadcasting, body. What this meant in practical terms was that there was no longer a body empowered to insist on a certain level of documentary provision.

The market was enabled by cable and satellite channels. Although they took some time to gain a foothold each represented ways in which television was soon to become fragmented. They offered a testing ground for new documentary producers which would help change the climate for factual television.

We have to acknowledge also the arrival of the camcorder, which fed into myriad new formats and helped demystify the production process (Humm 1998). As chapter 1 shows, CCTV footage came to have an important role in the remodelling of documentary (Palmer 1998).

Media education played a part in informing a generation about the processes by which documentary operates. A distinctive sort of knowledge is generated by the revelation of 'fakes' perpetrated by documentary producers (Roscoe and Hight 2001) More recently, docu-soaps and other pop-docs have helped diminish the sobriety of the genre (Bruzzi 2000).

What these changes amount to is a new media environment, one more finely attuned to the market but offering few certainties for viewers or programme-makers (Kilborn 1996) The relationship documentary has with its audience has changed as citizens came increasingly to be addressed as consumers. Documentary's project of increasing viewers' understanding and its historical bond with citizenry are now transformed.

The debate

Given the long and cherished history of documentary in Britain, these changes were bound to engender something of a divide between those who argue that the pursuit of ratings has led to a focus on the lowest common denominator and those who celebrate the new pluralism. One producer anonymously remarked: 'What you'll find is that there'll be less content and more hype, entertainment, infotainment value in which investigation takes the . . . stunt approach. A sort of manufactured journalism, rather than reporting what's actually happening in our names behind closed doors' (quoted in Barnett and Seymour 1999: 29).

Concerns about the state of documentary are periodically expressed at conferences, in the trade press and at launches of the quarterly schedule. A crude equation is often made suggesting that the serious is good and the frivolous bad. The new populists query the golden-age-of-television thesis often propounded on these occasions, arguing that the documentary enterprise has been opened up in a way which is both empowering and exciting. Liberals of varying persuasions can find much to celebrate in this new broadcasting environment. Peter Bazalgette, creative director of Endemol UK and the man behind such formats as *Ready Steady Cook*, *Body Spies* and *Big Brother*, is perhaps the best-known exponent of this view: 'Programmes and programme choice are better than they have ever been. Now is the true golden age' (quoted in Aldridge 2001: 37).

The new populists argue that docu-soaps and reality TV formats are changing documentary in very positive ways. In terms of viewing figures, new formats have stimulated public debate and made headlines. The greater volume of viewer response and number of column inches generated are indicative of an increasing interest on the part of both the viewing public and the television critics in the new documentary forms, and the documentary project may be viewed as going through a rebirth. Documentary now experiments stylistically in a way that was previously unthinkable. One symptom of this is that some narrators have dropped the sober consistency of tone which offered so much gravitas. The narrator can now be frivolous, sober and then sarcastic within a single text, sometimes within a single sequence.

Whatever one's point of view, it is certainly the case that 'documentary' *per se* has expanded into a wider field of documentary practice. The stylistic lexicon, the 'realistic subject' and the legitimising aura of the genre have been taken up by many new communities of documentary-makers whose work has keyed into issues of identity, citizenship and nationhood in novel ways. As a result the genre is less wedded to the past and seemingly more ready to experiment (Corner 1999).

Running alongside this fresh experimentation is a change in the role of *expertise*. Traditionally concerned with truth and accountability, documentary has been both the product of expertise in terms of journalism, directing and editing, and a legitimate space for the illustration of expertise in terms of accredited sources, the involvement of academics and other contacts and connections. The expertise within documentary was central to its authority; expertise was a crucial element also in the construction of responsible citizenship. The governmentality of which documentary programmes were a part 'has come to depend in crucial respects upon the intellectual technologies, practical activities and social authority associated with expertise. It argues that the self-regulating capacities of subjects, shaped and normalised thorough expertise, are key resources for governing in a liberal democratic way' (Miller and Rose 1993: 75).

Expertise has become an expensive commodity and one whose desirability is no longer universally felt. The decline in the attractiveness of expertise has been matched by a new and calculated estimate of the market. Ideas are more keenly pursued if they are perceived to have a target audience. Research is now undertaken within tighter working schedules by individuals whose decisions have to be informed by a hard-headed consideration of career progress and the monthly cheque. In place of the documentary-maker working within a tradition we now have the director who may focus on style at the expense of content because the former is likely to make a more impressive showreel for commissioning editors. This generation of programme-makers has to pursue subjects likely to attract audiences rather than admirers in the high-brow press.

Of course, broadcasting is not a monolithic institution but one peopled by diverse individuals, many of whom are passionate about their work. It is not the case that the quality sought by the old school has disappeared. Both the BBC and ITV can still produce documentaries and drama–documentaries imbued with all the crusading spirit of the past. The populace is not yet so fragmented by multi-channels that people are incapable of uniting around programmes such as *Sunday, Bloody Sunday* (2002). It is clear both that research still goes on and that some expertise is valued. The notion of public service has made something of a recovery under Greg Dyke at the BBC. Yet the inroads made by market forces dictate that such television 'events' are rare. The expertise that could be generated and developed in large institutions is in short supply, with programme-makers seeking short-term rewards in a broadcasting environment keenly attuned to the market. At worst, expertise has no place; at best, 'experts are relocated within a market governed by the rationalities of competition, accountability and consumer demand' (Dean 1993: 285).

The new populism

Stupid Behaviour Caught On Tape (hereafter *SBCOT*) is a perfect example of the new brand of documentary. A brief discussion of its form and content serves to illustrate the more extreme forms of contemporary factual television as well as to introduce themes which inform the chapters that follow.

The programme's title is indicative of its market in that it is straightforwardly simple and offers the potential viewer glancing through the hundreds of programmes on offer absolute clarity as to its content. It also stands out in that crowded marketplace. The programme is in three segments, each of which features preview clips, reassuring the viewer of what follows. This is also economical in that some clips are shown five times – at the introduction to the show and at the introduction to each segment, and usually in slow-motion repeat.

Economy is important here, for the show itself and its title are designed to entrance the viewer. The clips have all been bought in and may well have their point of origin elsewhere – perhaps in local news outputs or in similar US shows. The only identity the show would appear to have derives from the off-screen narration, which is sarcastic and cruel – providing a series of puns and witless links, rather like the drunken commentary of a friend sitting down alongside you on the sofa. When an unlocked van crashes into a supermarket we hear of 'cereal killers'; when someone falls asleep we hear night-time sounds from a cot; an amateur bullfighter is caught on the 'horns of a dilemma'. In short, the commentary and the music are very crude and designed solely to help us see the funny side.

The programme's style consciously apes American programmes – for example, when we hear the narrator intone 'And more of the same when *Stupid Behaviour Caught On Tape* returns', followed by an American-style graphic – seemingly situating the product for sale to the American market.

Nothing is ordered or structured; there are no clear-cut thematic sections, no captions. The police get as much time as anyone else. The objective is merely to amuse. Everything is shown, and nothing is explained. *SBCOT* could not be further from the traditional documentary. It consists of compilations requiring very little in the way of skill. No research has been undertaken beyond finding the clips. Episodes have no argument to make beyond the implied proof that 'people are funny'. They do not seek to engage with educated viewers but rather to encourage the lowest common denominator in *schadenfraude*.

SBCOT is the television equivalent of a high-fat snack – something we should feel ashamed about enjoying because it is undoubtedly bad for us. But programmes of this type rarely generate any critical attention because they are so obviously lightweight. Yet the clones of *SBCOT* make up a considerable part of television's new diet and are revealing about the ways in which documentary has become a space for experiments in behaviour.

Behave

Since the early 1980s various agencies of the State have exhorted us to report crimes or any behaviour which look suspicious. A whole series of campaigns has been launched directed at licence fee avoidance, tax evasion, crime and, latterly, benefits fraud. The authorities have been anxious to spread the message that constant surveillance equates with good citizenship. Since coming to power in 1997 New Labour has shared this perspective, the latest campaign for benefit fraud explicitly suggesting that those falsely claiming benefit are effectively stealing from 'the rest of us'.

Rather than standing apart from this process the expanded field of documentary practice is now part of it. Myriad new formats line up the irregularities and incivilities of everyday life to enable us to pass judgement on fellow citizens 'caught on tape'. Although many of these programmes appear as one-offs, the hit-and-run specials suited to the age, it may be possible to understand them not in isolation but as part of a vast unco-ordinated project of looking at behaviour.

Behaviour as the subject of scientific study finds expression in new television experiments such as *Big Brother* and *Lie Detector*. Behaviour is monitored in the great variety of talk-shows in which audiences are encouraged to make loud and aggressive condemnations of inappropriate conduct; it is now recorded by innumerable camcorders producing footage of innocent suspects being subjected to police brutality and is the subject also of compilation shows featuring the public misbehaving in common scenarios. This focus on behaviour, when coupled with the massively increased use of CCTV, has created a climate in which there are many more opportunities than before for us to be 'caught on camera'.

The documentary project needs to be reconsidered in this new context. Documentary belongs to a tradition of media which took as its subject the problematising of certain institutions, issues and situations. It performed the vital function of keeping the citizenry informed as part of its public-service orientation. A generation ago this orientation might have led it to examine the rise of CCTV and connected this to the unregulated development of private security forces. Documentary played an important role in balancing the news media's work of legitimising such developments. It represented a space wherein we might go beyond the headlines to learn of the complexities of the news story dealt with quickly in the bulletin. From this relatively safe institutional space, documentary-makers could offer critiques within the confines of the liberal consensus. The deployment of CCTV and the footage it generates are now uncritically accepted as part of the language of documentary, but there is far less in the way of joined-up critique (Raphael 1998). The expanded field of documentary practice provides an increasing number of platforms on which different types of behaviour can be seen, scrutinised and dissected. Documentary is now keyed in to a surveillance culture which is supposed to provide useful knowledge: 'Government that is to say is always dependent on knowledge, and proponents of diverse programmes seek to ground themselves in the positive knowledge of that which is to be governed, ways of reasoning about it, analysing it, and evaluating it, identifying its problems and devising solutions' (Miller and Rose 1990: 6–7).

Documentary has been informed by a fluid discursive formation. During the 1980s and 1990s new statements emerged on, among other things, the role of the citizen, the meaning of *community*, the use of surveillance and the function of law and order. Such statements destabilised documentary in that they altered the perspective from which it had worked in the past. People were offered new ways of thinking through their mediated relation to the world. Thus a story that might have raised civil liberty issues now finds itself interpreted as one of risk management. A series that might have looked at the social factors moulding young offenders now recommends target hardening of the home. Documentary now stands uneasily between communities. It has learned to speak in new ways that are in keeping with the times: 'Advanced liberal rule depends upon expertise in a different way, and articulates experts differently into the apparatus of rule. It does not seek to govern through "society" but through the regulated choices of individual citizens' (Rose 1993a: 285).

Perhaps the most striking change in terms of factual representation is that which can be seen in the new police documentaries (Oliver 1994). What law enforcement has come to mean is the patrolling of human behaviour. These new documentaries are not much given to analysis but choose instead to focus on target-hardening of the home and encouraging the community to become active by phoning in their suspicions. Programmes on risk management jostle for space with those illustrating the brutally effective techno-policing that is attempting to keep the streets safe and protect us all from shadowy *homo criminalis*. The commentary in these programmes is often provided by the police, and it goes entirely unremarked upon. The only expertise on show here is that of the police. No commentary intervenes to put into perspective changes in the law and the increase in police powers. It is clear what good citizens should do (Schlesinger and Tumber 1994). New police documentaries extol the virtues of the authorities and request that we all play a part in law enforcement. We are to take up the invitation to become one with the authorities – a strategy which is integral to the work of governance. Simon (1997: 178) argues that the 'new strategies aim to hold individuals more accountable or to "responsibilize" them. Governing through crime is also a way of imposing this new model of governance on the population.'

Although some analytical work on the police is still aired, the vast majority of the new police documentaries are sympathetic and free of any sort of critical impetus. They provide short-term excitements without bothersome analysis. Yet questions still need to be asked, especially given the increase in police personnel and the greater powers of arrest bestowed by new legislation. The police have made significant investments in new technology, the effect of which has been their withdrawal from the streets in many areas. Furthermore they have been subject to new managerial pressures seeking to increase their accountability. Unfortunately, these subjects do not seem to have excited much interest in programme-makers, who tend to reflect a new paradigm impatient with complexities. A new discursive formation which brings together governmental anti-crime campaigns, the news media and myriad dramatic representations of crime has helped feed the public's appetite for quick-fix solutions rather than those generated by protracted analysis. The modes of address adopted by programme-makers to reach the public help accentuate this quick-fix response. Criminal activity can be caught on camera, the efficiency of the technology demonstrated, the response of the good community vindicated in the detention of the perpetrators, and their sentencing reported – all in thirty minutes.

These new police documentaries are best understood as part of a wider web of discourses from organisations concerned to promote good behaviour and the correct use of authority. What this means is seeing the text as one which gives space to different rhetorics and which links up discourses on law enforcement with those on punishment, connects explicit lessons in responsible conduct with new sound-bite sentencing policies, describes the rise of security cameras and then joins that to electronic tagging and shaming policies.

It is because the new documentaries are uncluttered by critical impulse that documentary is losing the oppositional force it once had. It is now open to a complexity of voices seeking to assert authority. But while documentary's faint aura of expertise remains, it can be used by producers to help us read their programmes as independent productions rather than promotional material. Thus it is within this framework that we are offered the new messages from authorities in law and order – police officers, security officers and other new specialists in crime. In describing these voices in a range of formats a new discursive formation will be seen to replace concern for fellow-citizens with concern over improved security, which substitutes treatment for discussion and offers slogans in place of debate – all at a time when documentary's intellectual base is being displaced by the rise of the market. The new emphasis is a *practical* one – how we should behave and how we expect others to behave. In what follows I look at these various forms of television, describe the new programming strategies that contribute to the new common sense and reconsider their role in fashioning who and what we are.

> By making explicit the forms of rationality and thought that inhere in regimes of practices, by demonstrating the fragility of the ways in which we know ourselves and the tissue of connections between how we know ourselves and how we govern and are governed an analytics of government can remove the taken-for-granted characteristics of these practices. (Dean 1999: 36)

Television remains the chief focus of leisure for millions of people, but few critics seem to spend much time looking at how social and political changes work their way through the texts. Now that documentary has opened up, it may be useful to look at how its various discourses struggle to direct human conduct. This is particuarly pertinent at a time when the issue of good and proper conduct has become an overt theme in *governmental* discourse and has recently issued in such initiatives as introducing the subject of citizenship into the school curriculum.

Television is seen here as part of the work of culture-as-management, where culture is a set of *practices* aimed at producing – in line with governmental objectives – self-regulating, self-governing individuals. Documentary still signifies as a discourse of sobriety. Its still 'speaks' of a principled opposition. But what has changed fundamentally in the past twenty years is the context in which citizenship is made and understood. Documentary has always sought to define us. Yet our relationship with this project has been massively complicated. The public's greater understanding of the media has led to increased cynicism about television. The revelation of fakes and the cult of celebrity have informed documentary as much as they have any other genre. As a result documentary has a new relationship with the citizenship project on which it once depended. A wider field of documentary practice has far less to tie it together. In place of a shared understanding many documentaries now focus on particular behaviours and the punishments meted out to those who dare to be different. A wide variety of new and hybrid formats use the technology of discipline to produce confessions, revelations and transformations which render citizens more transparent than ever. This new visibility is central to the efficient governance of both ourselves and others.

To be precise, then, governmental self-formation concerns the ways in which various authorities and agencies seek to shape the conduct, aspirations, needs, desires and capacities of specified political and social categories, to enlist them in particular strategies and to seek definite goals . . . (Dean 1995: 563)

Bibliography

Aldridge, J. (2001) 'Why this is now the golden age of TV', *Observer*, 9 September.

Barnett, S. and Seymour, E. (1999) *'A Shrinking Iceberg Travelling South. . .'. Changing Trends in British Television: A Case Study of Drama and Current Affairs*, London, University of Westminster Campaign for Quality Television, Ltd.

Bell, E. (1986) 'The origins of British television documentary: the BBC 1946–1955', in J. Corner (ed.) *Documentary and the Mass Media*, London, Arnold.

Boyne, R. (2000) 'Post-panopticism', *Economy and Society*, 29, 2: 285–307.

Brown, M. (2001) 'Is there a documentary in the house?' *Guardian*, 27 August.

Bruzzi, S. (2000) *New Documentary: A Critical Introduction*, London, Routledge.

Burchell, G. (1991) 'Peculiar interests: civil society and governing "the system of natural liberty"', in G. Burchell, C. Gordon and P. Miller (eds) *The Foucault Effect: Studies in Governmentality*, Hemel Hempstead, Harvester Wheatsheaf.

Corner, J. (ed) (1986) *Documentary and the Mass Media*, London, Arnold.

Corner, J. (1999) *Critical Ideas in Television Studies*, Oxford, Clarendon Press.

Danaher, G., Schirato, T. and Webb, J. (1997) *Understanding Foucault*, London, Sage.

Dean, M. (1993) 'Government, authority and expertise in advanced liberalism', *Economy and Society*, 22, 3: 285–303.

Dean, M. (1995) 'Governing the unemployed self in an active society', *Economy and Society*, 24, 4: 559–83.

Dean, M. (1999) *Governmentality*, London, Sage.

Dovey, J. (2000) *Freakshow: First Person Media and Factual Television*, London, Pluto.

Dreyfus, H.L. and Rabinow, P. (1982) *Michel Foucault: Beyond Structuralism and Hermeneutics*, London, Harvester Wheatsheaf.

Fishman, J. (1999) 'The populace and the police: models of social control in reality-based crime television', *Critical Studies in Mass Communication*, 16: 268–88.

Foucault, M. (1980) *Power/Knowledge*, ed. C. Gordon, Hemel Hempstead, Harvester Wheatsheaf.

Foucault, M. (1991) 'Governmentality', in G. Burchell, C. Gordon and P. Miller (eds) *The Foucault Effect: Studies in Governmentality*, Hemel Hempstead, Harvester Wheatsheaf.

Franklin, B. (1997) *Newzak and News Media*, London, Edward Arnold.

Hardy, F. (1979) *Grierson: A Biography*, London, Faber & Faber.

Humm, P. (1998) 'Real TV: camcorders, access and authenticity', in C. Geraghty and D. Lusted. (eds) *The Television Studies Book*, London, Edward Arnold.

Kendall, G. and Wickham, G. (1999) *Using Foucault's Methods*, London, Sage.

Kilborn, R. (1996) 'New contexts for documentary production in Britain', *Media, Culture and Society*, 18, 141–50.

McNay, L. (1996) *Foucault: A Critical Introduction*, London, Polity.

Miller, P. and Rose, N. (1990) 'Governing Economic Life', *Economy and Society*, 19, 1: 1–31.

Miller, P. and Rose, N. (1993) 'Governing Economic Life', in M. Gane and T. Johnson, *Foucault's New Domains*, London, Routledge.

Mills, S. (1997) *Discourse*, Cambridge, Routledge.

Newman, J. (2001), *Modernising Governance: New Labour, Policy and Society*, London, Sage.

O'Malley, T. (1994) *Closedown? The BBC and Government Broadcasting Policy, 1979–92*, London, Pluto.

O'Malley, P., Weir, L. and Shearing, C. (1997) 'Governmentality, criticism, politics', *Economy and Society*, 26, 4: 501–17.

Palmer, G. (1998) 'Surveillance and documentary form', paper presented at the 'Governmentality' conference at Liverpool John Moores University, June 1998.

Pasquino, P. (1991) 'Criminology: the birth of a special knowledge', in G. Burchell, C. Gordon and P. Miller (eds) *The Foucault Effect: Studies in Governmentality*, Hemel Hempstead, Harvester Wheatsheaf.

Raphael, C. (1998) 'Reali-TV', *Jump Cut*, 48: 102–9.

Roscoe, J. and Hight, C. (2001) *Faking It: Mock-Documentary and the Subversion of Factuality*, Manchester, Manchester University Press.

Rose, N. (1993a) 'Government, authority and expertise in advanced liberalism', *Economy and Society*, 22, 3: 283–99.

Rose, N. (1993b) 'Governing the enterprising self', in P. Heelas and P. Morris (eds) *The Values of the Enterprise Culture*, London, Unwin Hyman.

Rose, N. (1995) *Governing the Soul: The Shaping of the Private Self*, London, Routledge.

Rose, N. (1996) 'The death of the social? Re-figuring the territory of government', *Economy and Society*, 25, 3: 327–56.

Schlesinger, P. and Tumber, H. (1994) *Reporting Crime: The Media Politics of Criminal Justice*, Oxford, Oxford University Press.

Simon, J. (1997) 'Governing through crime', in L.M. Friedman and G. Fisher (eds) *The Crime Conundrum: Essays in Criminal Justice*, Boulder, CO, Westview Press.

Swann, P. (1989) *The British Documentary Movement 1926–1946*, Cambridge, Cambridge University Press.

Wykes, M. (2000) *News, Crime and Culture*, London, Pluto Press.

Reality bites back

In the future everyone will be ordinary for fifteen minutes. (Collins 1998: 8)

It might be instructive to begin this discussion by looking at those programmes which are part of the expanded field of documentary practice. These programmes best exemplify the impact of the rise of the market as well as energising consideration of the role and function of documentary. The focus here is 'reality TV'.

It is not easy to encompass reality TV within a definition. For those in the industry it is a term so awkward as to have no value; and, as a result, some claim that there is no such thing. But 'reality TV' is used as shorthand to describe titles as diverse as *Nannies from Hell*, *Beware! Bad Drivers*, *Busted on the Job*, *999* and *The Secret World of Hidden Cameras*. In the late 1990s the term's denotation was extended to cover the real-life dramas of *Big Brother* and *Survivor*, as well as encompassing quiz shows with a focus on behaviour such as *The Weakest Link*, *Popstars* and *Pop Idol*, among others. It has begun to look as if the term 'reality TV' could be applied to any use of cameras which seeks to produce realistic effects.

Some saw reality TV as an American innovation. In a 1991 issue of *Variety* John Dempsey wrote of the

> sheer volume of reality TV shows [which] has multiplied exponentially over the last few years to the point where the shows now saturate network prime-time, first-run syndication and cable TV schedules. There are now nearly two dozen reality-based shows on TV and over a dozen waiting in the wings. (Dempsey 1991: 7)

Chad Raphael (1998) has identified the commercial imperatives behind such programming innovations: 'reali-TV', as he dubs it, came into existence during the writer's strike in the USA, when many producers began to consider formats which would not depend on writers. He also noted their 'low-end production values', which further endeared such formats to programme-makers. HBO's former head of original programming, Sheila Nevins, pointed out that the cost difference between drama and reality programming could be 'millions of dollars'. Furthermore, '[t]here are no stars. You have John Q. Public spilling his guts, literally spilling his guts on some shows[,] and John Q. Public doesn't demand a high price (quoted in Offil and Abramovich 2000: 1).

In the UK reality programmes proliferated on cable and satellite channels showing US imports, before infiltrating prime-time on the terrestrial channels. At first, reality TV attracted much critical attention because it's programmes tested the limits of the law and the accepted traditions of documentary. One example was Barrie Goulding's 1995 *Caught In The Act*. Goulding is an entrepreneur who first came to notice with *Executions* – footage of real people being put to death. He gained wider public attention when *Caught In The Act* was condemned by the police and by individual MPs. The programme featured people undressing in changing rooms, a couple having sex in a lift and reckless driving, and it gave rise to questions about what could legally be broadcast. What seemed at the edge of acceptability in 1995, however, has now found its way into everyday schedules, with a series using the same title and others, like *Kirsty's Home Videos* and *Tasteful Television*, offering similar material. Rather than pursuing subjects in a balanced and rational manner, reality TV looks to develop brands and to maximise audiences. As *Big Brother* 'creator' John de Mol declared, 'when you simply look at the ratings . . . you say that eight million people can't be wrong' (Snoddy 2001: 24).

UK producers of traditional factual programmes have been quick to distinguish what they do from what they regard as the cruder excesses of reality TV. For example, Robin Paxton, a former controller of features at London Weekend Television, referred to 'a genre of reality television that's extraordinarily sleazy' (quoted in Hill 2000: 17). Hill has interviewed other producers working in news and current affairs who are anxious to disassociate themselves from other types of reality TV, 'a type of TV that is metaphorically associated with sordid and venal sexual encounters' (Hill 2000: 17).

But it is precisely the crudity of reality TV, its odd hybridity, that makes the sub-genre worthy of discussion, for such programmes illustrate what happens when documentary is loosened from its moorings in public service and is informed by new and aggressive discourses on law, order and the importance of good conduct.

A great deal of reality TV depends on the use of CCTV footage. For some, use of CCTV material poses the issue of propriety, one summed up by a producer of *Dispatches* (an investigative series in the traditional mould): 'Appropriate use of CCTV would be presenting a robbery and using the footage for people to identify the robber . . . But it is only a small step to irresponsible use – using CCTV footage to excite, with footage of car accidents for example (Carter 1998). That was in September 1998. Since then reality TV has unashamedly adopted CCTV to entertain and shame in equal measure.

Reality TV's excited and sometimes shrill tone signals a break with traditional documentary's balanced approach to its subject. It is clear from the opening credits that the material to come lacks the sober discourse which has long informed documentary and given it status and prestige. Both *Chopper Coppers* and *Police Videos* open with clips of what is to come in the attempt to snare drifting viewers. As the titles suggest, these are straightforward and exciting quasi-documentaries on the work of the police, distinguished by a lack of critical distance. No time is spent in considering the tactics of those doing the chasing or in developing the background of those being pursued.

While the subjects covered by reality TV is varied, the content of its programmes does have characteristics in common: for example, use of music to add to the dramatic effect. In *Fear Factor* a number of individuals submit themselves to a range of unattractive alternatives designed to test their fears. Our emotional responses to the subject are guided by music at every opportunity. Reality needs a good soundtrack.

Another deviation from the traditional form comes in the narration. Because the narrator has no need to hold together a main argument in the course of a programme, his tone can vary from the jocular to the stern. The narrator does not represent an expert mediating and making sense of experience; his or hers is but a voice helping us to derive amusement from the clips. Programmes ranging from *Neighbours At War* to the recent (2002) *So You Think You're A Good Driver* feature a jokey narrator, whose attempts to amuse disinclines viewers to consider anything beyond the on-screen antics of the subject.

The contents of reality TV programmes are not the product of a team concerned with particular issues but are compilations, made by television's new entrepreneurs, that seek to engage our appetite for the titillating and exploitative. The footage belongs to a product–commodity aimed at consumers rather than images which appropriately illustrate a discussion about societal actors and citizens. The material is not sourced by a dedicated team in the field but collated from a range of disparate sources. *Stupid Behaviour Caught On Tape* has already been mentioned as typical of this new sourcing; *Scenes of Crime*, *Eyewitness Video* and *Police Videos* are other contemporary examples, all of them on offer on the same evening in December 2001.

Periodically commentators proclaim the death of reality TV and argue that the genre is tired and no longer of interest to commissioning editors. But the field of documentary practice is now so widely dispersed that it is difficult to imagine a television system that would not reserve significant space for such low-cost exploitative entertainments.

What distinguishes much of reality TV is a lack of human agency. Many of the programmes discussed in this book look at the ways in which the police seek to communicate with the public or how subjects come to terms with notions of identity, topics that will necessarily involve issues around citizenship and the community. Reality TV differs in that it pictures individuals who are citizens but also keys in to a scientific discourse on human behaviour: in its lens, people are both recognisably human and oddly mechanical.

The world of reality TV is flattened out. Little is done to anchor the material in particular contexts. The subjects are simply flickering images with no hinterland, nor any sort of life beyond the on-screen incident. Subjects very rarely get the chance to speak, and if they do it is only to illustrate their stupidity or naïvety. For what reality TV does is to share the gaze of CCTV and new surveillance technologies in focusing on people's behaviour in the steady gaze of the lens. Those trapped there rarely emerge as anything more than bodies. They do not speak outside of the clips and their cases are never developed. They are products of the technology. What we have to consider is how such programmes became acceptable – both as productions and as messages to be understood and consumed by the public.

The many answers to that question are considered throughout this book, but the most pertinent one here concerns the rise of CCTV – a technology central to the success of reality TV and one which offers a distinctive view of the human subject.

CCTV

In Britain in recent years, politicians, police, security pundits and media personnel have all contributed to an uncritical discourse on the need for, and unproblematic effectiveness of, CCTV systems. (Coleman and Sim 1998: 28)

It is not often acknowledged that England and Wales are the most spied on and pryed into population in the 'free' world (Morrison 2001). These two countries 'have more wide-area CCTV systems, geared towards surveying the public behaviour of citizens in public spaces, than any other advanced capitalist nation' (Graham, Brooks and Heery 1996: 1). Through a combination of statal and commercial forces both countries are criss-crossed by myriad networks of cameras. In 2000 it was calculated by the *Index on Censorship* that £385m was spent on CCTV in Britain in 1999, and the provision has increased considerably since. Simon Davies (1999: 8) of Privacy International writes:

Many people now expect to be routinely filmed from the moment they leave the front gate. Hidden cameras – once frowned upon – are now being installed unhindered in cinemas, police helmets, pubs and changing rooms; in 15 years we've come to see CCTV as a benign, integral part of the urban environment, despite little evidence that cameras cut overall crime.

Furthermore, while individuals may have some idea of where the cameras are, and might even hazard a guess as to why they are being filmed, they will have far less idea where the footage is going. CCTV has become an established presence all around us, but it is not one which is widely understood.

To some extent the spread of CCTV use can be attributed to the fact that it has a very high degree of fit with the Conservatives' strategies of the 1980s and 1990s. The first CCTV cameras were installed in the 1970s, when the police experimented with hidden cameras at the side of the road. These soon proved very successful, and there are now more than 6,000 cameras located along the roads of England and Wales measuring our speed – and, according to police research, working as a powerful deterrent (Ford 2000: 11; Wintour 2001) Not only are these useful silent policemen but they provide a very substantial income for the Treasury. But it was in the 1980s that use of CCTV cameras became widespread, as part of the Conservative administration's investment in making cities safer for consumers and communities.

The installation of CCTV offered a sense of security. The technology was part of a refocus and reinvestment in policing – a traditional Tory policy objective. CCTV was modern, clean and efficient – the 'magic bullet' solution to crime. Unlike a police officer, it worked twenty-four hours a day. It helped track the spread of incivilities at minimal cost. CCTV worked as a symbol to deter both planned and random crimes. Commercial forces obviously had an interest in the installation of CCTV cameras because they made environments safer for shoppers and people in general. Malls and stores which installed CCTV reported customers feeling more relaxed in their environments and therefore more willing to spend. Insurance companies provide a useful incentive to set up surveillance systems, offering up to '30% discounts on premiums to retailers who contribute towards the costs of wide-area CCTV' (Graham 1996: 58). Beck and Willis (1995: 161) reported that customers were keen to give CCTV 'a ringing endorsement'. In most of the places included in the study it was found that 'more than nine in ten members of the shopping public took the view that surveillance cameras in the shopping environment were acceptable – 91 per cent in town centres and 96 per cent in shopping centres'. CCTV cameras were there principally to guard the buildings, but they also served as a warning to potential thieves and sometimes even helped catch them.

The installation of CCTV brought together a series of policies and political objectives. A specific example of the way in which CCTV crystallised the value of new technology is its installation in football stadia. In the 1970s football was widely associated with hooliganism in the public imagination. Entrepreneurs in the UK noted, however, that several sports in America had greatly increased attendances by making stadia more family-friendly. These entrepreneurs saw the potential to increase attendances by widening clubs' fan-base so as to take in *families* rather than just male members, and the richer clubs began to redesign existing stadia, extending their grounds' capacity and introducing large all-seated areas to accommodate the increasing representation of women and children at clubs' games. CCTV became part of the architecture of these new stadia, in which everyone could be seen and monitored, where safety was of paramount importance. Its installation signalled to fans that a club was serious about 'controlling' its hooligan element. Football stadia, particularly of clubs in the upper leagues, became less attractive and, as a consequence of all-seated areas, less functional as arenas for battles. The decrease in violence worked for the Conservative Government, which, having advocated the increased use of CCTV, took significant credit for the improving safety of football grounds.

CCTV systems were integrated into multi-agency approaches to crime such as Neighbourhood Watch in the 1980s and 1990s. Law and order strategies in the 1990s were about 'responsibilising' the community. CCTV fits neatly with neo-liberal or advanced liberal strategies of rule that enable the State to 'set up' chains of enrolment, 'responsibilisation' and empowerment in sectors and agencies distant from the centre yet tied to it through a complex of alignments and translation (McCahill 1998a: 56).

Police forces have offered online advice for communities who wished to take up CCTV, giving tips on how to make best use of it, where to have it positioned and how best to protect it. The Crime Prevention website outlines the pitfalls of installing a system, and lists 'deterrence, detection, response and peace of mind' as the technology's main advantages (Peel Regional Police 1996).

CCTV's utility value, said its advocates, made it something in which we should invest. Typical of this support was a story that appeared in the *Sunday Telegraph* concerning a small group in Totnes, Devon, which had to dismantle its somewhat basic CCTV system because it violated 'the new code of practice produced by the EU commissioner to administer the 1998 Data Protection Act'. This was portrayed as a classic example of the law hindering the rights of citizens. Without such interruptions the community was said to be happy to come together around CCTV (Booker 2001). The installation of CCTV has offered opportunities for new alliances between local businesses, the police and citizens. Kings Lynn is often cited as a model case, for it installed CCTV before many other cities and thus has had more time in which to guage the success of its use.

> The surveillance system has grown because of the feel-good factor it creates among the public . . . Originally installed to deter burglary, assault and car theft, in practice the cameras have been used to target what town officials describe as anti-social behaviour . . . the system is administered by the local council, paid for by its residents and operated by a private security company. (Davies 1999: 177)

CCTV promised to reassert control over urban environments where fear of crime was on the increase; and because industrial sources

provided evidence that through CCTV fear of crime was decreasing it was allowed to grow unhindered by regulation. The CCTV companies themselves become exemplars of adventurous capitalism making substantial profits for their owners as they developed in a climate largely unrestrained by legislation. Such growth is part of the wider extension of surveillance and former military contractors into the privatisation of security.

A range of trade magazines soon burgeoned which featuring guest articles by esteemed figures such as New Labour's home secretary, Jack Straw. In *CCTV Today* Straw (1998: 3) wrote:

> The many thousands of people who make up the country's policing and security agencies are charged with the most exacting and sometimes the most difficult of responsibilities. In support of that the United Kingdom security industry plays a vital role and it is useful to have a communications medium through which information of news and developments can be exchanged.

CCTV also fitted into the managerialist ethic of the time by being an accountable, quantifiable way of contributing to crime prevention. It connected with new initiatives such as the *British Crime Survey*, which provided the Home Office (1999, 2001) with data for understanding both the incidence and the public perception of crime, and indicated public interest in CCTV's utility in the fight against crime. The *Survey* indicated that the installation of CCTV would appear to represent a perfect solution to crime – effective, efficient and popular with the public.

Use of CCTV is part of a long-term objective to impose order on urban environments. Historically, with the growth of population centres there was a clash between design and the influx of labour. The early industrial cities had to manage accommodation for the vast influx of new labour while also policing behaviour. In a period of unparalleled industrial expansion little time and energy were given to the relationship between architecture and the growth of crime. As a result some cities featured wide open spaces and boulevards where surveillance was relatively easy. Darker places remained, however, where surveillance was difficult, and these areas naturally became associated with the criminal element: 'The fear is that the machine is breaking down by itself, and that "outside" in the chaos of urban life, in the desolate city streets abandoned to the predators, lies the ultimate horror – chaos, disorder, entropy' (Cohen 1987: 210).

As urban crime proliferated the authorities looked into various means of illuminating these dark areas. Nightwatchmen and other licensed authorities could do only so much. Informers, then as now, were notoriously unreliable. Even the early policemen, themselves recruited from the criminal fringe, soon found themselves out of touch with the sources of crime. Given the limitations of information gained through contacts, it can immediately be seen how CCTV offers a new way to police the darkness – to bring everything before the light of the cameras. In this way, it was thought, everything can become knowable and the project of surveillance can end confusion and fear by 'distributing everyone into fixed spaces and rigid compartments' (Cohen 1987: 208). Robins (1996: 20) concurs: 'Through the principle of rational vision, aspiring to the ideal of universal panopticism, it seemed possible to achieve order, and consequently mastery, in the urban space.'

CCTV seems clean and efficient, and not liable to human error. As a scientific solution to the chaos of the city it extends administrative power both symbolically and as a tool of classification. Crime need no longer be unknown and frightening, but can be viewed as something manageable, even predictable:

> Surveillance as the mobilising of administrative power – through the storage and control of information – is the primary means of the concentration of the authoritative resources involved in the formation of the nation-state. (Giddens quoted in Barry 1995: 44)

CCTV increases efficiency by providing data which can be useful in tracking the movements of stock, machinery and citizens–consumers. From the traces we leave when making a credit-card purchase to the images of us recorded by CCTV cameras we offer ourselves up as data to be sorted. We are not at all surprised to see ourselves, as a result, targeted by mailorder companies – our identifiability has become part of what we are. 'I see the Panoptic sort as a kind of high-tech, cybernetic triage through which individuals and groups of people are being sorted according to their presumed economic or political value' (Gandy 1993: 1–2).

Similarly, we will accept and even welcome CCTV as the price to pay for safety and predictability. It is fundamental to the new 'discipline' of town centre management. We are able to appreciate CCTV when it works to improve our health and productivity, and to protect our children.

Thus, given the congruence of commercial interests, administrative directives and political objectives, it is hardly surprising that by the mid-1990s all the major cities' centres in England and Wales had CCTV systems and that all major shopping-centre premises have installed systems. It is estimated that there are 150,000 CCTV cameras in London alone (Conrad 2000).

A further boost to CCTV was the Tory Government's 1995 'City Challenge Competition' which granted a total of £15m to councils which used CCTV to improve security. Indeed as the Home Office's *Crime Prevention News* (April–June 1996, cited in Norris 1999: 27) makes clear, 'CCTV plays an identifiable and central role in the government's law and order strategy'. These developments were not opposed by the Labour Party. In the lead-up to the 1997 election, which New Labour was expected to win, the shadow home secretary, Jack Straw, made no distinction between Labour's policy on CCTV and that of the Tories. The civil liberties' framework, that once had informed left-wing discourse, was now clearly seen as inappropriate, if not old hat.

There are now very few spaces in the urban landscape unmonitored by CCTV cameras. In 2001 New Labour launched the biggest single investment in CCTV. A £79m plan 'will set up or expand nearly 250 CCTV schemes across England and Wales' (*Guardian* 2001). There was, remarkably, an almost total lack of critical response to the launch from the media. CCTV has transcended civil libertarian concerns, perhaps, because it has the magical qualities of being a deterrent to crime and popular with the public.

An account of the remarkable expansion of CCTV use should consider also the role of the media in propagandising for the technology. It is certainly the case that most reports concerning the use of CCTV highlight only its virtues. A simplistic response, though one not entirely without merit, would be that, so far as the popular press and commercial television are concerned, CCTV solutions to criminal behaviour are to be welcomed because they work in the interests of efficiency by restricting damage, and because they contribute to the safety of individuals – and their accountability – and are economical.

Yet there are cracks in this facade. Perhaps the most infamous instance of CCTV footage moulding the public imagination was in the case of Jamie Bulger. In 1991 the 2-year-old was led away from a shopping centre by two 11-year-old boys. He was taken to a disused railway line and there killed by the boys in a re-enactment of a scene in *Child's Play*. The case generated considerable publicity in which the two boys were positioned at the heart of a moral panic concerning 'our' children.

That one CCTV frame of Bulger being led away by Venables and Thomson has become a metonym for the endangered family, its mere presence working as a warning and a threat. But, as Sarah Kember (1995: 119) has noted, 'as presented in the reports, this crime seems to unsettle the whole process of surveillance and classification'. Some of the inhabitants of Bootle felt themselves to have been failed by this 'security system'. The technology failed to police our own boundaries; the system had failed to 'protect one of its most vulnerable members'. As Melanie Phillips and Martin Kettle (1995: 120) wrote, the CCTV images caused us to be 'doubly affronted, both by being made complicit in this terrible tragedy and by the demonstrable fact that such "security devices" are anything but'. Other reports in the press focused on the use of the technology. *The Times*, for example, claimed that one of the CCTV images had been 'subject to computer enhancement' which was 'a vital and unexpected source of information in the investigation of James's murder' (quoted in Kember 1995: 120).

One consequence of the death of Jamie Bulger, however, was a dramatic increase in Liverpool's investment in CCTV.

> Liverpool Council is hoping that the cameras will bring people back into the city. Eric Nolden, manager of Liverpool Councils' Traffic Control Systems division, says he hopes the CCTV initiative will make people feel safer when they walk the streets. The Liverpool authorities are so happy with the public response to the CCTV initiative that they plan to expand it to a 65 camera system covering a large section of Liverpool. Since the shattering effect of the Bulger trial, the cameras have received almost universal approval by Liverpool residents. (Davies 1999: 175)

It would be unsafe, however, to infer that CCTV use in the UK has met with universal acceptance. Short and Ditton's research (1998: 404) in Glasgow revealed a 'rich and broad diversity of views, which, in turn, serve to defy any obvious or common-sense categorisation of offender reaction to CCTV surveillance'. Furthermore Ditton's study for the Scottish Office discovered that one of the great motivating myths of CCTV may be flawed because 'the cameras had not proved cost effective, producing just one arrest every 40 days . . . The report said that there had been no sign of the investment, jobs or visitors it was promised the cameras would generate' (Ditton quoted in Flett 1999: 2).

Although they found a high degree of acceptance for CCTV in shopping centres and malls, Beck and Willis (1995: 177) found grounds for concluding that the 'rise and rise' of CCTV has been largely predicated on little more than a presumption of benefits which do not need to be made the subject of formal enquiry.

Other writers have raised important questions concerning freedom and public space to which the technology gives rise. Writing in the *Guardian*, Peter Preston (2001: 18) warned: 'We are never alone. We are always under surveillance.' David Lyon (1992: 169) contends that increased surveillance is a life-long threat:

> There are less places to hide; constraints on privacy invasion evaporate and anonymity is lost. Stigma clings to us more tenaciously and we may be reluctant to act in particular ways – apply for welfare, join a demonstration – for fear of it going on record.

A useful, if poignant, illustration of this is the case of Geoff Peck. In 1996 Mr Peck decided to take his own life by slashing his wrists with a kitchen knife. However, his attempt at suicide was monitored on CCTV by camera operatives who then sent a team of paramedics to his aid (Taylor 1996). Brentwood Borough Council sold the tape to television (it ended up on *Crimebeat*). In its defence the council argued that the footage would 'highlight the effectiveness of CCTV in deterring town centre crime' (Conrad 2000: 2–3).

The incident involving Mr Peck raises a significant and relatively unexplored issue concerning CCTV. Surveillance involves a degree of subjectivity. It is increasingly the case that cameras are not fixed in position but are moved by operators. What is rarely examined is the decision-making of those doing the moving and recording – the CCTV operatives who decide whether or not to call the police. In an ESRC-funded project Clive Norris and Gary Armstrong (1997) investigated the work of CCTV operatives in Hull's shopping centre. They discovered that these operatives worked with a very limited set of criminal stereotypes. As a result some groups, young men for example, were given a higher degree of attention than were others. This has been confirmed by Karen Evans, who found that 'black males already feel excluded from shopping malls where they experience intense scrutiny from security guards using CCTV systems' (quoted in Graham 1996: 58) These untrained, unlicensed individuals are reinforcing standard discourses on lawless youths by the mere process of acting on their stereotypes.

Mick McCahill (1998b) has called into question the efficiency of interconnected CCTV systems by noting the personal relationships that obtained between the operatives. Whatever the cameras showed became subject to the interpretative tendencies of this group of acquaintances (in some cases relatives), whose personal predelictions undermined the efficiency of the technology.

CCTV has been said to offer the prospect of better managed urban environments. Has its promise been realised? The new themes central to various authorities on law and order are management, security, safety, predictability and accountability. It is said that we work better in an ordered environment. Thus CCTV records the movements of people in shopping malls so that it may help in the more efficient use of floor-space. In America 8 million people live in gated communities. (Humphrys 2002). Private guards and security patrols offer the reas-surance that the hard-pressed police are unable to provide. In such ways we can become defined by our environment, and we take on that definition because it promises us the order which enhances our drive to be more efficient. But not everyone benefits from these new or enhanced patterns of exclusion created by CCTV. Zygmut Bauman (1998: 89) has suggested that two worlds now co-exist: that of cosmo-politan businesspeople, global culture managers and global academ-ics in which territorial borders present no barrier; and the 'second world', for whose inhabitants

> the walls built of immigration controls, of residence laws, and of 'clean streets' and 'zero tolerance' policies, grow taller; the moats sep-arating them from the sites of their desire and of dreamed-of redemp-tion grow deeper, while all bridges, at the first attempt to cross them, prove to be drawbridges.

The drive for order and predictability has repercussions, many of which are socially divisive. CCTV is more likely to be installed where the authorities believe it can do the most valuable work, and this often involves the monitoring of the poor, the dispossessed, the lost. Good citizenship is the face we present to the cameras which can be checked against other data to prove our value as good consumers.

CCTV is now an instrument in the ordering and classification of citizenship, but in the making of such distinctions it further margin-alises the 'bad' consumers: 'The poor, especially poor people of colour, are increasingly being treated as broken material or damaged goods to be discarded or sold at bargain prices to scavengers in the marketplace' (Gandy 1993: 2). In terms of the concerns of this book, however, it is their images that are being sold to the producers of reality TV.

The real thing?

One of the great successes of reality TV has been *Nannies From Hell*. This programme used footage from hidden CCTV cameras of nannies, their faces blurred, slapping their charges. Also featured were interviews with the agencies that supplied the nannies, though we did not hear from the nannies themselves (Blackstock 1998). Judgement had already been passed on them by the incriminating video footage. To have allowed the nannies to speak would have been to add a level of complexity that is beyond reality TV. *Nannies From Hell* also gave strong hints that 'mum' should be at home looking after her children. To drive home the point the programme featured mothers who expressed regret over leaving their children with nannies in order to work and who now promised to remain at home. As documentary *Nannies From Hell* is of questionable value; but as a television product it was guaranteed to succeed. Huge audiences were drawn to this emotional subject and, as a result, there was considerable debate in the media over the role and function of the modern mother. Programmes of this sort, however, can engender a general and unwarranted mistrust of the featured subjects; and it should, perhaps, be borne in mind that many nannies and child-care workers belong to a large and much-exploited new underclass, with ties to other workers who find themselves victimised by the lens, such as waiters, salespeople, attendants and other manual workers.

Questions might be asked concerning the rights of those captured by CCTV on-screen. It is often the case that the subjects of reality TV are those who can least afford to initiate legal proceedings against corporate interests. Reality TV takes the perspective of the authorities by focusing on the lives of those people who are least able to fight back: 'Under the institutions of bio-power it is those who are to be disciplined, observed and understood who are made the most visible' (Dreyfus and Rabinow1982: 191).

Reality TV contributes to the exclusion of those who are not performing well as consumers, who are not behaving correctly in the spaces provided, who are not, in short, acting predictably. But these are precisely the people on whose behalf documentary used to speak.

The use of CCTV footage by reality TV indicates that surveillance is on the increase, that more cameras are in place than ever before, that more agencies are now involved and that there are fewer spaces closed to scrutiny. While we may be justifiably apprehensive that our workplace and home life can come under scrutiny, we have no need to worry as long as we abide by the law. So although it seems to be frivolous fodder, reality TV is illustrative of ways in which criminality is being extended. As such these programmes excite, in equal measure, the fear and the excitement crucial to self-government. In this manner we pass on the message of policing. We become vigilant, for ourselves and others.

> The force field with which we are confronted in our present is made up of a multiplicity of interlocking apparatuses for the programming of this or that dimension of life, apparatuses that cannot be understood according to a polarisation of public and private or state and civil society. In the name of public and private security, life has been accorded a 'social' dimension as a result of the formation of a complex and hybrid array of devices for the management of insecurity and risk comprised by practices of social work and welfare, mechanisms of social and private insurance, and a range of other social technologies. (Rose 1993: 286)

CCTV is part of the technology of social control. The way in which it operates to link together information is by no means always to our advantage. As Graham (1996: 60) has pointed out: 'There are clear dangers that existing and emerging technologies will be implemented by powerful interests set to gain most without the visibility and democratic debate such applications clearly warrant.'

Christopher Dandeker (1990) has investigated the deep connections between military and other forms of bureaucratic organisation during the nineteenth and twentieth centuries. He relates CCTV to spy satellites and the passing of information through security networks set up between countries. GCHQ, Echelon. BT's System X, customs and excise, MI 5 and the National Criminal Intelligence Service are just some of the organisations sharing information about us without our consent. But to make programmes analysing such subjects would not be as exciting (or as easy) as showing security footage of someone doing something wrong.

Reality TV specials such as *I Spy* and *Shops, Robbers And Videotape* invite us to share the perspective of other watchers, to be in the viewing booth with the other instruments of authority. The very idea of taking a critical distance on the institution doing the surveying is becoming untenable. Such an approach might risk alienating those supplying the footage as well as introducing a level of complexity to an audience becoming unused to debate. As a result it is unlikely that we would link CCTV to the construction of a transglobal surveillance infrastructure. Such overarching perspectives have no degree of fit within the frame of reality TV. The footage we see does not constitute evidence on the basis of which we consider whether or not a subject is guilty. The footage proves the subject's guilt – that's why it is there. The lack of any real context means that what we are presented with is not information about which to think but simply images of incidents to which we react.

Reality TV diffuses the potentially troubling implications of total surveillance by the light commentary that accompanies the footage. The narrator is not an expert but a friendly voice whose words are informed by common sense tinged with outage. Such an approach mobilises the audience against those unfortunate enough to be caught on camera – whoever they may be. The overriding message of these documentaries is that CCTV is working for us, catching people engaged in anti-social acts and helping to prosecute them. CCTV helps to protect our children from malevolent nannies and dangerous youths. In learning to see these miscreants as 'other', we ourselves become subjects, written into discourses as watchful citizens, grateful and obedient to the authorities. In this way we help to disseminate a different understanding of the safeguards of privacy: rather than having to trust others we can look to the comforts of technology.

Whether directly engaging with surveillance technology, as in *Snoopers At Work* and *I Spy*, or whether the relationship is more oblique, as in *Neighbours From Hell*, such television programmes both contribute to and key into the current emphasis on security, surveillance and privacy. Reality TV is part of the evolving discourse in which the line between *public* and *private* is being re-drawn: 'the increasing prevalence of surveillance technology exposes private acts to public scrutiny and also renders any fleeting moment subject to both the permanencies and inaccuracies of recording' (McGrath 1998: 1). To give some examples of this new ethic of surveillance:

- Some hospitals have now begun the practice of covertly recording the behaviour of parents with their new-born babies to monitor any threat to their well-being.

- The Police Act of 1997 allows the police to enter citizen's private property with fewer guidelines than ever before. But this is seen as necessary because criminals are becoming adept at using new technologies such as the internet to evade detection. For example there are now sites where specific information about police informants and the identities of officers working undercover is disclosed.
- Advertisers are evolving new methods of tracking and surveying web customers without their knowing. The use of 'cookies' helps to render up the online customer as a mass of data for exchange and sale to interested parties.
- The very act of making a purchase by credit-card discloses information which can be utilised to gain access to house-holders via mail-shots and telephone 'cold-calling', thus problematising the 'private–public distinction' (Smart 1992: 59; Bogard 1996).
- Aggressive government campaigns such as that on fraudulent claimants launched by the Benefits Agency urge citizens to inform on suspects. We are offered symbolic and financial rewards – as well as the necessary anonymity.
- Employers have gained new powers to 'snoop' on their employees. (McCahill and Norris 1999). The Regulation of Investigatory Powers (RIP) Act of 2000 'allows security services and the police to "listen in" on e-mail and Internet traffic by means of "black box" surveillance systems attached to Internet Service Providers'. Police and employers can now read traffic data – 'a complete readout of all the internet sites that a user has used' (Henderson 2000). The utopian space which the internet once represented has been corrupted not only by its use by paedophiles seeking to ensnare children but by the operations of various agents of the state.
- Both Arriva and Stagecoach bus companies have installed cameras on their vehicles 'in the interests of security'.

Thus from the banal to the profound a whole panoply of measures are creating a discursive formation in which reality TV uses CCTV and in doing so 'fits' perfectly with the *zeitgeist*. What is less often depicted are the hostile ways in which people are responding to security measures. The *Observer*, for example, advises that employees can request details of any surveillance in place and that the Human Rights Act obliges employers to let employees know if workplace surveillance is in progress (cited in MacErlean 2001). This is backed up by a ruling from the European Court of Human Rights 'which determined that workers have a "reasonable expectation" of privacy in making and receiving calls at work' (Boughton 2000: 3).

Police cameras are sometimes challenged by motorists. Some drivers have covered camera lenses with pieces of paper or sprayed them with paint. One driver even ripped a camera down by tying a towrope from its pole to his car then driving away . . . In a recent Dutch case a motorist dismantled a device and threw it into the sea from a coastal road. Challenges are being made also to the legality of the police use of cameras. Although the 1988 Road Traffic Act makes it a criminal offence for motorists not to tell the police who was driving at the time of an alleged offence, this 'contravenes the right to silence and the right against self-incrimination' enshrined in the European Convention on Human Rights (Dougherty 2000).

Surveillance can work in the other direction because of the ubiquity of the cam-corder. Perhaps the most infamous use of video by a member of the public came in the recording of the Rodney King beating, which led to the trial of various police officers (if not their conviction). Cases such as this have occurred in Britain as well as America. For example, as Mr May was being threatened by police officers in January 1999 one of his neighbours, disturbed by the noise, switched on his security camera and captured enough footage of the event for one officer to be suspended from duty and others disciplined.

Reality TV highlights the potential of CCTV to reassure the public in an age of high risk and an increasing fear of crime – a fear that such programmes necessarily engender even as they claim to be dispel it.

What we are unlikely to see on television is anything critical of CCTV. It is worth noting that television has made little effort to investigate the practices of the security profession. Jones, Turner and Hiller (1997) have noted that CCTV may contribute to the displacement of crime away from city centres. They also point to how CCTV is part of the new behaviourism concerned with changing our conduct in ways directed by the authorities but which we are nevertheless invited to take up. Also worthy of note is that very few programmes have discussed the general effectiveness of CCTV – an issue worthy of investigation given the considerable sums of public money and the faith invested in such systems. 'Although [CCTV] probably does have some utility for the police it does not have these wonderful great societal benefits, so we really question whether the benefits it does bring us justify photographing everybody who goes into the city every day' (Ditton 1999: 1).

Simon Davies spearheads a growing number of people who are

deeply sceptical about the effectiveness of CCTV systems, the benefits of which have been presumed rather than established by formal
enquiry. And yet reality TV's presentation of CCTV's efficacy in
recording all manner of criminal activities cannot help but send the
message that the system works and that complaints along the lines
of cost-ineffectiveness or infringements of civil liberties are of little
consequence.

It is not easy to be optimistic about the world as presented by
reality TV. Across a wide range of subjects these programmes illustrate that we have less control than ever over our public and, increasingly, our private identities. We have less reason to trust our friends,
our environment and our employers. It is unsettling is that CCTV's
extraordinary infringements of civil liberties are hardly ever presented as such. Indeed the extension of surveillance is invariably justified by a 'means–end' argument: bad nannies or nasty perverts get
caught as a result of its use. This will occasionally be the result, but
such 'effective' CCTV footage represents only a tiny fraction of the
millions of hours taped every day. As thousands of cameras record
our motions reality TV shows us simply instances of anti-social behaviour and its effects. In place of debate is spectacle.

While the public tunes in to these pranks, attacks and disasters,
the authorities make greater inroads into our civil liberties.

> The boundaries which have defined and given integrity to social
> systems, groups and the self are increasingly permeable. The power
> of governmental and private organisations to compel disclosure
> (whether based on law or circumstance) and to aggregate, analyse and
> distribute personal information is growing rapidly. (Marx 1998: 2)

Reality TV generates a great deal of scepticism and hostility
among the 'old guard' of documentary-makers. Its obvious bid for
ratings' success at the expense of debate is seen as somehow distaste-
ful. But the producers of these programmes meet such accusations by
an appeal to the good judgement of the viewing audience: 'I don't
think these programmes work if we look deliberately cruel and upset
people, the audience don't like it . . . We are only making telly' (Znak
in Brown 2001: 8). And in this finance-driven age, they can always
point to the ratings.

Television which utilises CCTV helps to create victims, most of
whom have no right of reply. Thus individuals who are increasingly
spatially remote now appear on our screens behaving in ways which

would seem to justify their exclusion. It is not just the 'stars' of these clips who suffer. The industry guidelines do not protect those 'innocent' parties captured on film who are peripheral to the action. Permission has to be gained only from those who are prominent. It is also indicative of a time which gives little consideration to offenders that those convicted for the crimes recorded are offered no discretion. If they are pronounced guilty of the crimes shown then their permission is unnecessary, and thus their liberties are further eroded.

Reality TV is what happens when documentary is unhampered by a sense of balance or a need of argumentation. As a sub-genre it is part of the expanded field of practice which uses the legitimising aura of the documentary form to parade random images of unfortunates behaving badly. In place of argument it jeers; in place of discussion it threatens. For many critics it represents the genre's low point:

> Once the documentary stood alone from a privileged vantage point and eavesdropped on the public at play and at war. No longer . . . Nothing is too sacrosanct, too simple, to warrant the surveillance of the documentary in its current form. (Collins 1998: 8)

It would be unfair, however, to argue that reality TV represents the dominant trend in factual programming.

Chapter 2 considers the incorporation of CCTV and other surveillance technologies into narratives concerning the police and the public.

Bibliography

Ahmed, K. and Doward, J. (2000) 'Britain hunts net paedophiles', *Observer*, 28 May.

Armstrong, G., Moran, J. and Norris, C. (eds) (1998) *Surveillance, Closed Circuit Television and Social Control*, Aldershot, Ashgate.

Ball, G. and Routledge, P. (1996), 'A nation of snoopers', *Independent on Sunday*, 29 December.

Barry, A. (1995) 'Reporting and visualising', in C. Jenks (ed.) *Visual Culture*, London, Routledge.

Bauman, Z. (1998) *Globalization: The Human Consequences*, Cambridge, Polity Press.

Beck, A. and Willis, A. (1995) *Managing the Risk to Safe Shopping*. London, Perpetuity Press.

Bogard, W. (1996) *The Simulation of Surveillance: Hypercontrol in Telematic Societies*, Cambridge, Cambridge University Press.

Blackstock, C. (1998) 'Parents spy on nannies with secret cameras', *Independent on Sunday*, 29 March.

Booker, C. (2001) 'Surveillance stymied by privacy law', *Sunday Telegraph*, 12 August.

Boyne, R. (2000) 'Post-panopticism', *Economy and Society*, 29, 2: 285–307.

Boughton, I. (2000) ' No such thing as private e-mail', *Guardian*, 4 September.

Brown, M. (2000) 'Reality bites the dust', *Guardian*, 26 June.

Brown, M. (2001) 'Reality bites,' *The Producer*, summer (Sony Corporation).

Burzych, J.M. (2001) 'Uncovering the dangerous truths of public surveillance', Department of Criminal Justice, Northeastern Illinois University; available online: www.tryoung.com/journal-grad.html/4Shon/burzych.html

Carter, M. (1998) 'Time for a reality check', *Broadcast*, 18 September.

Cohen, N. (2000) 'Our zero privacy', *Observer*, 18 June.

Cohen, S. (1987) *Visions of Social Control*, London, Polity.

Coleman, R. and Sim, J. (1998) 'From the dockyards to the Disney store: surveillance, risk and security in Liverpool city centre', *International Journal of Law, Computers and Technology*, 12, 1: 27–45.

Collins, M. (1998) 'Media: is nothing sacred?' *Guardian*, 2 March.

Conrad, P. (2000) 'The all-seeing eye that understands nothing', *Observer*, 10 December.

Corner, J. (1999) *Critical Ideas in Television Studies*, Oxford, Oxford University Press.

Dandeker, C. (1990) *Surveillance, Power and Modernity*, Cambridge, Polity.

Davies, S. (1998) *Big Brother: Britain's Web of Surveillance and the New Technological Order*, London, Pan.

Davies, S. (1999) 'It's not just Big Brother – we'll all be watching you', *Daily Telegraph*, 'Connected' (supplement), 10 June.

Dempsey, J. (1991) 'Hot genre gluts TV market', *Variety*, 3 June.

Ditton, J. (2000) 'Crime and the city', *British Journal of Criminology*, 40: 692–709.

Dougherty, H. (2000) 'Law challenges driver's victory over speed traps', *Manchester Metro News*, 9 February.

Dreyfus, H. and Rabinow, P. (1982) *Michel Foucault: Beyond Structuralism and Hermeneutics*, Hemel Hempstead, Harvester Wheatsheaf.

Flett, R. (1999) 'CCTV out of focus with crime', BBC News Online, 14 July, available: http://news2.this.bbc.co.uk/hi/english/uk/newsid%%F394000/394021.stm

Ford, R. (2000) '2000 cameras to catch a speeder with every flash', *The Times*, 8 December.

Gandy, O. (1993) *The Panoptic Sort*, Boulder, CO, Westview Press.

Graham, S. (1996) 'CCTV – Big Brother or friendly eye in the sky?' *Town and Country Planning*, February: 57–60.

Graham, S., Brooks, J. and Heery, D. (1996) 'Towns on the television: closed circuit TV in British towns and cities', *Local Government Studies*, 22, 3: 1–27.

Guardian (2001) 'Government unveils biggest ever Big Brother investment', 29 October, available online: http://society.guardian.co.uk/Print/0,3858,4242807,00,html

Henderson, M. (2000) 'Big Brother is reading you', *The Times*, 16 June.

Hill, A. (2000) 'Crime and crisis: British reality TV in action', in Ed. Buscombe (ed.) *British Television: A Reader*, Oxford, Oxford University Press.

Home Office (1999) *1998 British Crime Survey (England and Wales): Technical Report*, London, SCPR.

Home Office (2001) *2000 British Crime Survey (England and Wales): Technical Report*, London, National Centre for Social Research.Humphreys, J. (2002) 'Nobody's safe and sound in a world of private police', *Sunday Times*, 10 February.

Index on Censorship (2000) 'The Privacy Issue', 3.

Jones, P., Turner, D. and Hillier, D. (1997) 'Someone is watching over you', *Town and Country Planning*, October: 268–9.

Kember, S. (1995) 'Surveillance, technology and crime: the Jamie Bulger case', in M.Lister (ed.) *The Photographic Image in Digital Culture*, London, Routledge.

Laurence, C. (1999) 'Nursery spy keeps an eye on nanny', *Daily Telegraph*, 27 November.

Lyon, D. (1992) 'The new surveillance: electronic technologies and the maximum security society', *Crime, Law and Social Change*, 18: 159–75.

MacErlean, N. (2001) 'How to tell if Big Brother is watching you', *Observer*, 13 May.

MacKenzie, D. (1997) 'Privacy police cautions Big Brother', *New Scientist*, 12 April.

Marx, G. (1998) 'An ethics for the new surveillance', available online: http://socsci.colorado.edu/_marxg

McCahill, M. and Norris, C. (1999) 'Watching the workers: crime, CCTV and the workplace', in P. Davies, P. Francis and J. Urry (eds) *Invisible Crimes: Their Victims and Their Regulation*, London, Macmillan.

McCahill, M. (1998a) 'Beyond Foucault: towards a new contemporary theory of surveillance', in G. Armstrong, J. Moran and C. Norris (eds) *Surveillance, Closed Circuit Television and Social Control*, Aldershot, Ashgate.

McCahill, M. (1998b) 'The surveillance web' – paper presented at 'Surveillance – An Interdisciplinary Conference', at Liverpool John Moores University, June 1998.

McGrath, J.E. (1998) 'After privacy: surveillance, sexuality and the electronic self', paper delivered at 'Surveillance – An Interdisciplinary Conference', Liverpool John Moores University, June 1998.

McNamara, J. (2001) 'Trapped by the cameras', *Manchester Evening News*, 23 March.

Messenger Newspapers (2001) 'Candid camera catches crooks', *Sale & Altrincham Messenger*, 13 December.

Morrison, R. (2001) 'The British public is now the most spied-upon, pryed into population in the 'free' world', *The Times*, 19 April.

Norris, C. (1999) 'The selling of CCTV: political and media discourses' (draft version), in C. Norris and G. Armstrong, *The Maximum Surveillance Society: The Rise of CCTV*, Oxford, Berg.

Norris, C. and Armstrong, G. (1997) *The Unforgiving Eye: CCTV Surveillance in Public Space*, Hull, Centre for Criminology and Criminal Justice, University of Hull.

Norris, C. and Armstrong, G. (1999) *The Maximum Surveillance Society: The Rise of CCTV*, Oxford, Berg.

Offil, J. and Abramovich, A. (2000) 'The human show: I spy', available online: wysiwyg://85/http://feedmag.com/documentary/doc_dr.html

Palmer, G. (1998) 'Surveillance and documentary form', paper presented at 'Surveillance – An Interdisciplinary Conference', Liverpool John Moores University, June 1998.

Peel Regional Police (1996) 'Closed circuit television: big bucks – big bust', available online: www.peelpolice.on.ca/cctv.html

Preston, P. (2001) 'Blunkett's Bill will end up with his besieged police force', *Guardian*, 10 December.

Raphael, C. (1998) 'Political economy of reali-TV', *Jump Cut*, 41: 102–9.

Repeal of Investigatory Powers Act (2000) 'Commentary', available online: www.magnacartaplus.org/bills/rip

Robins, K. (1996) *Into the Image: Culture and Politics in the Field of Vision*, London, Routledge.

Rose, N. (1993) 'Government, authority and expertise in advanced liberalism', *Economy and Society*, 22, 3: 285–99.

Short, E. and Ditton, J. (1998) 'Seen and now heard: talking to the targets of open street CCTV', *British Journal of Criminology*, 38, 3: 404–29.

Smart, B. (1992) *Modern Conditions, Postmodern Controversies*, London, Routledge.

Snoddy, R. (2001) 'Reality television with added fiction', *The Times*, 'T2' (supplement), 24 August.

Straw, J. (1998) 'Foreword' to *Public Security*, 1, March: 3.

Sweeting, A. (1998) 'Provocations: lights, camera, act natural', *Guardian*, 10 January.

Taylor, R.N. (1996) 'Man who attempted suicide can sue over film', *Guardian*, 19 October.

Wintour, P. (2001) 'Review of "covert" speed cameras', *Guardian*, 23 July.

Tough policing

> The police are an integral aspect of the presentation of society as governed by the rule of law . . . the architects of the British police tradition were concerned to construct an image of the bobby as both effective and the embodiment of impersonal rational–legal authority. (Reiner 1985: 136)

The image of the police is integral to the processes of governance. Police officers are the most visible representatives of the law, traditional symbols of authority. Programmes about the police are here discussed in the context of an evolving discursive formation which has changed how we are governed and what we are invited to understand as *good governance*. This discussion takes into account the transformations in policing practice and broadcasting over the past twenty years which have changed the relationship we have with the authorities, with the community and with ourselves.

A great deal has been written on the relationship between the police and the media, much of it concentrating on the sociology of journalism and the relations obtaining between reporters and their sources (Erikson, Baranek and Chen 1989; Schlesinger and Tumber 1994). Another area of focus concerns the moral panics occasioned when the work of police, journalists and experts reinforces or helps to produce cycles of deviance (Cohen 1972; Hall, Crichter, Jefferson, Clarke and Roberts 1978; Sparks 1992). The larger framework in which the police are studied identifies them as agents of the State struggling to deal with a 'crisis of legitimacy' which is now at least thirty years old. This work has recently been supplemented by studies of the police's own efforts to improve their public image following high-profile events, such as the Miner's Strike, in which they have not been seen to their best advantage (Graef 1999). This work has provided valuable insights on the issue of control over information and the claims of both the media and the police to be working in the public interest. It is not my intention to dispute the findings of these studies, my aim being rather to look at how the police–media relationship has found expression in documentary. What I am arguing is that the critical function once central to the genre has been superseded by a new generation of programmes which not only celebrate the police but extend the work of policing into more areas than ever before. 'The police are either seen as a reactive force (the so-called "fire-brigade" model) or as a pro-active service (the community policing model), or as some, usually pathological, combination of the two' (Johnston 1991: 18).

In this and the following chapter I divide police programmes into those two kinds: the fire-brigade model, which take its lead from fast-paced action dramas showing the police in a variety of exciting scenarios doing battle with criminals; and the community policing model, which emphasises the police's role in helping communities to protect themselves, by target hardening their homes and by assisting the police and their affiliated agencies. Programmes of both kinds can be connected to inter-governmental and other mechanisms which extend the work of governance. This is not to say that such programmes play a part in any keenly engineered conspiracy, but rather that they present, somewhat uncritically, the work of governance as part of the policing message. Such programme will be seen to contribute to the evolving policing strategies – either by sharpening viewers' awareness of crime, and so of the need for a strong police force, or by motivating viewers to develop the neighbourliness of the ideal community. Programmes of both kinds offer models of policing practice for our consideration, and this is one means by which the work of the authorities informs the way we conduct ourselves. It is important to bear in mind, however, that such programmes are keyed into an economic climate where the short-term rewards of ratings are more important than discussion or analysis.

Aspects of a changing discursive formation: the police

The police represent the last resort in a long process of social control, the 'thin blue line' which is breached only when civility is breaking down. But it is precisely because most people encounter the police only in highly charged situations where they have powers of arrest that, for them, the authority of the police outweighs that of the other professions. The police are always symbols of authority whether or not we connect them with the government and other systems of authority. However the maintenance of this authority will always be a struggle. News media are focused on the day-to-day workings of the police and they often report stories which present the police in a less than favourable light. The recent past has seen the police come under increasing attack over charges of bribery and corruption and allegations of entrenched racism. The case of Stephen Lawrence is the most high-profile recent instance of the media highlighting racism as endemic, or institutional, within the police force.

The police are aware of their need to cultivate a positive image. This is a crucial issue not only for their symbolic value as authority figures but for the purposes of crime detection, for it is estimated that the vast majority of offences are brought to the attention of the police by reports from victims and witnesses. In this light it is important to consider the work the police have done to cultivate relations with the media and to project the right image.

Any recent history of the media representation of the police would have to mention how the industrial conflicts of the 1970s and 1980s saw police forces deployed in situations where they had a quasi-military role. Memorable images from the news such as mounted police charging the miners at Orgreave 'politicised [policing] in new and dangerous ways' (Heidensohn 1989: 119). This sort of coverage indicated that the tradition of police impartiality was under threat. As Roger Graef (1989: 72) wrote: 'Even for viewers with pro-police sympathies it was a disturbing sight.'

Historically the police and the media have had a rather antagonistic relationship, one characterised by mistrust. The police have been accused of adopting a fortress mentality in their dealings with the media. For their part, the media have asserted their right to information in the public interest. The police have expressed their reluctance to release information for fear that it would be misused. This well-rehearsed exchange is indicative of the police's reactive, rather than proactive, role in the processes of news production.

However, over the past twenty years the police have come to appreciate that negative publicity is rather more significant for them than it is for other professions. If the police are thought to be unreliable and corrupt, the public will be reluctant to help them by phoning in information about crimes: 'when public trust and confidence in the police fall so do the levels of co-operation and information, which, in turn, make it harder for the police to detect and solve crime' (Stephens and Becker 1994: 223). The police need the public to respect them as symbols of authority and to feel comfortable in approaching them. This support becomes particularly important when new measures are introduced which might easily be misconstrued as infringements of civil liberties. The full review of police–media relations that Robert Mark instituted situates him as the first police commissioner in the UK to take the media seriously. In 1988 Wolf Olins produced *A Force for Change*, which comprised an audit of existing police relations with the media. This began a lengthy process of change which has seen the police and the media working together more co-operatively. Ericson, Baranek and Chen (1989: 11) noted a similar process at work with Canadian police forces:

> In the face of being used at the forefront of public debates about the relation between the individual and the state, and as a sign of govern-mental accountability, the police recognise the importance of allow-ing reasonable access to the news media and the accountability allowed by its discourse.

One response to this new climate was the Metropolitan Police's news-paper *The Beat*, which at its height had a readership of 1.25 million and was designed to counteract the overdramatisation of crime.

The Metropolitan Police developed a more professional news operation than had been in place by hiring civilian press officers to deal with the media and to present the work of the force in media-friendly language. Forces around the country followed suit. It is now estimated that more than half of all police forces in the UK have civil-ian press officers whose principal role is damage limitation. It is because they understand how the media operate that they can help police forces to present themselves in media-friendly ways. Many forces also monitor the media and are proactive in writing stories tailor-made for media consumption. In the new and demanding media environment press officers now find it increasingly easy to place their stories and have them reproduced verbatim by hard-pressed journalists (Mawby 1999).

Since 1985 all senior officers have had to undergo media train-ing at the Police Staff College, Bramshill. Individual commands sometimes supplement this training with their own courses. The Association of Chief Police Officers (ACPO) set up a Media Advisory Group. Its opening recommendations made clear its desire to con-tinue the free flow of information between police and media, though its principal concern is to protect potential victims (ACPO Media Advisory Group 1999).

In 2000 John Stevens of the Metropolitan Police issued a new policy for dealing with the media. On the Met's internet site (www.met.police.uk) Stevens (2000a: 11) made it clear that

> we needed to improve our relationship with the media. As an organ-isation we have so many good stories to tell but far too many fail to reach the viewers, listeners and readers or those who report on the Metropolitan Police Service . . . We therefore need to take a new approach to our working with the media by developing more effec-tive and positive relationships with journalists.

Stevens went on to list three criteria which would govern the infor-mation the Met released to the media:

> We will tell the media things which:
>
> - are in the best interests of the public to know about
> - help to show the public the way in which the police go about their work
> - help to build public confidence in the police.

In America the role of the press information officer (PIO) is crucial. The PIO is fully prepared to used the media in the interests of the force, and has assisted with the preparation of programmes such as *Most Wanted Men*, *Inside Edition* and *Hard Copy*. Although the rela-tionship with the media is not entirely harmonious and varies from office to office, it is clear that for the most part the PIOs understand the importance of good media relations – little wonder when the resulting programmes are so fulsome in their support of the police. It is also the case that little fraternising goes on between journalists and police in America, though relations are for the most part conducted professionally. US police forces have their own journalists and photographers who record stories for police usage.

The British police's 'Could you?' recruitment campaign is the latest step in defining modern policing in the UK. The 2001 campaign cost £7 million and featured a small selection of celebrities each of whom sits on an empty chair ruminating on a particular scenario. These scenarios are realistic depictions of situations faced by police officers, such as a riot at a football match and informing a man of the death of his wife. Following these scenes, the celebrities declare that while they may be capable of 'heroic' deeds on the screen or in the ring they doubt their own capacities for the everyday heroism that is part of police work.

The choice of celebrities for the campaign is instructive. Among them were Lennox Lewis, world heavyweight champion, and Falklands War veteran Simon Weston – two men who have been through extreme challenges and whose inclusion demonstrated also how open the police are to mixed-race entrants. Patsy Palmer, an actress, was perhaps representative of the working-class from the ranks of which the majority of police officers are recruited. In these commercials the routine work of the police comes across as a kind of everyday heroism beyond the resources even of those who have achieved celebrity status by their endeavours.

The police themselves are not shown in these dramatic reconstructions. Instead the viewer is asked to adopt the point of view of the police officer confronted with one or other of these demanding situations. The question 'Could you?' is really asking 'Do you have it in you?', so that only those with the requisite inner resources will answer affirmatively. As one analyst has put it, 'The ads are based on an interesting approach, which is to ask a question that forces the viewer to self-select themselves either into or out of this advertisement – and therefore into or out of the potential for being a recruit' (Pringle 2000).

The policy of demonstrating a range of tasks that the police are routinely required to engage in was inspired in part by an awareness that many new recruits have a preconception that the work is continually exciting and dangerous – an impression they may well have derived from the media. The advertising campaign shows the importance of those resources traditionally coded 'feminine', such as the capacity to empathise.

The information pack (Home Office, nd) which supports the advertising campaign reflects the aspirations of the police to recruit more women and people from all sectors of the community. Of the nine officers profiled in the pack, four are women and three are from ethnic minorities. In this booklet entitled 'Not everyone can be a police officer. Could you?', designed to support the television and internet campaign, potential recruits are asked about their physical fitness and powers of observation, but also about their sensitivity. Superintendent Brian Langston of the Thames Valley Police is quoted as saying

> To create a police service that reflects the community it serves, forces encourage women and people from the ethnic minority communities

to apply for jobs. Of the 126,000 or more police officers in England and Wales, more than 20,000 are women and more than 2,500 are from ethnic communities. (www.policecouldyou)

The most important of a police officer's capacities have always been the ability to see both sides of a situation and the interpersonal ability to defuse a conflict. We now operate in a problem-solving culture that calls for greater powers of analysis, flexibility and creativity. This applies as much in dealing with local nuisances as it does in serious crime investigations (Langston 2000).

An awareness of the need to represent the police in a good light is increasingly important, not because of the damaging critiques of documentary programmes but to counter the many negative representations which have emerged in television dramas and even the news. The 'Could you?' recruitment campaign is only one platform, a small space in the televisual environment where the police have an opportunity unequivocally to define themselves.

Aspects of a changing discursive formation: the media

The public's understanding of the police is informed by a mixture of fictional and factual representations. Although the two are rarely confused by the viewing public, the extraordinary drive for realism which has characterised many British and American representations of the police need to be considered in any assessment of their image.

In traditional fictional representations, the British 'bobby' was very much part of the community and was a kindly force for order. British television fiction certainly played a part in reinforcing this image through characters such as Dixon of Dock Green and the affable bobbies of *Z-Cars*. The fictional British policeman was tough but fair, and the force in general was made up of principled men (police officers were invariably men) with safe and comfortable private lives. Storylines set out to prove that crime does not pay – in *Dixon* this message was driven home almost didactically in the prologue and epilogue to each episode.

British producers of fiction have, since the early 1960s, introduced an element of documentary realism into their work. *Z-Cars* was developed by the BBC's Documentary Unit, and ITV's *The Bill* is the latest in a long tradition of dramas which have sought to root their narratives in everyday reality. The producers 'emphasise the research incorporated into [the programmes], and the deliberate immersion of its writers, actors and creative personnel in the world of real policing, with attachments to police stations and the like' (Reiner 1991: 21).

Most drama series present the actual operations of the law as

> an abstract embodiment of a natural justice, morally incontrovertible, which often has nothing to do with the rules for its enforcement . . . [Furthermore this law is] separated out from the social and political structure which is inscribed in it. (Hurd 1981: 66)

It was only the documentary which threatened to disrupt the benevolent image of the police by revealing the darker side of the profession with portrayals which illustrated that all was not straightforward and above board down at the station. The genre's leftist critical stance may have made the police wary of co-operation.

The past twenty years have produced in the UK and the USA a wide variety of police dramas distinguished by an increasing level of documentary realism. In the UK Tony Garnett produced *Cops* in 2001, 'where bent and racist coppers are to be found but with the inevitable implication that such disgraces to the uniform are only fictional' (Lawson 2001: 17). Even *The Bill* has introduced corrupt policemen. American series such as *NYPD Blue* and *Homicide: Life On The Streets* feature accounts of police officers' lives in which fragile personalities struggle with alcoholism or teeter on the edge of mental and physical breakdown. The realism of these programmes has been achieved by importing documentary techniques. Sudden camera movements, apparently unedited speech and improvised dialogue give the dramas an edge of gritty realism. Although it is understood that these programmes are merely dramas, when their images of despair are followed by news reports of police corruption and racism the public may be forming a view of the police as all too susceptible to human frailty.

In these modern dramas the officers generally remain on the side of right: although tempted by bribes and other inducements, they remain true to the law they have sworn to uphold. But the drive for realism has required representations of the police as increasingly complex characters in testing circumstances. What is missing in the modern television landscape is a pointed and sustained critique of the force.

Over the past twenty years both Britain and America have produced a huge number of programmes offering viewers access to the world of the police. Series ranging from *America's Wildest Police Chases* to *Crimewatch, UK* offer the viewing public unprecedented opportunities to be 'up close and personal' with the police.

There are 126,000 police officers in England and Wales, approximately one officer in every 400 people (www.policecould you). Given the proliferation of new police documentaries this makes the police the best-represented profession on television. The reasons for this are complex. In the first place such programmes satisfy a hunger for issues relating to law and order which is at least as old as the popular press and continues unabated. If further evidence were needed new magazines discussing crime and the role of the police were introduced in the late 1990s and continue to proliferate. Second, the changes in the funding structure of broadcasting has meant that both independent and institution-bound producers are more likely to make a series on a reliably popular subject such as the police than to risk their resources on something new. Third, the introduction of lightweight portable technology makes it more feasible than ever to film the police performing their most exciting role – as crime-fighters. These factors warrant further discussion.

As we saw in the previous chapter, many documentaries are made by personnel contracted for short periods of time. With such an arrangement it is impossible to rely on experience 'in depth' because such depth is economically prohibitive. Expertise is rare and expensive, where available, and represents a commodity in decline as new producers wonder to what extent it is useful. Furthermore, workers on short-term contracts are under new time pressures and may be more than usually dependent on the public relations units and press releases of organisations such as the police. Another consequence is that researchers tend to rely on well-known figures, so that the same faces and the same views and stories get repeated time and again. Independence and critical distance become more difficult because the structures that made critique possible are changing. Parallels may be drawn with the decline of specialism in the local press where efforts are underway by employers to create generalists rather than specialists. This is, perhaps, even more significant in the case of the police.

Ericson, Baranek and Chen (1989) studied conflicts between the police and the media around access to information. Of particular relevance here is the divide between those journalists who take on the values of the police and those who display greater journalistic autonomy. Ericson *et al.* found that the former were less inclined to file copy critical of the police, and that the latter were treated by the police with

a corresponding level of suspicion. Even the more autonomous journalists can find themselves sidetracked by the police: 'By keeping
reporters preoccupied with things they are bound to be interested in,
and by easing their workload in the process, sources can offset the
likelihood of incursions into private spheres (Ericson, Baranek and
Chen 1989: 18).

Chibnall (1977: 146) said that crime reporters are 'like golfers'
who prefer 'to keep to the fairway, avoiding sand traps', and he
emphasised the 'need to become aware of the bonds which bind
together reporter and police'. He recognised that there are tensions in
the relationship between the two, but claimed that this is not necessarily a bad thing for democracy as it may be useful and healthy for
the media to have a certain suspicion of police activities.

Although the press occasionally offers critical comment and
dramas sometimes present the police in a negative light, it is over-
whelmingly the case that the *new* police documentaries are sympathetic and unquestioning to the point that they risk being read as
public relations exercises. The new economic constraints have accen-
tuated those inclinations detected by Chibnall who wrote that 'it is the
reporter's world which is drawn towards that of the policeman rather
than vice versa'. Chibnall discovered many reporters were anxious
not to upset the police. Indeed 'most crime reporters see their professional responsibilities towards the public as entailing the support of
the police in their battle against crime'. A parallel example was provided in article on reality TV in the trade journal *Broadcast* in which
it was reported that producers of police documentaries were unashamed in their desire to help rather than criticise the police (cited in
Carter 1998).

Many producers find they are pushing against an open door
when it comes to working with the police. The Met's Commissioner
Stevens has said:

> I am keen to see more media being taken along on police operations.
> This will give a good insight into policing and how we are tackling
> crime. Officers planning such operations should always consider the
> media as part of their overall strategy. (Stevens 2000b: 3)

But such a proactive policy on the part of the police has to be understood in the context of a threat from the private sector. Articles in
Police Review have long expressed the fear that security firms and
others could soon be used to replace the force in areas where their

limited numbers make it difficult to patrol, such as the streets around 'clubland'. For example, in Nottingham there are now more bouncers than there are police. Although the two are working together it is not difficult to imagine a time when such patrolling duties are officially franchised to private security forces. The onset of the commercial sector is apparent also in Home Secretary David Blunkett's plans to publish league tables showing the performance of regional police and in the threat to appoint managers from the commercial sector to take over failing forces. The police argue that low recruitment, an unprecedented level of early retirements and increased paperwork has made their job increasingly difficult. They argue that New Labour does not understand the complexities of modern policing when it presents managerial dictats and policies which are difficult to enforce, such as 'spot fines' for miscreants.

> The political logic is simple: behind the twitching curtains of suburban Britain, the feeling is that yobbery is on the march, unchecked by a lily-livered Government. So what better way to reclaim the law and order initiative agenda than by tossing the tabloids the juicy bone of summary justice? (Hall 2000: 22)

The new police documentaries work in just such a way – presenting the work of law and order as a matter of summary justice. They do not explain or probe the difficulties of modern policing. While some work on the fringes (by the UK's Channel 4) does investigate the complex range of tasks that new policing involves, the vast majority of representations are simplistic. Criminals are treated either as evil and beyond rehabilitation or as nuisances who have to be dealt with summarily. And while the police find broadcasters willing to assist they might perhaps consider the value of such crude representations. There has always been a space for pro-police programmes; but what is notable today is how rarely one finds anything at all critical of the force.

Aspects of a changing discursive formation: police and media

Modern factual representations reveal a rather closer working relationship between the force and the media. This reflects in part a mutual desire to prove their value to the audience, but this mutuality is underscored by economic rather than ideological factors. Despite the rising costs of purchasing CCTV and other footage from the police it is still less expensive and easier for programme-makers to create programmes which showcase the police than make those with an independent critical voice. As a result, the police, perhaps more than any other public service, have been the beneficiaries of this new market-driven climate in television.

It is certainly the case that the police are co-operating with the media more than ever before and that the mistrust which used to characterise their relationship has been replaced by a mutually supportive relationship. As Peter Ainsworth (1995: 221) suggests: 'It is essential that the police win over the media if they are to make a start in reassuring the public that they really are trying to provide society with what is needed, and in a way that is professional, caring and sympathetic.' Presenting such a favourable image is particularly significant at a time when the police's presence on the streets is increasingly slender. Modern policing strategies aim at increasing the technological presence on the street at the expense of the human. Police patrols may represent good PR but they are not cost-effective. A great deal of energy is expended on demonstrating the cost-saving benefits of CCTV and associated technologies, and much police programming is dedicated to illustrating how efficient this technology can be, while actual analyses of this claimed efficiency is missing.

When the new documentaries about police work use footage and in-car commentary sourced from the police, a double function is served: such material provides income (users have to pay the police every time they use an image or clip) as well as helping to present the police in a strongly favourable light – naturally the police release only footage in which their endeavours are successful. CCTV has become a crucial component of programmes about police work, in some cases occupying more than 60 per cent of the total content. Its use in these programmes excites fears of misrecognition, extends shame and helps the spread of a disciplinary technology. In short, it serves to normalise surveillance because it is embedded in a discourse which proves its value in catching criminals.

It is also useful to remind ourselves that what we see on screen of the police is always a performance. When watching programmes involving the police we are judging their performances in a variety of situations – performances that are aimed at us, the viewing public, the officers' superiors, the criminals and even, to an extent, their fellow-officers. This performative dimension illustrates that the police, as public servants, have to be aware that their actions will be 'read' by

others. What we see on screen is a performance conveying the authority of the police in relation to the citizenry as well as the officers'
powers of self-governance necessary to modulate their own behaviour. When we see the police involved in a car chase what we overhear
is a commentary that necessarily involves a degree of self-editing.
What the officers say and do is in part a performance which will be
monitored by their superiors as well as providing footage for potential television audiences. When programmes present items on road
safety a different degree of self-scrutiny is at work. Furthermore there
are occasions when the programme-makers ask the police to play
themselves, and that involves yet another kind of performance which
will have to be considered. In short, what we see is how the police
want themselves to be understood (Palmer 1999).

The most important and interesting finding of the *Operational
Policing Review* was the apparent mismatch between the public's perception of what the police role should be and that of the police themselves. Specifically the police placed a high value on law enforcement
and crime control, with their concomitant reliance on such aspects as
technology and fast response times. On the other hand, the public
generally was much less enthusiastic about these tactics and methods,
wanting instead a community policing style of approach – policing
with a human face, as it were (Ainsworth 1995: 216).

The police themselves feel that 'good' policing is that which
matches the dramatic role – car chases and action – while 'bad' policing consists of dealing with the miscellaneous minor incidents which
mark a policeman's life. These views reflect in part the machismo
ethic which still informs the profession, despite the efforts made to
eradicate it. They also indicate that coping skills have a low priority
in a profession in which women remain under-represented. It is only
recently that programmes about the police have reflected this split
between domestic and action-oriented policing – although they have
made little comment on the divide and have not revealed how the
police feel about this divide.

The new police documentaries appeal to a sense of responsibility
in the imagined community, which may have lain dormant but which
can become activated by feelings of shared outrage, which are more
easily stirred by showing crimes which target the innocent. Although
their methods and modes of approach are markedly different, both
action- and community-oriented programmes seek to connect with
the audience. This attempt to fashion communities is central to the

work of governance for it offers communities standards and parameters within which they may choose to act.

> [T]he ties of community – real or imagined, traditional or contrived – come to form the image of the good society. Community becomes the means of denoting legitimacy in associations as diverse as state, church, trade unions, revolutionary movement, profession and cooperative. (Nisbet 1966: 47)

As part of the changing discursive formation it is worth noting how new trends in criminology have a high degree of fit with the new police documentaries. As Cohen (1987: 176–7) puts it:

> In criminology, cognitive passion used to be directed towards causation. To be sure, the quest was utilitarian (the correctional attitude was to find out the cause of crime in order to do something about it). But appreciation was also possible: it once seemed intellectually interesting to know why people committed crime. Now the Holy Grail of causation has been displaced by the Holy Grail of evaluation. Disillusioned with basic research and the quest for root causes, prepared to settle for limited intellectual horizons and constrained by the demands of funding agencies, criminologists started a decade ago asking the question, What works?

Garland (2001: 15) also has noted the change of perspective, from one which looked on criminality as deviance rooted in social deprivation to one which focuses on 'control theories of various kinds that deem crime and delinquency to be problems of inadequate controls'. In place of what are called the criminologies of the welfare state are control theories which 'assume individuals will be strongly attracted to anti-social and criminal conduct unless inhibited from doing so by robust and effective controls such as family, community and state'.

In this new climate we might also consider the extent to which such new police programmes may be contributing to the fear of crime. It has been repeatedly found that the fear of crime is invariably out of proportion to the actual incidence of crime. Indeed fear can outstrip incidence by as much as 50 per cent. But it has proved difficult to say with real confidence what the media contributes to such fear. While news programmes report that actual incidence of crime has decreased in nearly all categories of crime over the past ten years the *British Crime Survey* reports that the fear of crime shows no signs of declining. It is reasonable to argue that, while an earlier tradition of documentaries sought to inform the public on the incidence of crime, the more sensationalist

techniques of the new police documentaries are less interested in analysis (Home Office 1999a, 2001). It is hardly surprising to read that the
British are by far the largest household investors in security equipment.
The home fortress is made stronger while an understanding of the
offender declines. Action-oriented police documentaries suggest that
the world is a violent place while community-centred programmes
teach us to be on our guard. The result is anxiety.

Despite occupying the high moral ground programmes such as
Crimewatch, UK are typical in their stated desire not to increase the
fear of crime while creating reconstructions which cannot help but do
so. Indeed surveys have produced evidence that such public awareness programmes can increase the fear of crime (Schlesinger, Dobash,
Dobash and Weaver 1992). In a recent (13 February 2002) *Crimewatch,
UK* we heard from a distraught mother and child about a recent car-
jacking. Statements like 'I needed to save my children' and 'Thank
God you're ok' were followed by the presenter declaring reassuringly
that there is no evidence of an increase in such crimes and that claims
to the contrary were but examples of media hype, as if *Crimewatch,
UK*, a programme watched by millions, was above such tendencies.
But this moment encapsulated the dilemma. While the public service
interest of the broadcasters is to reduce unjustified fear of crime the
aggressive impulse of marketplace insists that they produce material
likely to have exactly the opposite effect.

Garland (2001: 20) has spoken of 'a perpetual sense of crisis' that
marks our age, and of a new outlook according to which the old
arrangements for crime control involving specialist agencies of the
criminal justice system are no longer valid, having become increasingly incoherent: 'In this period the public has increasingly lost confidence in criminal justice and politicians have become more and more
unwilling to entrust decision-making to criminological experts or
criminal justice personnel.'

It is suggested in what follows that new police programmes
present an image of the police which is uncomplicated, propagandist
and likely to spur the public to support an expansion in the force and
an extension of policing to the wider community. The affinity that
exists between media and police, while not extending to the ideological, is based on the same notions of governance and is fashioned by
the same discursive formation. It serves the interests of both to
produce messages which depend for their impact on a shared understanding of good and orderly conduct.

In what follows I discuss American and British action-oriented programmes as both products of and contributions to the changing discursive formation

Police! Cameras! Action! in the USA

When the danger's real, when the stakes are high, when there is no turning back, that's when the law puts it all on the line. (*World's Scariest Police Chases*, 2001)

In America a new breed of documentary has radically transformed the television landscape. New action-oriented series such as *LAPD*, *Justice Files* and *America's Dumbest Criminals* are prime-time shows representative of successful brands with uncomplicated accounts of police work. These programmes share many characteristics, in that they are aired at peak viewing-time, offer narrative resolution (out of all proportion to actual cases of capture and arrest), are dramatic and exciting in a particularly flashy style, and depend for *gravitas* on the sober contribution of news anchors. Their relatively low production costs and high ratings make them successful brands perfectly tailored for what Kilborn has called the new broadcasting ecology (Kilborn 1996; Palmer 1998).

Programmes like *Cops*, now in its eleventh series, are forthrightly unapologetic in offering themselves as platforms for the police. As Jessica Fishman has pointed out this type of programming uses 'old myths to construct models of law and order based on the power of a paternalistic state and, alternatively, civic agency' (1999: 269). *Cops* emphasises a public that is subordinate to those who have been invested with the power of the state and thus deemed responsible for maintaining law and order (270). In one sense *Cops* appears to be as unguarded a representation of the police as is imaginable. The footage we see is roughly shot as if by an officer. The police confront the public in a wide variety of conditions. In one oft-repeated and famous sequence an officer stops a man he suspects of driving under the influence of alcohol. Their exchange is noteworthy, not only for the abusive tone of the accused complaint but for the stoical calm demonstrated by the officer.

The work of James Q. Wilson has resonance here. In his study of various police patrol behaviours Wilson (1968) noted that people in urban environments respond differently from those in rural environments. For example, according to his 'broken windows' hypothesis, once an area shows signs of decline people begin to retreat into their homes while outside criminal elements are attracted by the signs of decay. He recommended that policing strategies take account of deterioration in urban environments, and efforts should be made to keep living environments ordered and predictable. This work has since been described as the inspiration for the 'zero tolerance' policing that became popular in the 1990s in New York and other American states (Wilson and Kelling 1982). Variations on the approach have been attempted in Britain. Thus when officers are shown policing acts of casual incivility the current discourse on strict law and order helps us to see their responses as attempts to halt the spiral of decline affecting the area.

Cops has a particularly realistic feel because so much of the programme consists of raw footage with minimal commentary. We are given the police officers' point of view throughout. The audio track is taken up with suspects' defences or the emergency calls and operators' responses. Each programme ends, as do so many of this subgenre, with an expression of gratitude to all the police forces who contributed to its making.

In demonstrating the bravery of the police, *Cops*, *LAPD* and *Real Stories Of The Highway Patrol* endorse the role of the police as authoritarian agents of criminal control. In *World's Scariest Police Chases* any pretence of objectivity has been cast aside. The presenter is seen at a 'drugs bust', handling one officer's weapon and chatting with others. He later refers to one officer as a 'living legend'. Even police propaganda would never be so crude as is this use of television to proclaim 'Criminals beware!'

A more confrontational approach can be seen in *Real Stories Of The Highway Patrol*, which informs viewers 'What you about to see is real' over the dark, low tones of the audio track. In exciting stories, played out by the state troopers themselves, suspects are aggressively apprehended. Here policemen act as anchors to the show, while our role is to be 'prepared to assist' – although we are simultaneously told that police work of this kind is very dangerous and should not be attempted by the public. Such programmes have as one of their functions the winning of public support for aggressive policing: 'The maintenance of public order depends on the perceived legitimacy of control measures and therefore also on the way in which disorder is represented, so any analysis of disorderly public must include work on representation' (Wykes 2000: 60)

In *Justice Files* we are told: 'These officers often live twenty-four hours in a world they wish did not exist.' This programme also offers police officers a platform from which they can express their frustration with the constraints on what they can lawfully do in pursuing suspects. Their views are not framed by critical debate; this is simply their opportunity to speak in the absence of any opposition. The programme boasts of the new and intrusive technologies the police can use to catch suspects. The justification is simple – 'It works.' The commentary helps paint a one-dimensional picture of criminals, one of whom is described as 'epitomising evil'. It need hardly be said that this represents a rather backward step in our understanding of offenders. As the programme bluntly puts it: 'Rehabilitation appears to have been a myth.'

> And since the criminal predator is usually presented without personal history or any semblance of having come from a normal social milieu, since they are depicted, in short, as abstract threats divorced from the rest of society, their punishment is hardly likely to prompt sympathy or regret. The messages that these images convey is clear. Criminals aren't like the rest of us. They are the deviant ones among us. (Sherwin 1999: 10)

These programmes represent the police as the human agents of a new technology which is working to make law enforcement more efficient. Indeed it is that same technology which brings those programme's images to viewers' screens. But it is also the case that sane, rational and tolerant police officers remain in control, thus tempering the frightening implications of techno-policing in dystopian fantasies such as *Robocop*.

Perhaps the most humane and comforting representation of the American police officer can be found in the hugely popular *America's Dumbest Criminals* (*ADC*, hereafter), a programme at the other end of the scale from public service broadcasts like *Crimewatch, UK. ADC* features a series of humorous acts committed by dim criminals. It is a light entertainment, disconnected from any project aiming to generate understanding and a classic example of what happens when the field of documentary practice is opened up to new practitioners. *ADC* is a hybrid, combining elements of light entertainment with comedic clips from reality TV and actual police footage. At work here is an almost biological imperative to represent these criminals as foolish children. *ADC* suggests that crime is something to laugh about.

Devised by Daniel Butler, *ADC* was an attempt to turn police officers' amusing stories of their encounters with the underworld into entertainment. In the first series he used a mock-serious news-style format in which soberly suited presenters gave grave accounts of crimes committed by the incompetent. The second series was made with a far bigger budget and featured the very excitable Debbie Allen with whom Butler presided over a set decorated with captions, cartoons of inept burglars and car parts protruding from odd corners. Set in a studio and aided by regular bursts of canned laughter, Allen and Butler introduced a range of segments with titles like 'We're not making this up' and 'Stories torn from the back of your local paper'.

Such was the success of the series that Butler was able to launch a book based on the programme which has since gone into six editions. Nevertheless to amuse is not the sole aim. Butler has a sober purpose: 'What makes it so appealing is that we finally get a chance to laugh at the bad guy, nobody gets away and the cops get them almost immediately' (Butler quoted in Mendoza 2000).

The programme is made with the co-operation of the police who provide the narratives linking the stories. It should go without saying that the clips offer a 'fun' side to law enforcement by presenting the officers in a good light as amenable fellows. The criminals, however, are depicted as mere objects of ridicule. They do not speak: they are silenced (dumbed) by their shame.

In the third series Butler appeared to be broadcasting from the *ADC* 'Mobile Command Vehicle', a mobile home made to look like a police van. From this 'covert operation' he introduced a series of clips of foolish criminal behaviour. The majority of the scenes shown are reconstructions, though this is not made explicit. As a result we are presented with a very simplistic view of law and order in which criminals are for the most part quite literally 'dumb'. When footage of real events is used, for example in the case of a student who had stolen a book, no attempt is made to blot out the miscreant's face. Thus the individual is humiliated on a nationally syndicated programme instead of having his or her shame limited by locality. It is the police who have made this footage available and who therefore help in extending this punishment symbolically. The producers serve only to amplify the shame as a lesson to the rest of us.

Extending shame in this way has become part of the repertoire of some judges in the USA, as later chapters show. In some states, shaming penalties rather than the more traditional punishments are being imposed, with judges recommending that those found guilty should not take up expensive jail space but instead must don signs indicating the nature of their crimes to their community. *ADC* extends this shaming nationally, with its humorous context defusing any civil liberties' issues we may have.

ADC programmes close with 'A big thank you' to all the police involved in helping to make the series, and their names are listed in the extensive end-credits. Debbie Allen used to end the show with the words: 'As always we hope we've learnt from the mistakes of others.'

This programme is perhaps the most unapologetic space imaginable for the presentation of law enforcement messages. Such positive publicity for the police works in a context which largely defuses criticism and dismisses criminality as little more than a series of pranks perpetrated by dumb misfits.

These action-oriented programmes help us to make sense of the criminal underworld from the perspective of the police. Furthermore, by offering these law enforcement platforms the media have become an institution trusted by the the police and of use to them in future collaborations.

Police! Cameras! Action! in the UK

> It increasingly feels, though, that the Metropolitan Police is subletting premises within Television Centre. (Lawson 2001: 17)

Documentaries about law enforcement in the UK are produced against a background in which the media have been critical of the police. But, as we have seen, the new discursive formation has meant a declining investment in critical perspectives, so that UK programmes now have more in common with American police documentaries than ever before. Thus when the BBC launched *X-Cars* it was perhaps making a subtle reference to *Z-Cars*, though the officers who featured in *X-Cars* were given nothing like the same 'depth' as their fictional counterparts. *X-Cars* also featured a community of officers but this time the focus was not crime and the community but the exciting business of catching car thieves in and around Manchester. This is perhaps the sort of ride-along television envisaged by Commissioner Stevens, discussed above.

In *Blues And Twos* producers focused on the work of the emergency services. In these programmes the narrator took on the language of the officers involved, sometimes without explanation or translation.

One episode showed a very dramatic street scene involving firearms – a scene with a particular resonance in the UK where police officers are rarely armed – over which the narrator intoned: 'What you are about to see could happen in any street . . . in any town . . . in accordance with strict police rules on the use of firearms'. But, having shown how efficiently the officers deal with the situation without using firearms, the narrator concludes reassuringly: 'No-one has ever been shot by an ARV officer.' Yet we are aware that police officers are ready for such situations and we are suitably impressed – and perhaps alarmed.

Again a reading of Wilson's work proves instructive as the police patrol 'tipping points' (places people use to tip domestic rubbish) before an area enters a spiral of decline and becomes 'lost'. Policing is seen to be about maintaining social order.

A large proportion of the new programmes about UK police work uses footage supplied by the force, which, like CCTV footage, provides photographic evidence of wrong-doing. Such footage bears all the hallmarks of proof – after all, 'the camera never lies'. This may in turn halt the declining faith in documentary realism. This reading may be supported by the fact that the police exercise 'considerable care and oversight of film-work' (Mawby 1999: 282). This form of documentary differs from the older documentary which would offer contextual information of some kind. Here, however, the offender is beyond consideration – he has vanished from the frame, obliterated as a shadow.

The ITV programme *Police! Cameras! Action!* offers a compilation of CCTV and police footage of UK motorists making a series of errors on the roads. The programme was perhaps inspired by the commercial *PoliceStop!* videos, compiled from traffic footage 'handed to the [video] company by various forces'. As the ACPO Media Advisory Group (1995) reported: 'It became apparent that in many cases material had been handed over without the knowledge of senior officers and/or force media advisors.' The sale of footages to television companies was left in the hands of individual commands. In the case of *Police! Cameras! Action!* Alisdair Stewart, a broadcaster of national standing, was recruited to link series of clips and to provide the requisite *gravitas*. The police retain an awareness of the programme via the ACPO press office which will 'make arrangements for relevant police officers and expertise to be involved in the editing of any national programme' (ACPO Media Advisory Group 1995).

Given this press office-mediated relationship with the police it is hardly surprising that *Police! Camera! Action!* comes across as a gritty public service announcement. In one edition Stewart talks of how the Highway Code 'is as relevant today as it was sixty years ago'. The only sounds we hear are a mix of Stewart pointing out the stupidity of these drivers and background comments by police officers. Stewart's commentary provides no real critical distance. Indeed, he joins in with the police in making remarks like 'Can you believe how stupid that is?' Bad drivers are described as 'suicidally impatient' or 'unbelievable'. Stewart is not afraid of utilising clichés to help reinforce these everyday dramas. Criminals have 'nowhere to hide', they will be 'caught and punished', a fire is not merely alight, it is a 'raging inferno'. In sharing the voice and perspective of the police Stewart abandons the role of dispassionate newsreader, although our reading of his words may retain some association of him with 'the news'.

An entire episode of *Police! Cameras! Action!* was given over to the journey of a parcel containing a human liver for a transplant operation. This trip had to be accomplished in thirty-six minutes. Although exciting, this offered little other than showing all fifty officers involved in the mission coordinating their efforts wonderfully well – a propagandist rather than a documentary purpose.

Programmes of the late 1990s, anxious to capture crime on camera, tended merely to reinforce the importance of surveillance. A notable example was Granada's *Rat Trap*. This series was based on local intelligence: the police knew certain crimes were being committed in certain parts of town. The *Rattrap* crew took themselves to these areas, where cameras were hidden and the criminal activity awaited. The offenders' timely capture on film was seen as proof both of the police's good intelligence and that the public interest was served by the programme-makers. *Rat Trap* did little, however, but confirm what the police and the local people already knew. In its use of grainy CCTV images to picture car theft and vandalism it simply reinforced stereotypes about criminals. It is certainly a long way from the noble traditions of Granada's *World In Action* – a series which was cancelled due to its low ratings.

I began this chapter by noting that the police constitute an important symbol of authority. New police documentaries in the UK and the USA rarely question the exercise of that authority. What is significant now is that we, the viewers, are asked to take a small measure of share in that authority as part of the project in which we are disposed to govern ourselves and our communities. This is the result of a govern-mentality which 'constructs individuals who are capable of choice and action' but which seeks to shape them 'as active subjects, and seeks to align their choices with those of governing authorities' (Garland 1997: 377).

Many of the crimes that feature in UK and US police programmes highlight precisely the need to restore order rather than impose the law. We can see for ourselves the signs of this disorder and can appre-ciate the ways in which the police are seeking to restore it for the rest of the citizenry. As the police employ a 'softly-softly' approach we have reason to believe that their actions are guided by common sense and a degree of autonomy and sensitivity which makes them recog-nisably human rather than agents of remote authorities.

The co-operation of the police with the media has been secured at a high a price in terms of editorial emphasis, but misgivings in that respect perhaps reflect the concerns of previous generations within an earlier discursive formation which accorded importance to the critical voice constructing the argument. Important questions concerning the extension of police powers, the presence of corruption and other lin-gering scandals have become not so much uninteresting as unthink-able.It is now more important to see the evidence of wrong-doing for ourselves. Why complicate the case?

Although it is fashionable to write of the polysemy of the text where meaning is made by each viewer interacting with the onscreen materials, most of these documentaries offer explicit instruction and guidance in the fight against crime and so work to close down meaning. These new programme-makers are helping to construct citi-zenship by enabling discourses around crime which activate the *zoon politicon*. But it needs to be stressed that the crimes we see on television tend to be the more sensational ones, whereas much police work is of a pedestrian kind. Under an increasingly managerialist culture the police have to be responsive to a vast administrative apparatus. There is now such a degree of paperwork involved in logging and recording crime, officers claim, they are being prevented from doing important investigative work . This is an interesting subject and one which would help us to picture how complex modern policing and crime-fighting have become. Alas, the new discursive formation means that we are spared analysis and instead are offered more 'gripping' car chases.

It was not long ago that documentary film-makers were feared by the police. Roger Graef's *A Complaint Of Rape*, made in the early 1980s, served to bring a change in the law, yet it also ruined the career of at least one individual. Similarly Channel 4's *The Nick*, an insightful consideration of how modern police officers operate, illustrated also the machismo culture pervading police forces. When Graef returned to make *Police 2001*, he found the police overstretched and understaffed:

> Each call to the station requires a response, but most of the resulting staff-hours go unlogged, because they don't lead to an arrest. With the police's role being extended to counsel offenders, contain demonstrations, monitor domestic violence and basically wipe the arse of every snot-nosed car-thief in town it was little wonder that there are not enough bobbies on the beat. (Smith 2001:18)

It is a sad commentary that, at a time when the police are experiencing an extension of their powers as well as an unprecedented level of criticism from government and a recruitment crisis, new documentaries on the police offer such a limited and limiting picture of their work. Such television is not good for the media, for the police or for democracy: 'it is . . . vital that the police are not allowed to manipulate public attitudes and to present an image that is largely devoid of accuracy and truth. In respect of all police operations there should be a proper and effective system of police–public consultation and accountability' (Crandon 1995: 226).

Bibliography

ACPO Media Advisory Group (1995) *Release to the Media of Police Held Video Footage: A Practical Guide*, London, ACPO.

Ainsworth, P.B. (1995) 'The police and the media', in P.B. Ainsworth (ed.) *Psychology and Policing in a Changing World*, London, John Wiley & Sons.

Bennett, T. (1990) *Evaluating Neighbourhood Watch*, Aldershot, Gower.

Carter, M. (1998) 'Time for a reality check', *Broadcast*, 18 September, 16–17.

Chibnall, S. (1977) *Law and Order News*, London, Tavistock.

Clarke, A. (1991) *Television Police Series and Law and Order*, Popular Culture Series Unit 22, Milton Keynes, Open University Press.

Cohen, S. (1972) *Folk Devils and Moral Panics*, Oxford, Martin Robertson.

Cohen, S. (1987) *Visions of Social Control*, London, Polity Press.

Crandon, G. (1995) 'Public information management – a comparative analysis of three law enforcement agencies in the State of Texas, USA', *Policing and Society*, 5: 233–47.

Ericson, R.V., Baranek, P.M. and Chen, J.B.L. (1989) *Negotiating Control: A Study of News Sources*, Milton, Keynes, Open University Press.

Ewing, K. and Gearty, C. (1997) 'History of a dog's dinner', *London Review of Books*, 6 February, 7–9.

Fishman, J. (1999) 'The populace and the police: models of social control in reality-based crime television', *Critical Studies in Mass Communication*, 16: 268–88.

Garland, D. (1997) 'Governmentality and the problem of crime', *Theoretical Criminology*, 1, 2:173–214.

Garland, D. (2001) *The Culture of Control: Crime and Social Order in Contemporary Society*, Oxford, Oxford University Press.

Goodchild, S. (1999) 'Club bouncers "taking over" from police', *Independent on Sunday*, 5 December.

Grabe, M. (1999) 'Television new magazine crime studies: a functionalist perspective', *Critical Studies in Mass Communication*, 16: 155–71.

Graef, R. (1989) *Talking Blues: The Police in Their Own Words*, London, Collins Harvill.

Graham, A. (1997) 'Smile, you're on police camera', *Radio Times*, 10 May.

Greater Manchester Police (nd) 'Are you ready for something different? (promotional leaflet for GMP).

Hall, A. (2000) 'Are we really a nation of yobs?' *Observer*, 2 July.

Hall, S., Critcher, C., Jefferson, T., Clarke, J. and Roberts, B. (1978) *Policing the Crisis*, London, Macmillan.

Heidensohn, F. (1989) *Crime and Society*, Basingstoke, Macmillan.

Home Office (1999a) *1998 British Crime Survey (England and Wales): Technical Report*, London, SCPR.

Home Office (1999b) *Government Crime Reduction Strategy*, London, Communications Development Unit.

Home Office (2001) *2000 British Crime Survey (England and Wales): Technical Report*, London, National Centre for Social Research.

Home Office (nd) 'Not everyone can be a police officer. Could you?' London, COI Communications (promotional booklet).

Hurd, G. (1981) 'The television presentation of the police', in T. Bennett, S. Boyd-Bowman, C. Mercer and J. Wollacott (eds) *Popular Television and Film*, Oxford, Oxford University Press.

Johnston, L. (1991) 'Privatisation and the police function: from "new police" to new policing', in R. Reiner and M. Cross (eds) *Beyond Law and Order: Criminal Justice Policy and Politics into the 1990s*, Basingstoke, Macmillan.

Kilborn, R. (1996) 'New contexts for documentary', *Media, Culture and Society*, 18: 141–50.

Langston, B. (2000) 'Not everyone can be a police officer', Report CY 1, Home Office Communications Directorate, London, COI Communications, August.

Lawson, M. (2001) Column, *Guardian*, 'Media' (supplement), 26 February.

Maguire, M., Morgan, R. and Reiner, R. (1997) *The Oxford Handbook of Criminology*, Oxford, Oxford University Press.

Mawby, R.C. (1999) 'Visibility, transparency and police–media relations', *Policing and Society*, 9: 263–86.

Mendoza, N.F. (2000) 'Stupidity gets them nowhere: "America's Dumbest Criminals"', available online: wysiwyg://13/http//tv.zap 2it.com

Nisbet, R.A. (1966) *The Sociological Tradition*, London, Heineman.

Ollins, W. (1988) *A Force for Change: Report on the Corporate Identity of the Metropolitan Police*, London, Metropolitan Police.

Palmer, G. (1999) 'The new spectacle of crime', in D. Thomas and B.D. Loader (eds) *Cybercrime*, London, Routledge.

Pantazis, C. (2000) '"Fear of crime, vulnerability and poverty": evidence from the *British Crime Survey*', *British Journal of Criminology*, 40: 414–36.

Pringle, H. (2000) 'Police ads: an expert's verdict', BBC News Online, available: http://news.bbc.co.uk/hi/english/uk/newsid_902000/902853.stm30/08/2000

Rawlings, P. (1991) 'Creeping privatisation? The police, the Conservative Government and policing in the late 1980s', in R. Reiner and M. Cross (eds) *Beyond Law and Order: Criminal Justice Policy and Politics into the 1990s*, London, Macmillan.

Reiner, R. (1985) *The Politics of the Police*, Brighton, Harvester Wheatsheaf.

Reiner, R. (1991) 'The dialectics of Dixon: the changing image of the TV cop', in R. Reiner and M. Cross (eds) *Beyond Law and Order: Criminal Justice Policy and Politics into the 1990s*, London, Macmillan.

Reiner, R. (1997) 'Policing and the police', in M. Maguire, R. Morgan and R. Reiner (eds) *The Oxford Handbook of Criminology*, Oxford, Oxford University Press.

Riddell, M. (2002) 'Teach us all to be British', *Observer*, 27 January.

Schlesinger, P., Dobash, R.E., Dobash, R.P. and Weaver, C. (1992) *Women Viewing Violence*, London, British Film Institute.

Schlesinger, P. and Tumber, H. (1994) *Reporting Crime: The Media Politics of Criminal Justice*, Oxford, Clarendon Press.

Seddon, J. (2002) A fair cop? Not for the police, *Observer*, 6 January.

Sherwin, R.K. (1999) 'The jurisprudence of appearances: when law plays the media game the media win', paper presented at the conference 'Visible Evidence', University of California at Los Angeles, CA.

Smith, R. (2001) 'The beat generation', *Guardian*, 26 November.

Sparks, R. (1992) *Television and the Drama of Crime*, Milton Keynes, Open University Press.

Stephens, M. and Becker, S. (1994) 'The matrix of care and control', in M. Stephens and S. Becker, *Police Force, Police Service: Care and Control in Britain*, London, Macmillan.

Stevens, J. (2000a) 'Relations with the media: the Metropolitan Police's new policy statement', Editors Inc., available online: www.ukeditors.com/articles/2000/October/Acpo325.html

Stevens, J. (2000b) 'Speaking up for the Met . . . a new policy for relations with the media', available online: www.met.police.uk/mps/press/mediapolicy.htm, 22/09/2000

Thompson, T. (2000), 'Police numbers crash', *Observer*, 9 April.

Walklate, S. (1998) 'Excavating the fear of crime: fear, anxiety or trust?' *Theoretical Criminology*, 2, 4: 403–18.

Wilson, J.Q. (1968) *Varieties of Police Behaviour*, Cambridge, MA, Harvard University Press.

Wilson, J.Q. and Kelling, G. (1982) 'Broken windows: the police and neighbourhood safety', *Atlantic Monthly*, March: 29–38.

Wilson, D. and Ashton, D. (1998) *What Everyone in Britain Should Know About Crime and Punishment*, London, Blackstone Press.

Wykes, M. (2000) *News, Crime and Culture*, London, Pluto Press.

Young, J. (1997) 'Left realist criminology', in M. Maguire, R. Morgan and R. Reiner (eds) *The Oxford Handbook of Criminology*, Oxford, Oxford University Press.

Website addresses

www.policecouldyou

www.met.police.uk

3

Police and the community

The community provides a palatable collective imagery for those aspects of government through individuals that cannot be rendered satisfactorily to the individual level . . . The community as a collective appears as an outcome of private relationships formed through the coalescence of mutual desires articulated with a consultative expert organisation. (O'Malley and Palmer 1996: 148)

This chapter considers programmes which look at community-oriented policing. Once again it will be seen that new discursive formations help create the circumstances in which such programmes are made, understood and responded to. The BBC programmes *Crimewatch, UK, Crimebeat* and *Crime Squad* are discussed as examples of justice at an emotional level where the emphasis is on empathy and spectacle in place of analysis and investigation. In these programmes the police are presented not as instruments of discipline but as agents working with communities to empower them. This is of course not a new departure – the police have often been represented as part of the community. What is different is the greater number of opportunities given to the police to demonstrate their capacity for care as distinct from control, a capacity which according to Reiner (1997) serves as a central legitimising myth of the British police.

Also new is a focus on the *victim*. Crime programming which concentrates on victims reflects a trend to shift the public's attention away from the inexplicable nature of the offender, and his or her social origins, and towards the responsibilities of the community. Television has to be effective in creating a shared sense of community in order for this strand of programming to work. The stronger their feeling of community the more readily will viewers feel the pain of the victim and connect on an emotional plane. Offenders are excluded. Barbara Hudson (2001: 7) sums up the dilemma:

The predatory animal needs to be caged, restricted or at least kept out in the wilderness beyond the bounds of society; it is the fellow-citizen who needs to be re-integrated, re-settled and included. If criminal justice policies are to play their part in the reduction of social exclusion, therefore, the sine qua non is that they should recognize at all times, in all processes and practices, that they are dealing with fellow-citizens.

Before I discuss these programmes it may prove useful to consider how a new discursive formation, including trends in criminology, community policing and debates on citizenship, provides enframing devices.

Crime and the community

As was noted in chapter 2, trends in criminological thinking have shifted so that there is less interest in causes and social origins than in quick solutions: 'Since the mid-1970s legislatures have increasingly reclaimed the power to punish that had previously been delegated to experts, thus reversing the historic pattern that had accompanied the rise of the penal-welfare framework' (Garland 2001: 151).

The new actuarial approach to the problem of crime is sometimes known as administrative, or neo-classical, criminology. This view became popular in the 1980s as a result of the belief that traditional strategies and approaches were ineffectual in reducing crime. The rehabilitation thesis had failed to provide any real solutions to the rise in crime. Public surveys indicated that most people were fearful of crime and disenchanted with wrong-headed 'soft' welfare, social service professionals with vested interests and out of touch liberal elites. What was new in the 1980s and 1990s, according to Garland (2001), was that the experts who had once been responsible for designing these 'liberal' rehabilitation schemes were themselves experiencing, close to their own neighbourhoods and their children's schools, an intimacy with crime uncomfortable enough to inform new and draconian strategies.

Administrative criminology justifies policies by the use of statistics. Crime is made something measurable, calculable, definable. The *British Crime Survey* is a clear example of this – a device designed to provide an accurate picture of crime and which can work also to reassure the public about the true nature of crime (Home Office 1999, 2001). In this way an irrational 'fear of crime' might be effectively countered by presenting people with the facts. An actuarial approach takes a scientific view of crime and combines this with a cost–benefit analysis to measure and monitor behaviour. A typical example of this new strategic thinking is situational crime prevention, an approach which 'rests on two assumptions: that the criminal is a rational decision maker who only goes ahead with a crime where the benefits outweigh the costs or risks; and the opportunity must be there' (Geason and Wilson 1988: 1).

Over the past twenty years, radical shifts in the criminological understanding of victims have entailed a move away from a focus on the social structures that form crime situations to a focus on individuals within communities. The so-called new realism appears to take a public-view approach to crime by focusing on the victim: 'The new realist is concerned to see crime through the eyes of the public; to take what the public defines as a problem as being the points to take. Policy initiatives and suggestions flow from this view of the world' (Walklate 1989: 23).

Another dominant trend in policy thinking in the 1980s and 1990s was to increase the involvement of the community. Under the Tories the claim was made that social disorganisation played an important part in escalating levels of crime. What was needed was for the community to reassert itself as a moral force, as 'active citizens'. A newly enfranchised generation of home-owners created by the boom (and bust) of the 1980s was particularly keen to protect its newly acquired property. Ian Taylor, in a study of south Manchester (1996), pointed to the burgeoning power of suburban social movements whose concern with quality-of-life issues made them a force to be reckoned with. It is the fear of 'encroachment and containment' which frightens these groups.

> In policy discourses 'community' usually denotes the desire to foster close human links within troubled and fragmented populations, within alienating and fragmented bureaucracies and bureaucratic agencies of collective security and external social groups. (Stenson 1993: 373)

'Community' is not a term with an objective denotation, but one that needs to be persuaded to fit policy objectives while also encouraging membership and a sense of belonging. Thus administrative, or neo-classical, criminologists look to *communities* in reducing the costs of crime by involving them in the monitoring of criminal behaviour. The responsible community, integrated with the work of associated inter-governmental authorities, provides the reception context for police programmes.

The Tories' strategy of reinvigorating the community did not involve funding. Indeed between 1979 and 1997 local authorities were starved of precisely those resources which would have helped crime prevention 'if only because it was closest to those who experienced victimisation or high levels of fear of crime' (Loveday 1998: 113). Nevertheless, the community was evoked in rhetoric and integrated with various multi-agency strategies, such as Neighbourhood Watch, to fight crime alongside lawyers, interest groups and the police. Police consultative committees were set up to 'allow general policies to be adapted to meet identified needs in the light of the expressed wishes of the local community (Home Office 1985: 3).

Local newspapers often lead on stories which either praise or abuse the local council work's in the community. One recent example of a council's efforts to help the disadvantaged involved the use of tiny surveillance cameras to spy on problem landlords. 'The equipment, including miniature cameras and telephone microphones, was bought by Manchester City Council 12 months ago to investigate allegations of harassment and illegal eviction by private sector landlords' (Palmer 1998: 9). So successful was this initiative that other councils are now considering adopting the same measures. In such ways are communities of interest formed. As Geason and Wilson (1989: 9) put it:

> The general public's apathy about self-protection arises mainly from ignorance of the means of protection, and a perception that some-body else – 'the Government' or insurance companies – bears most of the cost of theft and vandalism. The community is beginning to realise however that crime levels are rising despite increasing penalties, that the judicial system cannot cope, and that it is the individual who eventually foots the bill for crime through increased taxes for expanded police forces and more jails and through increased insurance premiums.

When it took office in 1997 New Labour was determined to follow its election promises to be 'tough on crime, tough on the causes of crime'. Since then, a series of policies have been enacted which are indeed tough in terms of sentencing, and the prison population has undergone an alarming expansion under New Labour. But it is more difficult to see what has been achieved in terms of tackling the root sources of crime. Nevertheless the policy of community involvement established by the Tories remains significant under New Labour. Home Secretary David Blunkett (2001: 18) is as insistent on the central significance of the community to crime limitation as were any of his predecessors: 'To successfully bring down crime the community must be part of the solution. We must all play our part and work together – government, local authorities, police, community groups and individual citizens.'

Citizenship has been recognised as a priority by New Labour, which signalled its desire to reaffirm the principles of citizenship at the heart of national life in its declaration, in February 1999, that citizenship lessons would be compulsory in all secondary schools by 2002. Debate around citizenship was also sparked by Blunkett's toying with definitions of 'Britishness' when he spoke of helping people newly arrived in Britain to commit 'to the family and draw that out into the wider community so that people can identify with their neighbourhood and, ultimately, their country' (quoted in Gerard 2002: 5).

But how is citizenship to be articulated to adults, especially in a climate where this concept is poorly defined? Mrs Thatcher had a clear idea of how the 'active citizen' could engage in good citizenship in a private capacity. As Hall and Held (1990: 174) pointed out: 'In this discourse citizenship is detached from its modern roots in institutional reform, in the welfare and community struggles, and rearticulated with the more Victorian concepts of charity, philanthropy and self-help.'

One of the ways in which the good citizen can demonstrate commitment to the community is by responding to government's appeals for information. It is the good community member who phones in suspicions of a neighbour who might or might not be working fraudulently. Campaigns targeting cheating rail users, TV-licence dodgers and other defecting consumers request that community members exercise responsibility by identifying the transgressors. In the winter of 2001 the British police announced a new initiative: those who suspected car-drivers of having imbibed more alcohol than legally permitted were encouraged to ring Crimestoppers to report such irresponsible behaviour.

> One of the central concerns of the police agencies, and indeed other agencies of social regulation within a liberal framework, is the attempt to create citizens who are reflective and self-policing, behaving in ways which are broadly acceptable to a range of authorities. (Stenson 1993: 375)

Such campaigns spread policing functions throughout the community. By framing their appeal for co-operation so that the transgressor is seen to be endangering *our* lives or stealing from *us*, community members are offered opportunities to exercise a righteous sensibility.

The definitions of 'community' presented in such public appeals enframe those made by community-oriented programmes about the police. For factual crime programming to succeed it has to marshal the efforts of the viewers so that they feel part of one of these communities. Community is defined here by function and is made to come into existence around certain acts, certain types of individual, certain crimes. Moreover, the increasingly interactive nature of television – its email, phone-in and vox pops functions – all help substantiate television producers' claim to be working in the public interest for 'the community'.

At the heart of the ideal community is the active citizen willing to involve himself or herself in the community's affairs – via the phone. Programmes such as *Crimewatch, UK*, *Crimebeat* and *Crime Squad* give this individual the opportunity to exercise commitment to the community while, via the anonymity of the telephone, protecting his or her identity. The reward is the apprehending of wrong-doers and a sense of having done his or her duty. Such a response is entirely in keeping with neo-liberal reform strategies to help the community 'take on greater moral and practical responsibility for the prevention and control of crime' (Stenson 1993: 383). In sharing the concerns of the authorities these individuals take part in the processes of governance. As law-abiding citizens they heed the exhortation to patrol the conduct of suspect others. In this way surveillance shapes the community.

> And as in our own lives, so with the assistance of the media, in the public domain, where we extend our anger to external representations of the things we refuse to accept in ourselves. (Upton 2000: 20)

The shifting emphasis of crime programmes

The three programmes on which I focus here – *Crimewatch, UK*, *Crimebeat* and *Crime Squad* – were developed in the 1980s and 1990s. Their shift of emphasis from social structures to individual citizens is enframed by the wider debate on the meaning of community. Each programme was produced at the BBC and as such also provides us with an example of how the corporation served the public service ideal during a troubled period of its history. How the different kinds of surveillance featured in *Crimewatch, UK* work to fashion the community is one focus. In discussing *Crimebeat* it will be seen how foregrounding the victim becomes a way of focusing the will of the community. In considering the most recent of the three series, *Crime Squad*, how situational crime prevention contributes to the making of the community becomes apparent. In all three programmes the community has a role to play which involves patrolling their boundaries and highlighting the criminal as a defective individual.

> A person who commits a crime, says Ferri, is a criminal: that is to say, a person whose psychic and moral constitution is not normal. There is no point in searching for the motive of his or her act: the reason for the crime is, precisely, the person's criminality. (Pasquino 1991: 236)

Calling for help: *Crimewatch, UK,* surveillance, community, citizenship

> 'To Hell with the criminal. What about the poor bloody victim?' (Chafer quoted in Schlesinger and Tumber 1994: 254)

> What is taking place here is an updating of a paternalistic public service discourse to include a more democratic selection of topics and voices outside the traditionally defined areas of public interest. (Bondebjerg1996: 36)

Direct appeals to the public for help in solving crime have been broadcast in the UK since the mid-1960s when Shaw Taylor introduced *Police Five* with the simple aim of asking the public to help the police with their enquiries. The simple format of the bulletin made it closer to a public service announcement than a television programme. The five-minute bulletin was presented by Taylor for more than twenty years.

During the 1970s, crime began to gain a separate space of its own in regional news programmes. These short segments provided regional police forces with a platform from which to appeal for the public's assistance in relation to particular crimes. There is no hard data on the success of these appeals in terms of viewer response, but they continued to feature in news programmes at least once a month. By the 1990s most regional stations in the UK had their own thirty-minute monthly crime programme.

There were also the Crimestoppers' short (half-minute and one-minute) appeals concerning particular criminal incidents. Although Crimestoppers, a registered charity which was set up in New Mexico in 1976, is often mistaken for a 'real' police initiative, it is not actually part of any police force, though it does pass on to the police information from the public. So important and useful has Crimestoppers proven over the years that the organisation is advertised on police vans. Crimestoppers offers callers complete confidentiality because not all members of the public wish to be involved directly with the police.

The direct mode of address was a common feature of crime documentaries and news programmes of the time, and was effective in representing crime as a close and real threat to the community. Citizens are told that they can make a difference by phoning in and reinvigorating the community.

In 1982 the BBC took these appeals to the public a step further when it launched *Crimewatch, UK*, which has become the best-known and most enduring of all the 'call-in crime' programmes. It operates by forging a bond between the police and the public. The show featured Nick Ross with co-host Sue Cook who was later replaced by Jill Dando until her murder in 1999. The current co-host is newsreader Fiona Bruce. *Crimewatch, UK* airs, now as then, once each month, usually on Thursdays at 9.30 p.m. The fifty-minute programme is followed by an 'Update' some thirty minutes later where the usefulness of the information phoned in can immediately be reported. *Crimewatch, UK* has run every month for twenty years and has become an important part of the BBC's public service mission.

Ross and his co-host are joined by regular police officers as well as the officers investigating the month's big crime. In using the same people every effort is made to give the impression of order and stability in the fight against crime. The set has not changed much over twenty years. The backdrop is featureless but for some desks and chairs where officers can be seen taking calls. Action and order are apparent. The voices in the background make it clear that members of the public are communicating with the police, so the programme is demonstrably 'working'. The 'Updates' endorse the claim of the presenters that information is coming in fast and action is being taken even as we watch. This plain and simple format aims to inspire us to join the community of concerned viewers.

Crimewatch, UK's format is now well-established: an introductory menu featuring the incidents which will follow; a 'rogues gallery' of faces in the 'e-fit'; a selection of CCTV clips; a discussion with officers of a certain crime or series of crimes; and, the centre-piece of the programme, dramatic reconstructions of particular crimes such as a rape or an armed robbery.

Two regular features of the show – the e-fit and the reconstruction

– merit special mention because of the way they tie in to current discourses on criminality and the role of the community. While they appear modern both recall older methods used by the police to jog the memory of the public.

Crimewatch's update of the photo-fit – the e-fit – recalls a time in the early days of photography when its practice was quickly assimilated by the police as one of its many mechanisms for measuring the criminal. Photography was written into a scientific discourse which was seeking to define the physical characteristics of the criminals. As such photography was part of the new disciplinary mechanisms for marking the criminal type.

> Photography as such has no identity. Its status as a technology varies with the power relations invested in it. Its nature as a practice depends on the institutions and agents which define it and set it to work. Its function as a mode of critical production is tied to definite conditions of existence, and its products are meaningful and legible only within the particular currencies they have. (Tagg 1994: 63)

Tagg here reminds us that photography can be adapted to make sense within certain discourses. The photo-fit and now Crimewatch's e-fit arrive before us with a particular history. The deviant code is already there in the framing. Although the individuals in *Crimewatch, UK* may be innocent until proven guilty, by presenting them in the e-fit they become instantly guilty: 'This is not the power of the camera but the power of the local state which deploys it and guarantees the authority of the images it constructs to stand as evidence or register a truth' (Tagg 1994: 64).

The reconstructions, the most expensive part of the programme, are very much the centre-pieces. The police have a long history of using 'official' reconstructions to jog the public's memory by restaging crimes in the original location. The *Crimewatch* team gains a great deal of access to police information here because of the value of publicity.

> According to the journal *Police Review*, concern about the use of dramatic reconstructions to jog the public's memory and at the same time 'entertain' the majority was allayed by the mutual formulation (by ACPO and *Crimewatch*) of two basic ground rules: first that anything filmed would be embargoed and could not be used again unless the force involved gave its permission; and second that the police must reveal all the known facts and their suspicions to the *Crimewatch* team – then the two parties must make a mutual decision about what is to be shown to the public. (Schlesinger and Tumber 1994: 255)

Such reconstructions are a complex and relatively expensive feature of programme making, involving the panoply of drama – actors and crew, locations, drama production personnel. In many ways the reconstruction is a mini-drama–documentary. But what is significant here is that such reconstructions present the community as a stable, integrated group of people held together by routine. Crime, in such reconstructions, is committed by *outsiders*, by those who have no place in the routines of community members. On the audio track real-life participants are heard to make comments such as 'X didn't look right' or 'Y usually delivered the bread on Thursday and anyway the van was making too much noise'. The point of reconstructions is that they define crime as a break in the community's routine.

In reconstructing such crimes the producers are using a mixture of techniques which demonstrate the virtues of surveillance. Actual CCTV footage of crimes is sometimes available and gives the programme a realistic edge. But in the reconstructions these fragments of the taken-for-granted represent what David Sibley (1997) has called organic surveillance. This unspoken but dimly understood 'feel' for a neighbourhood seems realistic because it is grounded in character and, unlike CCTV, arises from the residents themselves. Such a mix serves the aim of showing how both types of surveillance can and do work together. Even the fact that the crime can be reconstructed is testimony to how community surveillance can be made to work. Given its proven power in helping to identify perpetrators of crimes it becomes harder to regard CCTV as an alien technology implanted by remote authorities.

Crimewatch, UK demonstrates its value just thirty minutes after the main transmission when the hosts announce in the 'Update' how many people have called in with information. The programme attracts an audience of at least 7 million – a very respectable figure for the time of day. And it seems reasonable to assume that a percentage of these viewers transform into callers during the show and its immediate aftermath, especially after the passionate exhortations of the host to call in. The active audience beloved of television's ethnographers of the 1980s and 1990s here becomes involved in community policing via direct action – checking out the neighbourhood, phoning in their suspicions, etc.

These discourses stress that the 'community' needs to apprise the police of the services it requires in its specific locale, and needs to advise 'its' police on what are locally regarded as problems of order and security, and stress a correlative adaptability and accountability of police to local communities. (O'Malley and Palmer 1996: 142)

Such is the appetite for programming of this type that various *Crimewatch, UK* spin-offs have been attempted – the most obvious example of which is its sister programme *Crimewatch Daily* which sometimes emerges for a two-week block during which it is broadcast for an hour every weekday at 9 p.m. The format of this programme does not radically differ from *Crimewatch, UK*'s, although it features very few of the expensive reconstructions. It is clear that the information which might be gained here would depend on the kind of familiarity that many home-workers have of their community. It is also worth considering that a lot of daytime television is watched by older people who may have a different understanding of community and may welcome the opportunity of phoning in their suspicions. (This theme will be explored in the next chapter.)

Another way of measuring the impact of *Crimewatch, UK* is to consider how those on the commercial channels have responded to the programme. Perhaps the best-known attempt to ape *Crimewatch, UK* was Michael Winner's *True Crimes* (1992). Winner has had a long association with the police as a patron, and his films have often glorified the actions of the rebellious if righteous individual doing whatever has to be done for his family's safety (*Death Wish*, 1974). Winner's *True Crimes* series had none of the public service interest one might associate with *Crimewatch, UK*. Instead of reasoned requests for help in identifying miscreants, their crimes were recounted or depicted in gruesome detail; and the show quickly came in for criticism because of its gory content. More significantly, because the featured crimes had already been solved, it was asked what purpose was served by showing such material. To some, the programme seemed to be nothing more than propaganda for the police.

Crimewatch, UK does, however, feature some attacks which are at least as horrifically shocking as Winner's material. One could argue that the programme is even more frightening, bearing in mind that the perpetrators of crime are 'still out there' and thus remains an 'evil' in our midst. (This is the sort of language that the presenters use.) By focusing exclusively on the victim and offering little real background to the crimes, offenders are presented as essentialised evil – Evil as Other, as David Garland (1996) has put it. In a study commissioned by the Broadcasting Standards Council, '*Crimewatch, UK* was said by over half of its respondents to "increase" their fear of crime, with one-third saying that it made them feel afraid' (Schlesinger, Dobash, Dobash and Weaver 1992: 39–40). In this light it is interesting to note that when Nick Ross decided to conclude the show with words other than those he invariably used – 'These crimes are very rare ... Don't have nightmares now' – thousands of people are said to have complained. As a result of this the reassuring statement was reinstated. Such reactions tell us a great deal about people's fear of crime, as well as what they feel to be the responsibility of the public service broadcaster to its audience.

The murder of co-presenter Jill Dando on the doorstep of her Fulham home in 1999 occasioned a national outcry. Many press reports blended fear with fact. The cry went out – if someone as high-profile as Dando could be murdered 'in broad daylight', what hope for the rest of us? It was suggested that her role on television as a 'crime-fighter' had been a spur to some aggrieved villain. The killing of such a well-known figure became an occasion to debate the relationship of celebrity and public service. In some ways this made *Crimewatch, UK* more important than ever in uniting the community of law-abiding viewers against 'the others'.

Crimewatch, UK seeks to create or, rather, recreate the community idealistically, and it does so to mobilise citizens for the common good. Nick Ross is explicit on this. In an article written to celebrate *Crimewatch, UK*'s 150th edition he declared:

> Whatever the reasons the police themselves are convinced that *Crimewatch* has improved their image, and because of this the very language of the programme has evolved. In the old days it was always 'they', the police, who were trying to solve crimes. Now we as a community are all in this together. (Ross 1999: 27)

With its comforting blend of well-known presenters and familiar police officers, and its assurances that, although we may have been frightened, at least something is being done, *Crimewatch, UK* is close to the spirit of *Dixon Of Dock Green*, the comforting closing words of which were seen as essential to viewers throughout its twenty-five years on screen.

Crimebeat: victims and offenders

Even if we accept that in the law as in every other domain we are retreating from the precedence of general over individual interest, what is shocking is the rapidity with which the supremacy of the

victim or the bereaved has reasserted itself in the consideration of
crime. In the span of twenty years the call for revenge has begun to
undo the legal intricacies of centuries. (Upton 2000: 20)

Crimebeat began in 1997 on BBC 1 in the prime-time slot of Tuesdays
at 8 p.m. It ran for three series. The programme was hosted by Martyn
Lewis, a popular if rather controversial newsreader who had made
headlines in calling for more upbeat stories in the news.

Crimebeat featured a range of crimes which illustrated the technological capabilities of the police. But its guiding theme, victimhood,
keyed into the policy debates of the time by producing emotion-
centred television with which a prime-time audience was expected to
identify. As Upton (2000: 19) writes, 'for as long as political agendas
are based on focus groups and opinion polls, personal hurt threatens
to become an engine of public policy'. In its use of reconstructions and
its offer to help the public *Crimebeat* can be seen as a concentrated
version of *Crimewatch, UK*.

Crimebeat can be understood in the context of the victim's movement which, beginning in the 1980s, helped to displace interest in the
offender. The media and news indicate that the victim could be any
one of us. His or her hurt is something to which we could all relate. In
the world of *Crimebeat*, victimhood is open to anyone at anytime. As
a result we have to be on our guard against myriad tricksters, huck-
sters and common-or-garden conmen. But *Crimebeat* could avoid the
charge of sensationalism by explaining how to avoid becoming a
victim ourselves. Sometimes this means suggesting that individuals
are not entirely free of responsibility for their victimhood. 'Victim
blaming strategies presume that the key to understanding criminal
victimisation lies in the "precipitative" behaviour of the individual,
the community or the environment' (Walklate 1991: 206).

Crimebeat is never explicit in victim-blaming. It is for the viewers
at home, watching the reconstruction, to decide how inappropriate
the victim's behaviour is. For the most part, we are directed to the suffering of the victim. The context is secondary.

One episode illustrated how vulnerable are the elderly and frail to
con-men and exploitation. Narrator Lewis spoke of ways in which new
technologies could protect their money. The solution offered here is
identity cards of the type which are said to have 'eliminated credit-card
fraud at a stroke' in France. The apprehendion of miscreants through
surveillance technologies is presented here as advance on more tradi-

tional means of protecting people But what is also revealed is the complex web of surveillance technologies. The sinister implications of increasing surveillance do not enter the frame of the programme, and opponents of such measures are rarely given an opportunity to make their case. Instead we are offered a presentation which is uncritical of the police and which suggests, moreover, that those critical of such surveillance policing are in some way 'soft' on crime.

In another edition of *Crimebeat* the focus was victims of crime in the rural communities of Wales. One community's response had been to set up a rural security patrol at a monthly cost of £1,500. As a result crime in the area is now down 20 per cent despite such patrols having no legal status or powers of arrest. But *Crimebeat* suggests that the community has to come together because the police are struggling to patrol their territory with limited resources. There can be successes: environmental detectives are seen using the latest image intensifiers in tracking fish thieves. Without the help of the community, however, crime-detection becomes more difficult.

We are given insight, in one sequence, into a large operation to randomly check vehicles across a wide area of Cumbria. This is seen as tedious work, until one patrol apprehends a group of young men, whose reluctance to comply when asked to get out of a car quickly leads to their arrest. They complain that they are being filmed, and are mocked for being 'camera-shy'. To be shy of being photographed or filmed is now a universal signifier of guilt on television.

In another edition we are shown alarming footage of violence on the railways. Assistant Chief Constable Paul Nicholas of the British Transport Police informs us that the chances of being involved in a violent crime on the railways are '3 million to one'. Nevertheless the item goes on to illustrate that to avoid being a victim people can either form a community of interest, as indicated in relation to Neighbourhood Watch, or to feel safe under the eye of the lens. The police then go on to express their desire for even more CCTV cameras, a desire which is made obvious in the narrative but which is not supported by evidence of its efficacy.

Victimhood and all that it entails is an interesting and complex subject. A new set of commercial factors is acting upon the citizen, one which complicates his or her response to crime. The individual who is robbed might be deterred from reporting it because of the insurance implications. A neighbourhood house vandalised might not be reported because the owners do not wish the incident to reflect on the area and so drive down the price of property – this is one reason why they use private security firms to patrol and protect their properties.

Unfortunately the complexities of victimhood are unlikely to appeal to producers looking to maximise audiences at peak-time. In their place we are offered an emotional response to crime with practical assistance helpfully appended and extended in a free booklet.

Crimebeat presents us with a figure who might be described as *homo criminalis* (Pasquino 1991). The figure has easily distinguishable features. In the vast majority of cases he is male and seen acting in a hostile manner. His natural habitat is the city where he is apprehended by grainy CCTV cameras whose inability to render him in anything but black and white only serves to make him more alien. He is usually silent, but if he does sound it is to issue instructions or to make threats. This frightening, disconnected figure is made into a signifier of urban *angst*. It is only by reconnecting him to us, the watching community, that we can both control and humanise him. It is only by establishing connections that he, and the world of crime he represents, will be brought within the circuit of the law, to be governed, and we can avoid becoming victims.

> The sanctification of victims also tends to nullify concern for offenders. The zero-sum relationship that is now assumed to hold between the one and the other ensures that any show of compassion for offenders, any invocation of rights, any effort to humanise their punishments can easily be represented as an insult to victims and their families. (Garland 2001: 143)

Crime Squad: being helpful

> Governing as an interactive perspective is directed at the balancing of social interests and creating the possibilities and limits of social actors and systems to organise themselves. (Kooiman and van Viet quoted in Newman 2001: 15–16)

We have seen how in *Crimewatch, UK* and *Crimebeat* viewers are asked to become involved in community policing by phoning in their suspicions or by learning how technology can prevent them from becoming victims. *Crime Squad* advances the notion of citizenship in a more dynamic and proactive process.

It has already been noted that multi-agency approaches to crime were designed to extend policing to a public whose knowledge of their communities would represent a sort of expertise for collective use. *Crime Squad* continues this work of empowering the community by offering a variety of techniques and procedures to assist us in policing our conduct.

It was during the first New Labour administration in 1999 that BBC first broadcast *Crime Squad*. The programme aired at 7.30 p.m. on Tuesday nights on BBC1 in the slot usually reserved for consumer items. Its audience averaged 3.2 million.

The format of *Crime Squad* is similar to that of *Crimewatch, UK*. It features an esteemed public figure (Sue Lawley) who introduces a menu of items at the top of the show. However, the credits introduce the four expert presenters as 'characters' who are seen dynamically going about their work in the fight against crime. Each programme usually features four segments, giving each presenter an 'item' to front. Two police officers feature in the opening credits as well as a young and highly telegenic barrister Jess Radford and a former prison governor, now an academic, Professor David Wilson. It is interesting to note that one police officer is black and the other an attractive young woman – in an earlier series both of the featured police officers were black, which seems an almost unbalanced over-compensation for a force which has great difficulty in recruiting from the ethnic communities, though this may be an attempt by the producer to represent multi-cultural Britain. In this way *Crime Squad* is a model of the kind of co-operative expertise so badly needed to combat crime.

Rather than being studio based, Crime Squad is focused on a number of locations – such as a street for surveillance issues, a neighbourhood for vandalism and a nightclub for security matters – around which the programme's themes are developed. The *Squad*'s members show us how they work as a crime-fighting unit and in doing so illustrate that policing is a highly complex activity that involves the expertise of agencies beyond those staffed by police officers. 'Crime reduction was not solely the responsibility of the Home Office but a concern of central government departments. At a local level, so the argument ran, all agencies had a part to play, not only the police' (Pease: 1994: 686).

Episodes feature a mix of items, from testing herbal remedies (for their efficacy and compliance with regulations) to fingerprinting. What makes the programme distinctive, however, is its focus on crime *prevention*.

Crime Squad's focus on crime prevention reflects the belief that criminal behaviour – from victimisation to theft – can be controlled. If we can at least predict criminal behaviour, then we can manage our own risk in relation to it. To that end, a series of statistics and other survey results are presented. The more accurate our picture of criminal behaviour the better informed will be our efforts at prevention.

The police have mixed feelings about crime prevention initiatives. While there is a realisation that, in the long term, they may be of use, they are not given a high priority by many forces. Much of this lack of enthusiasm can be put down to the fact that it is not easy to show successes in the prevention of crime, and the demonstration of success is increasingly important in a managerial culture where everything has to be quantified.

The producers of *Crime Squad*, however, have realised that crime prevention is something that the public should know more about. The challenge is how to illustrate crime prevention and interest viewers at the same time. By demonstrating on screen the value of a particular strategy, the producers are involving the public in the efforts of the police to reduce crime, as well as giving the police an opportunity to present their 'human' face.

Perhaps the most significant distinguishing feature of *Crime Squad* is that it looks at crime from a perspective which envisages the viewer as both citizen and consumer. In subtle ways, such as in product-testing steeringwheel locks, it differentiates those with the resources to purchase their way out of danger. *Crime Squad* addresses the consumer–citizen. In this model crime can be prevented by investing in a range of technical solutions, as well as by bonding with the community. It is no accident that the programme occupies the slot usually reserved for consumer programmes such as *Watchdog, UK*.

Crime Squad's typical criminal operates by 'rational choice' theory, according to which

> offenders seek to benefit themselves by criminal behaviour . . . [which] involves the making of decisions and of choices, however rudimentary on occasion these processes might be, and . . . these processes exhibit a measure of rationality, albeit constrained by the limits of time and ability and the availability of relevant information. (Pease 1994: 664)

Thus *Crime Squad* is less about sensational crime than it is about individuals exploiting opportunities the public provides by insufficient care. The criminals here are not monsters. There are no reconstructions, no scary photo-fits. This is not simply a function of its 7.30 p.m. scheduling. *Crime Squad* does not posit some dark 'Criminal as Evil' but suggests a more mundane individual whose law-breaking 'tendencies' can be curbed or thwarted by wary householders working together and by investing in certain technologies.

In its drive to help the audience fashion more efficient responses to criminal activity, *Crime Squad* is firmly located in the field of new administrative criminology. In this new perspective situational crime prevention coupled with rational choice theory are the dominant elements. If opportunism is a feature of much criminal behaviour, then *Crime Squad* works by empowering viewers to reduce the opportunities they provide. As citizens–consumers we are empowered by the programme to reduce these opportunities.

The public service ideal lingers in the presence of officially sanctioned experts like Wilson and Radford. The producer of the series is anxious to illustrate that the programme is very different from shows on ITV such as *Rat Trap*. He makes it clear that the BBC would never use criminals to take part in the series. Furthermore he believes that the show has a positive value in that it provides practical aid to the viewers, an objective not always evident in ITV's crime programmes (Savage 2000: 1).

What *Crime Squad* shares with *Crimebeat* and *Crimewatch, UK* is its advocacy of increased surveillance. But, in directing so many items at the nuclear family and at those able and prepared to invest in the security measures it advocates, *Crime Squad* differentiates between groups of consumer–citizens:

> Of course what this kind of argument tends to forget is that user pays models generally disadvantage the poor. In keeping with the tendency to abandon social justice, crime preventionism – through the progressive under development of public sector services – tends to leave the weak to fend for themselves. (O'Malley 1992: 272)

Conclusion

Social historians remind us that, prior to the institution of organised policing and other instruments of authority, communities managed crime themselves. Wrong-doers within a community were punished by various processes which held the people together in mutually constricting bonds. To an extent, those same processes are at work still, today, in some inner-city communities, and they remain one of the more stubborn features of life in parts of Ulster. Such communities are held together by nothing other than mutual fear.

Britain's underclasses live in communities which have long been abandoned by the police. It seems they have also been abandoned by documentary-makers. These were the communities that felt the force of the Police and Criminal Evidence Act of 1984, legislation by which police officers were empowered to stop and search at will, though it also worked to stem the flow of information from the public to the police. Thus, gradually, low-level surveillance and informal links between police and community were replaced by high-profile and military-style policing (Kinsey, Lea and Young 1986). Rather than marshalling the community against crime, the heavy-handed use of 'stop-and-search' tactics has infuriated a great number of people, many of whom could have provided useful information to the police.

Although the three series discussed above are BBC productions, they are also programmes determined by market forces. They have survived because they have maintained their audiences. But their representations of the offender are as shallow as any being offered on the commercial stations. The criminals featured here have all the depth the market will stand. In keeping with policy objectives which bind the community and exclude the offender, the criminal becomes barely worthy of discussion.

Each of the series has presented a picture of the police as public servants doing their best to work in and for the community. If public confidence in the police is nearing crisis point, as Reiner suggests, then such factual programming is doing what it can to counter such disquiet.

> Community policing recognizes that such open control may be counter-productive and seeks to penetrate communities to break down community resistance, to engineer consent and support for the police and to reinforce social discipline. (Gordon 1987: 141)

It is the mode of address adopted by these programmes that invites the community to adopt such social discipline, to make it one of our choices.

These positive representations of the police are the best example of the new rapport between police and media. Police press officers, in tandem with an increasingly media-savvy ACPO, are making full use of the opportunities offered by public service broadcasters to boost the image of the force. For their part, producers are anxious not to endanger such close contacts within the police, for while they have this relationship they still have access to footage with the potential to generate high ratings.

Fundamental questions still have to be asked of the police, whether or not we retain our faith in the public service mission of the media. The police are part of the authority structure. They are able to control what information is distributed and how. Has the development of a market-led broadcast environment made unviable the very idea of critique? This would at least explain why pertinent criticisms of the police come only via dramatic representations.

New Labour continues to give rhetorical force to the notions of community and citizenship articulated by the Tory administrations of 1979–97. Tony Blair is said to have been influenced by a new communitarianism which makes its appeal to 'real people in specific bounded communities, rather than abstract notions of liberty and individual rights, thus its strong conservative appeal' (Hughes 1996: 20). As Etzioni has remarked: 'Communitarians call to restore civic virtues, for people to live up to their responsibilities and not to merely focus on their entitlements, and to shore up the moral foundations of society' (quoted in Hughes 1996: 21).

Recent Home Office research has concerned itself with strategies for crime reduction and with measures by which the community can be empowered. The Social Exclusion Unit at least acknowledge the difficulties New Labour faces in re-invigorating our communities. While the majority of communities may be assisted, there will be those that are left behind. As was noted in chapter 2, the police are sometimes outnumbered 'on the ground' by private security operations. Here the role of the police may be weakening because of their limited resources and changing tactical emphases. As Stenson (1993: 385) comments:

> [W]ith limited resourcing for the state police, the growth of commercial and community based policing strategies based on little commitment to any conception of a public interest or public sphere and sharpening conflicts between groups, there may be increased pressure on the police to align with pro-active initiatives from well-organized groups who have their own regulatory agendas.

Bibliography

Blunkett, D. (2001) 'Blunkett to "mobilise" the country to cut crime' (column), *Howard League Magazine*, 19, 3: 3.

Bondebjerg, I. (1996) 'Public discourse/private fascination: hybridization in "true-life-story" genres', *Media, Culture and Society*, 18, 1: 27–55.

Clarke, P.B. (1994) *Citizenship*, London, Pluto Press.

Evans, K., Fraser, P. and Walklate, S. (1996) 'Whom can you trust? The politics of "grassing" on an inner-city housing estate', *Sociological Review*, 44, 3: 361–80.

Garland, D. (1996) 'The limits of the sovereign state', *British Journal of Criminology*, 36, 4: 445–71.

Garland, D. (2001) *The Culture of Control*, Oxford, Oxford University Press.

Geason, S. and Wilson, P. (1988) *Designing Out Crime*, Canberra, Australian Institute of Technology.

Geason, S. and Wilson, P. (1989) *Crime Prevention: Theory and Practice*, Canberra, Australian Institute of Technology.

Gerard, J. (2002) ''Moving where other citizens fear to tread', *Sunday Times*, 1 February.

Gordon, P. (1987) 'Community policing: towards the local police state?' in P. Scraton (ed.) *Law, Order and the Authoritarian State*, Milton Keynes, Open University Press.

Hall, S. and Held, D. (1990) 'Citizens and citizenship', in S. Hall and M. Jacques (eds) *New Times: The Changing Face of Politics in the 1990s*, London, Lawrence & Wishart.

Home Office (1985) *Guidance on Arrangements for Local Consultation Between the Community and the Police in the Metropolitan Police District*, London, Home Office.

Home Office (1999) *1998 British Crime Survey (England and Wales): Technical Report*, London, SCPR.

Home Office (2001) *2000 British Crime Survey (England and Wales): Technical Report*, London, National Centre for Social Research.

Hudson, B. (2001) 'Time for joined-up thinking', *Howard League Magazine*, 19, 3: 6–7.

Hughes, G. (1996) 'Communitarianism and law and order', *Critical Social Policy*, 16, 49: 17–41.

Judd, J. (1999) 'Schools to teach citizenship lessons', *Independent on Sunday*, 21 February.

Kinsey, R., Lea, J. and Young, J. (1986) *Losing the Fight Against Crime*, Oxford, Blackwell.

Loveday, B. (1998) 'Local authorities and crime prevention' (review article), *Local Government Studies*, 24, 1: 113–18.

Newman, J. (2001) *Modernising Governance: New Labour, Policy and Society*, London, Sage.

O'Malley, P. (1992) 'Risk, power and crime prevention', *Economy and Society*, 21, 3: 252–75.

O'Malley, P. and Palmer, D. (1996) 'Post-Keynsian policing', *Economy and Society*, 25, 2: 137–55.

Palmer, L. (1998) 'Tenants spy on problem landlords', *Manchester Metro*, 5 June.

Pasquino, P. (1991) 'Criminology: the birth of a special knowledge', in G. Burchell, C. Gordon and P. Miller (eds), *The Foucault Effect: Studies in Governmentality*, Hemel Hempstead, Harvester Wheatsheaf.

Pease, K. (1994) 'Crime prevention', in M. Maguire, R. Morgan and R. Reiner (eds) *The Oxford Handbook of Criminology*, Oxford, Oxford University Press.

Reiner, R. (1997) 'Policing and the police', in M. Maguire, R. Morgan, and R. Reiner (eds) *Oxford Handbook of Criminology*, Oxford, Oxford University Press.

Ross, N. (1999) 'You've been nicked', *Radio Times*, 23 January.

Savage, C. (2000) Interview with author.

Schlesinger, P., Dobash, R.E., Dobash, R.P. and Weaver, C. (1992) *Women Viewing Violence*, London, British Film Institute.

Schlesinger, P. and Tumber, D. (1994) *Reporting Crime: The Media Politics of Criminal Justice* Oxford, Oxford University Press.

Sibley, D. (1997) *Geographies of Exclusion*, London, Routledge.

Stenson, K. (1993) 'Community policing as a governmental technology', *Economy and Society*, 22, 3: 373–89.

Tagg, J. (1994) *The Burden of Representation*, London, Macmillan.

Taylor, I. (1996) 'Fear of crime, urban fortunes and suburban social movements: some reflections from Manchester', *Sociology*, 30, 2: 317–37.

Upton, J. (2000) 'Crimewatch, UK', *London Review of Books*, 22, 18: 19–21.

Walklate, S. (1989) *Victimology: The Victim, the Criminal and the Criminal Justice Process*, London, Unwin Hyman.

Walklate, S. (1991) 'Victims, crime prevention and social control', in R. Reiner and M. Cross (eds) *Beyond Law and Order: Criminal Justice Policies and Politics into the 1990s*, Basingstoke, Macmillan.

Walklate, S. and Evans, K. (1999) 'Zero tolerance or community tolerance? Police and community talk about crime in high crime areas', *Crime Prevention and Community Safety*, Leicester, Perpetuity Press.

Worrall, A. (1997) *Punishment in the Community: The Future of Criminal Justice*, Harlow, Longman.

4

Local policing

> Crime acts as a surrogate for the failed social contract, offering instead the criminal contract; the imaginary space where crime is fought and vanquished . . . membership of the community is bought through fear of crime. (Young 1996: 4)

This chapter discusses the ways in which programmes about local crime, in particular Granada's *Crimefile*, seek to fashion the north-west community of England around concern over crime. The programme is seen as part of the process of governance in which the interests of the State and those of the individual are made to coalesce against the figure of the criminal. The discussion extends the notion of governance by looking at the work of the local press, in this case the *Manchester Evening News*, in shaping England's north-western community. I look in particular at the way in which the newspaper activates shame in the attempt to mobilise the community against individuals. In short: how do the local media bring the watching and reading community to an understanding of and an empathy with the law?

Crimefile

> The net of social control is thus thrown ever wider into the community, its thinner mesh designed to trap even smaller 'fish'. Once caught in the net, the penetration of disciplinary intervention is ever deeper, reaching into every aspect of the criminal's life. (Worrall 1997: 125)

Crimefile is produced by Granada, a company which has transformed itself over the past ten years from a purveyor of high-quality dramas and current affairs programmes into a multinational company with powerful interests in many areas.

Legend has it that Sydney Bernstein named Granada after his

favourite holiday resort. He chose to invest in the north-west of England because he believed its high rate of rainfall would ensure large stay-at-home audiences for his programmes. Granada's was one of the first commercial licences awarded, in 1955, and the company is the only one to have retained its licence from that time.

Granada soon established itself as one of the premier news and drama providers on the ITV network. It was behind *Coronation Street* and pioneered news and current affairs in series such as *World In Action*. Granada was bold in experimenting with new writers, and was responsible for much that was innovative and exciting in British television in the 1960s and 1970s.

The company continued to enjoy high-profile successes in the 1980s with classic dramas, *Jewel In The Crown* being one example, and gained prestige from its production of documentary–dramas like *Who Bombed Birmingham?* In the early 1990s, however, Granada's other business interests began to change the focus of its television work. The appointment of businessman Gerry Robinson to head the company in 1990 was greeted with surprise within the broadcasting community, though it was received rather better by the City, where Granada's share price began to rise. Soon after the resignation of David Plowright it was apparent that the 'old guard' would have to be replaced, and a new set of managers were appointed.

Granada now took a more robust attitude to 'the bottom line' and was soon axing those programmes which failed to attract the requisite number of viewers. Probably the best-known casualty of this time was *World In Action*, which was dropped because it was not generating enough viewers at prime-time on Monday evenings. Many industry commentators saw this as signifying the onset of the decline not just of Granada but of the documentary genre. Many of the old guard remain productive there, but can be depended upon to fire broadsides at a managerial culture which is said to be squeezing out programme-makers. It is noteworthy that the Campaign for Quality Broadcasting is led by former editor of *World In Action* Ray Fitzwalter.

Nevertheless, from a business perspective Granada is a very successful company. Its share value has risen more or less consistently over the past ten years. After a series of takeovers and mergers, it is now one of the two most powerful players in Britain's ITV network – and the one 'tipped' to take over the network when the rules on ownership change to allow a merger with Carlton. While Granada still produces award-winning drama, it is also responsible for the Men and

Motors channel – a programming strand that is as far distant from the high points of *World In Action* as can be readily imagined – but nevertheless maintains an impressive and cost-effective share of the market.

When the ITV franchises were awarded there was a clause which stipulated that the winning company had to demonstrate a commitment to the region. Granada expresses this commitment via its work with the local community and in schemes such as the Granada Education Partnership. It also serves the region through news and other programming.

Granada's *Crimefile* began life as a five-minute item within the regional news at 6.30 p.m. once a week. In this small feature viewers were presented with some details concerning local crimes and ways in which they could help identify the perpetrators. The popularity of this item persuaded the editor Sue Woodward to develop the segment into a programme. Another important factor in this development was her belief that five minutes was not sufficient time to 'take the fear out of crime', which was Woodward's understanding of *Crimefile*'s social action brief (Woodward 1998). The thirty-minute show was usually broadcast in the once-monthly regional drop-in slot at 11.10 p.m. on Thursday evenings, though it has recently been moved to 7 p.m. The presenter in So Rahman, a news-anchor at Granada, supported by another of the local reporters and regular crimedesk policewoman Marina Whittle. The format is not unlike that of *Crimewatch, UK*, although it has considerably less resources. Each month a reconstruction is featured; the newsdesk offers five or six crimes, the majority of which feature CCTV; and a section is regularly given over to foregrounding new police technologies. Programmes can include such other items as interviews with officers working on particular cases followed by calls for help, and consumer testing on locks, alarms, etc.

In designing the programme Woodward was anxious to distinguish it from *Crimewatch, UK*. Having noticed *Crimewatch*'s practice of inserting dialogue in the mouths of actors in reconstructions which 'they could not possibly have known', she insists that no dialogue is presented in the reconstructions unless it is factually based – a policy which would seem to restrict opportunities for the emotional involvement that *Crimewatch, UK* generates. Another distinction she made was in terms of viewer response. Woodward believes that many crime programmes trade on fear while doing nothing to help the viewer to move beyond fearfulness. In her view such programmes are entertainment barely disguised as public interest. *Crimefile*, with its primary objective of empowering viewers, was to be different. Indeed, in the course of a forty-minute interview with Sue Woodward, 'empowerment' was used seven times: 'This is not an entertainment programme. It's about empowerment . . . the feeling that [viewers] can do something . . . [We present] useful information . . . [to] empower the viewer' (Woodward 1998). Woodward's main aim with *Crimefile* is to give the community of viewers the feeling that people *can* do something. This aim is directly tied to Granada's social action project, which has community assistance as a specific objective.

How then does *Crimefile* reach the community? Woodward's use of 'empowerment' is interesting. The word was formerly associated with oppositional politics, more specifically the politics of identity, being concerned with the self-assertion of an individual in challenging an identity with which he or she feels uncomfortable. The talk-show was the television arena *par excellence* where such endeavour was highlighted and sometimes achieved. It is interesting to note how the word's meaning has lost its oppositional force (Shattuc 1997). Those on the right now use the term to describe the ways in which the 'silent majority' may now reclaim an identity lost under liberalism. Empowerment now permits them to stand-up for traditional values. In this way it is used to align the aims of the authorities with the needs of the free-thinking citizen. Empowerment has now become part of the work of governance.

The problem faced by *Crimewatch, UK* is that it has to build the national community around a few crimes based in different parts of the country. Because it deals only with the north-west region, *Crimefile* is likely to be more successful in targeting suspects. Indeed Woodward is keen to point out that it *is* more successful that *Crimewatch, UK* in terms of helping to clear up crimes, and this is a persuasive commendation of itself to viewers and a means if binding them into a community. The use of local presenters works to the programme's advantage because they are seen to speak directly to the needs of the region rather than as national celebrities.

Woodward believes the choice of presenters to be crucial. In deliberately choosing an Asian newsanchor, the programme sends out the message that it is not always black people who commit crime. Similarly in choosing a policewoman to front the newsdesk Woodward is attempting to break down the belief that police work is a male-only enterprise: she addresses the police with this message in the hope that they will increase their recruitment of women.

Crime committed within our region in a sense *belongs* to us, and *Crimefile* makes it our responsibility. A crime shown here is likely to have a bearing on people in the north-west and so will more readily engender a sense of community. As Rahman puts it: 'These are crimes only *you* have the answer to.' Crime is presented as a violation which can unite us and restore that sense of communality easily forgotten in busy day-to-day life. In the 'Crimedesk' segment, Officer Whittle deals with local crimes, most of which are supplemented with CCTV footage. These cold and harsh images of urban life are emblematic of the atomised community in which citizens are often seen as consumer-machines. The act of phoning in humanises the footage, grants identity to an anonymous figure, and takes the individual from the literally shadowy criminal community and places them within the nexus of the law. Their real origins, their base in families and 'real' communities, now come into play. The result, as we shall see, can sometimes be disastrous.

Woodward says that she chose not to use fear to bond this community. It was an astute choice. As many criminologists have pointed out, fear reduces both people's willingness to help others, as well as the responsibility they feel for their immediate space (Skogan 1990; Davidson and Locke 1992). The emphasis in *Crimefile* is on providing information and forestalling any emotional involvement. The programme realises that to 'shop' an individual is a very dangerous task. Marina Whittle always adds: 'Don't worry – we won't ask for your name.' The type of community that meets here has to remain faceless, just a series of disembodied voices united only by a rekindled sense of responsibility. It can, of course, also be the case that people call in for malicious purposes (falsely accusing someone), but that is an inevitable by-product of what the programme is trying to do. The programme offers a sense of community and the badge of citizenship for the price of a phonecall. Yet, given the wide use of the call-back facility allied to an increasing mistrust of the police, this use of the telephone as a mechanism of community-formation has to work not through the police but through Crimestoppers.

Woodward is very conscious of the complex relationship Granada has with the police. When the idea for the *Crimefile* item was first mooted, in 1991, Woodward encountered considerable mistrust from local police officers. As a result, she organised a meeting with the major police officers of the region at which she made clear her intention to maintain journalistic objectivity while arguing convincingly that *Crimefile* would prove useful to the police. Over the past six years the relationship has developed into one of mutual trust. The incidents featured on *Crimefile* are provided by journalists who encounter them in the normal processes of newsgathering. Only occasionally do the police themselves suggest an item, and when that happens the case is debated by the news team who decide whether or not it is to be aired.

I suggested earlier that *Crimefile* both foregrounds and is implicated in systems of governance. By helping to forge a self-managed community the programme contributes to the policing of the region in complex ways. It may be that *Crimefile* 'works' by activating those communities which the police no longer reach, though it is important to qualify this suggestion. The extent to which the programme 'succeeds', in terms of crime detection and conviction rates, is something beyond the remit of this book. Moreover, there is no suggestion of any collusion between police and journalists. Indeed it is important that both groups are not seen to be working too closely with one another. Granada claims to serve the community, and the police aid them in this. The programme's involvement in crime does not go beyond sending out factsheets. If viewers do have information, then they are recommended to call Crimestoppers (the telephone number appears many times throughout the show). It is only by the viewer making connections, via the call, that these various bodies are co-ordinated. Thus the viewer is made central in the act of forging a community against crime.

Crimefile uses its proximity to the police to demonstrate its contact with legitimate sources, but in displaying journalistic autonomy it stands apart from them and reaches out to the community, the community to which it belongs. Apart from the Crimedesk segment, in which Officer Whittle addresses the viewers, the police communicate to us via the presenter, So Rahman. The interviewee, who never addresses viewers directly, is introduced by Rahman; and, once the interview is over, it is Rahman who offers observations and invites us to phone in. Thus the police are at no point overtly instructing the viewer. The programme helps to bind the community together by extracting the required information from the police and using it to ask the viewer to take the initiative and call in.

The use of shame

The *Manchester Evening News* (hereafter *MEN*) and its associated regional 'freesheets' have a role to play in developing an understanding of crime in the local community. *MEN* is owned by the Guardian

Media Group (GMG). Although representing the more liberal wing of the national press, GMG seems to be part of the arrangements on the 'ownership' of certain areas, owning fourteen titles in the north-west region and easily dwarfing the far-smaller independents. It is curious that such hegemony has never been investigated. *MEN* is edited by Paul Horrocks, who has been with the paper since 1983 and was formerly its crime correspondent. Figures indicate that *MEN*'s sales have declined from 183,543 in 1996 to 170, 346 in 2001 (JICREG 2001). Nevertheless, it remains Manchester's only paid-for newspaper.

The largest free paper in the region (and one of the largest in the country) is *The Metro,* of which Paul Horrocks is also general editor. It has far fewer journalists than *MEN* and relies heavily on advertising (which takes up around 75 per cent of the paper). *MEN* has a direct relationship with its eleven free papers in the region, the total weekly circulation of which comes to 1.3 million copies, considerably greater that the *MEN*'s daily sale.

An understanding of how shame is circulated by these local papers can be gained by looking at the reports which they carry and considering how they may be understood by the various communities of the region.

Franklin and Murphy (1998) argue that the local press used to have a watchdog function in that journalists working close to the parish pump helped to preserve a degree of democratic accountability. However the past decade has seen a 'revolution in the production methods, the distribution and the possibilities for innovation in local and regional press'. In the mid-1990s large corporations bought into the market with the intention of exploiting the local press as profit-making ventures rather than investing in them as media which served the interests of the people.

Glover (1998: 112) contends that 'more than 90% of the British population read a local newspaper of some sort'. Pilling quotes Parkes arguing that 'people generally want to feel part of a community, they want to have some allegiance' (1998: 182). However local paid-for papers have seen a decline in circulation at a time when the free press, while not reaching the heights gained in the early 1990s, remain the most buoyant part of the sector. Whatever the sales, the local press still has an agenda-setting function, one which has inspired comparatively little study.

Significant changes in the ownership of local newspapers took place in the 1990s, one of the consequences of which has been that the new corporate owners see news items as data which can be repackaged and resold to a range of communities. The local journalist is becoming someone who contributes to an electronic database. The role of the specialist fades away as large corporations train journalists to be generalists. An understanding of and an empathy with 'the local' are in decline as lowly paid journalists seek greater remuneration and prestige elsewhere.

Local papers, freesheets in particular, treat readers as citizens *and* consumers. The strategies these papers adopt on crime attempt to mould readers into communities of interest. If journalists are correct when they say that truly 'local' stories increase sales, one can see whence comes this interest in crime. But critics suggest that changes in ownership have meant a decline in the *amount* of news in the local and the free press. Indeed Franklin and Murphy (1998) quote one freesheet editor as saying, anonymously, that his journalists are merely filling in the gaps between the advertisements. While it is true that a great deal of editorial is given over to lightweight stories of one kind or another, crime does play an increasingly important role in these papers.

In the mid-1990s *MEN* under Horrocks's guidance launched a 'shop-a-pusher' campaign, the aim of which was to involve the community in crime detection by asking readers to phone-in the names of those they suspected of dealing drugs. The strategy increased sales and won the support of the police; it also led to many 'dead-ends' and, unfortunately, wrongful arrests.

In 2001 *MEN* built on this strategy by working with local police to name and shame those who were convicted of kerb-crawling. *MEN* made its position clear by giving the police a platform to 'ensure that the identities were given the widest circulation'. The officer leading the new policy was Inspector Mike Schofield. Schofield was given a great deal of space in *MEN* to express his support for paper's stance on shaming. Indeed, the paper showed him with a camcorder in his hand to make the mission clear. Headlines such as 'OUR SHAME BY THE MEN CAUGHT TRYING TO BUY SEX' and 'CLEANING UP STREETS OF SHAME' (10 and 15 January 2001) indicate the intention to utilise the shaming tactic. At the same time, some of the reporting did show sensitivity to the prostitutes' plight. Another contradiction can be seen in the way that other European countries' laws on prostitution and the use of brothels are discussed as examplars of good practice (Swinden 2001). *MEN*'s principal concern, it seems, was with the impact of prostitution on the streets of residential areas. It may have had in mind Manchester's image – perhaps in the light of rising property values in the north-west and the city's hosting of the Commonwealth Games in 2002.

MEN is particularly harsh on those caught 'shopping for sex', reserving its venom for kerb-crawlers. These are precisely the targets of Inspector Schofield's campaign (Taylor 2001). Those arrested were paraded before special magistrates and were featured in the paper leaving court. *MEN* gave personal information on the men, extending their shame to their wives and children (Frame 2001). All of this is done for the public good, of course, and has the full backing of the police.

Shame is an attractive subject for the media because it is very much centred around individuals being put before the community. Such stories readily lend themselves to a dramatic frame, with 'in-built' victims, offenders and families in identifiable communities. Shame allows the media to legitimately reframe criminal acts as moral issues for the law-abiding public to involve itself with. Shame can also be connected to the widening of a technological network, as discussed above, when deployed by authorities to catch people 'in the act'. Shame reminds us of the responsibilities we have to one another, responsibilities which are monitored by community members watching out for each other – Sibley's organic surveillance.

Central to debates concerning social justice is the role of punishment. The right-wing neo-classical view advocates a policy of 'just desserts' in which punishments fit the crime. This perspective has found expression in a variety of ways, such as the dramatic increase in the prison population as well as the public shaming spectacles recommended by some American courts. Those on the left point to the social, economic and environmental factors which shape an offender's criminality. But what both camps are beginning to consider is the value of restoring power to the community through schemes which focus on the healing power of shame.

Writers such as Helen Lynd (1958) and Norbert Elias (1978) have reflected on the factors which have lowered the shame threshold over the past 150 years. While their emphasis differs they agree that as a method of social control shaming is most effective in traditional societies where a high value is accorded to personal relationships. They argue that the more individualistic cultures are characterised by a loosening of societal bonds. Furthermore, the legal process is experienced as a depersonalising process which has more to do with calculation than with morality. The label 'deviant' and the subsequent stigmatisation of its bearer can serve the purpose of creating 'communities' with alternative value systems according to which shame has a positive value in increasing the status of an individual among other law-breaking peers. The majority of law and order strategies fail to capitalise on the value of shame.

What distinguished the *MEN–Metro* coverage was how the shaming stories represented a new challenge to journalistic conventions. Rather than respecting the privacy of individual citizens to deal with 'criminal' status in their own way the papers extend the punishment meted out by the courts by shaming them. In publishing their names and addresses, photographs of them leaving court or police 'mug shots', they help activate a string of associations which can involve an offender's family, employer, friends and associates. *MEN* pursues this policy with a rhetoric which claims to speak on behalf of the community. Indeed, having thought 'long and hard' about this strategy, Horrocks feels that the community does have a role to play in being aware of its wrong-doers and perhaps in monitoring their conduct. Such a policy has a precedent in the *News of the World*'s exposure of paedophiles whose names are on the Sex Offenders' Register which led to several lynchings and vigilante activities across the country.

Since the early 1990s shaming has become the cornerstone of new police practices that reflect what was formerly known as *restorative* justice:

> In brief, this means that a police officer, prior to administering the formal caution, facilitates a discussion of the harm caused by an offence and how the offender might repair it. All those affected by the offence, including any victim, can be invited to attend and participate by explaining how the offence affected them. (Hoyle and Young 1999: 28)

The inspiration for much of this work has come from John Braithwaite. He thinks of such re-integrative justice as the apportioning of sufficient shame to bring home to the individual the seriousness of the offence, but in measures that fall short of humiliating and hardening the offender (Braithwaite 1989). This attempt to reaffirm the emotional interdependence of persons was behind New Zealand's Family Conferencing Act of 1989. This Act enshrined legislation designed to heal the community by creating a forum in which all the participants discuss the human cost of the offence before reparations are made.

The more recent research of Sherman, Strang and Woods (2000) has focused on the Canberra Re-integrative Shaming Experiment

(Rise). Their aim was to develop 'a strong scientific theory and practice of restorative community conferences'. 'Conferencing' is seen to have achieved a high degree of success, with all participants expressing satisfaction that the system dealt with them in a just manner. Furthermore the community is seen to have been restored by these carefully arranged interactions.

In 1999 the UK's Thames Valley Police began to use a restorative policy of shaming in place of cautioning (www.thamesvalley.police.uk). The aim was to transform what has been described as a 'degradation display' into something more constructive. Richard Young has noted how such work involves a considerable shift in the treatment of offenders. The experiment would seem to be a success in that greater general satisfaction is generated than is produced by cautioning.

The turn to shame is not without precursors, such as the victim–offender groups noted earlier which had the modest yet demonstrable effect of helping some victims come to terms with their experience. The Youth Justice and Criminal Evidence Act of 1999 also includes provision for restorative practices. These policies are significant for binding the community. As Young and Goold (1999: 138) have written:

> There is evidence that people obey the law (and co-operate with its agents) partly because they acknowledge legal institutions such as the police to be legitimate. Restorative cautioning sessions constitute important encounters between offenders, other members of the public and the police.

For policies such as shaming to be effective the community has to develop a sense of participation. The shaming function is a way of prompting 'organic surveillance' on the part of the community by encouraging it to take responsibility for its own members. As such it is of a piece with the 'responsibilising' strategies of the 1990s.

Support for restorative justice is gathering. It comes from a range of organisations such as HMP Grendon, the Howard League for Penal Reform and the NSPCC, as well as from those who have experienced the process themselves (www.rjkbase.org.uk). One young offender talks of how he feared conferencing because he knew he would be confronting someone whose understanding of him was derived from the media:

> I wanted her to hear my side of the story, then she could make her own mind up . . . It wasn't just a question of being sorry. I was sorry,

but that wouldn't bring her son back. I wanted her to see what sort of person I was. Not this psychopath that the papers had made out. (Sigler 2000)

David Rose writing in the *Observer* highlighted the dilemma faced by the police in utilising restorative justice. Although 'there is real evidence that it responds to communities' needs', it will do nothing for Thames Valley's detection rate (Rose 2001). The worry expressed by Rose and others investigating the field is that managerial pressures will make restorative justice 'uneconomical' and therefore liable to cancellation. Another reason for concern might be the lack of fit between this new and 'sensitive' policy and existing news paradigms. For example, it is hard to see how *MEN*'s policy of naming and shaming those it considers morally culpable will help the community to rebuild itself and develop a rapprochement with the offender.

Both *MEN* and *Crimefile* give rise to an understanding of criminality the utility of which depends on communities rejecting those who fail to observe their standards. It sometimes happens that the definition of community is contested. 'What greater example of privatisation can we find than the argument that the solution to crime lies in self-control and that self-control is the result of the processes of socialisation of familial institutions without any contextualization of this process?' (Morrison 1995: 460).

On 12 December 1998 the front page of *MEN* featured the McGinty family. Mr and Mrs McGinty had been watching 'a TV *Crimefile*' and had recognised their son on CCTV footage committing an armed robbery. The parents took their son to the police, and as a result had been ostracised by the local community and the family forced to move. As far as *MEN* was concerned these were good parents upholding the rule of the law in an attempt to help their offspring. Indeed the report was headlined 'The Price of Courage'. The local community, however, saw their act as one of betrayal. In this manner are battle lines drawn up between the good and law-abiding and the bad. The story is presented so as to elicit our sympathy. The front page carries a picture of the parents in traditional 'victim' pose, united but alone and now forced to seek a life in a new community. In the middle of the block headline is a colour photo of their son as a child. At the bottom of the page is a blurred still of him 'in action', robbing a shop, from CCTV footage. In this piece alone we can see how the family, the core unit of the organic community, has been broken by lawlessness. This family, led by the father, had sought to use the law to bind together its members. The outlaws are those who choose to live beyond the law, or, rather, within their own law – a sort of north Manchester *omerta*.

This leads us to consider what we know of the viewing community. *Crimefile*, like much other regional programming, is watched mainly by 'older' viewers. The figures indicate a rise in groups over 45 years of age and are highest for those over 65. (It is interesting to note that the readership of *MEN* is also predominantly older.) It may be that this generation has a different relationship with the media than do younger people. The latter are often described as a new media-literate generation with a less trusting view of television. They are growing up in a climate in which documentary fraud is uncovered and they are becoming jaded with the medium. It may be that older people are more ready to trust television, regional television in particular. Their own sense of community was formed under circumstances in which the media played a far smaller role than it does today. We might speculate that is to the media that they are now turning to rebuild this lost ideal, although only further research will clarify this.

What is crucial to the McGinty report, and to so many of the narratives illustrative of the law, is the focus on the victim(s) – a focus, long established in media usage, which serves to engineer an emotional response. New policies such as restorative justice may not lend themselves to such straightforward representation.

Woodward's *Crimefile* does not engage in exploitative presentations of victims in this manner. Her aim is to diminish in viewers' minds the liklihood of their becoming victims and, to some extent, to 'take the fear out of crime'. However Woodward has to work within the logic of mainstream television. It is almost inevitable that any programme on crime will engender some level of fear. It has to be seen in context. Fear can be increased or decreased from a variety of sources external to the medium.

One item from the autumn of 1998 illustrates the dilemma . This segment was designed to increase public awareness of victimisation. It revealed that the group most at risk from attack on the streets are young men. To illustrate this statistic it offered a visual reconstruction over which two young men described their mugging. This was done in 'voice over', according to Woodward's principles, not by way of dialogue. Shown in black and white, the slow-motion approach of the attackers, while artistically satisfying, was nevertheless still frightening. This reconstruction was followed by a short lesson in self-defence involving the presenter and a professional trainer, a vox pop and some words of advice from a psychologist. Here the stated aim was to make it clear that machismo behaviour by the target only exacerbates the violent intent of the aggressor. Perhaps it is only by presenting stereotypes that the programme can challenge them. Yet the segment works within a format which reinforces the view, established by other television programmes, that we have to be on guard against the dangers of criminal behaviour that are all around us. Furthermore, *Crimefile*'s focus on attacks carried out by men on strangers in public reinforces certain stereotypes about criminality, while ignoring both white-collar misdemeanours and violence against women in the private domain (Stanko and Newbury 1994).

Conclusion

According to Downes and Rock (1998: 96), Durkheim suggested that rituals which process and punish crime have a function in constructing a society's morality, promoting cohesion among its members by publicising violations of a given code and, by implication, teaching its members to abide by certain codes. As we have seen, the police and the media have a mutual interest in reaching out to members of the community to gain their trust and support. But at a time when journalists are not held in the highest esteem, and when mistrust of the police may be on the increase as a result of the negative publicity produced by certain high-profile cases, securing public support is no easy task. Yet it is the case still that the media and the justice system constitute two institutions jointly responsible for much of what we learn about the social order. When these two institutions are shown to be acting co-operatively the public is presented with a marriage of moral entrepreneurs which can be very powerful. Alternatively, this collaboration may be seen as an unholy union, and that would provoke a greater degree of mistrust and unease than previously obtained. 'Public knowledge and opinion about criminal justice is based upon collective representations rather than accurate information, upon a culturally given experience of crime rather than the thing itself' (Garland 2001: 158).

Both *Crimefile* and *MEN* are actively working with the police in ways that benefit the interests of all three parties. Although both programme-makers and police are seeking to reach the community, each retains a level of autonomy in the production of the text, an autonomy that each requires in order to generate the respectful co-operation of the community. (It remains to be seen whether this autonomy is perceived as such by the public.) The independence of *Crimefile* is safeguarded by a policy of non-interference on the part of the police, resulting in the production of the triad of community–victim–criminal, which is one of the new trends in criminology discussed in the previous chapter. *MEN* demonstrates less in the way of such critical distance and is more open to providing the police with space in which to express their views. Neither *Crimefile* nor *MEN*, however, expends much effort in considering the contexts of the offences they feature. This approach is perfectly in keeping with a new discursive formation which sacrifices analysis for the spectacle of improper behaviour.

Crimefile and *MEN* work in circuits of governance by providing lessons about appropriate behaviour within moral and legal frameworks. In looking at the co-operation between police and media we engage with what Goode and Ben-Yehuda (1994) call 'interestgroups', those on the middle rungs of power and status hierarchies who have an independent stake in bringing their chosen issues to the fore. These interests express themselves in the material generated by the relationship between police and the *MEN–Crimefile* teams which takes place within a culture of management. In this way shame becomes a tool of organisation. The shaming campaigns of Granada, via *Crimefile*, and *MEN* seek to define good citizenship in ways which have a high degree of fit with governmental and other licenced authorities' interests, as well as those of the commercial sector. Self-management becomes a matter for individuals and communities, and it is this unity that we are asked to key into by responding. In this model shaming is a tool of sound (self-)governance which, in turn, links to responsible citizenship. Self-management 'refers to the targeting of population as an object of government at both the collective and individual levels, in order to foster human wealth, economic efficiency and so on . . . the management of persons in relation to each other' (Stenson: 1993: 379).

One of the reasons why schemes such as re-integrative shaming are taken seriously by New Labour is that they fit in with its understanding of how a community should be empowered. This in turn connects to the 'responsibilising' thesis which underpinned the multiagency approach to crime outlined by the Tories in the late 1980s and the 1990s. But while there may now be cross-party agreement that the problems of criminality will not be solved without the consent and active participation of the public (Kinsey, Lea and Young 1986; Johnston 1991), it is not yet clear that the public is being made ready for re-integrative justice.

Thus far we have seen how most new crime programmes, at international, national and local levels, key into a discourse which largely excludes the offender. He or she has become the forgotten element in much media discussion, unless he or she can be painted in extreme colours and made into a menace to society. Shame is very much part of the new working vocabulary of the media, nationally and locally, as the recent series of campaigns to expose Britain's paedophiles by the UK's press has indicated. And while re-integrative or restorative justice attempts to bring the offender back into consideration the media's current use of shame is unlikely to generate increased understanding. It is because the media have portrayed law and order issues in such simplistic and emotional terms that it is difficult to be optimistic about the reception of restorative justice initiatives. But re-integrating the offender depends upon the community's degree of receptivity to the possibility that people can change, that they are not fundamentally and irreparably flawed. As Morrison (1995: 260) has observed: 'A locality that does not provide the material and psychological resources for self and group growth provides instead messages which are disorientating and confusing.' It is hard to see how the shame that *MEN* invites for offenders will help the project of understanding or aid the healing process so necessary for civil progress.

Changes in law and order over the past twenty years have been both complex and significant in eroding certain basic civil liberties and altering the meaning of public space. In neglecting those changes in favour of emotion-generating programmes, television has helped to engender systems of governance in which the rule of law works only when it is challenged. *Crimefile* has striven to break away from such a tendency, but it has to work within the logic of a commodified broadcasting system. *MEN*, on the other hand, has abandoned journalistic objectivity in working alongside the police to target criminals. Behind these initiatives is the changing status of the law. As people form relational communities and struggle for the right to assert their own values, lifestyles and ideals, the law seeks to constrain their efforts. By appealing to the community of shared interests, the law seeks to assert and legitimise itself as a valuable force for an unquestioned 'good'. It is only by examining this evolving relationship that we can see how government seeks to work via the law – 'that discreet yet uninterrupted threat which acts through the medium of representations on that particular form of mental representation which forms the "calculus of the goods and evils of this life"' (Pasquino 1991: 22).

Bibliography

Armstrong, G., Moran, J. and Norris, C. (eds) (1998) *Surveillance, Closed Circuit Television and Social Control*, Aldershot, Ashgate.

Barnouw, E. (1974) *Documentary*, Oxford, Oxford University Press.

Berko, L. (1992) 'Surveying the surveilled: video space and subjectivity', *Quarterly Review of Film and Video*, 14, 1: 61–91.

Braithwaite, J. (1989) *Crime, Shame and Reintegration*, Melbourne, Oxford University Press.

Bright, J. (1991) 'Crime prevention: the British experience', in K. Stenson and D. Cowell (eds) *The Politics of Crime Control*, London, Sage.

Corner, J. (1996) *The Art of Record*, Manchester, Manchester University Press.

D'Agostino, F. (1998) 'Two conceptions of autonomy', *Economy and Society*, 27: 1–31.

Davidson, N. and Locke, T. (1992) 'Local area profile of crime', in D. Evans, N. Fyle and T. Herbert (eds) *Crime, Policing and Place*, London, Routledge.

Ditton, J. (1998) 'Public support for town centre CCTV systems: myth or reality?' in G. Armstrong, J. Moran and C. Norris (eds) *Surveillance, Closed Circuit Television and Social Control*, Aldershot, Ashgate.

Downes, D. and Rock, P. (1998) *Understanding Deviance*, Oxford, Oxford University Press.

Elias, N. (1978) *The Civilizing Process: The History of Manners*, trans. Edmund Jephcott, Oxford, Blackwell.

Ericson, R.V., Baranek, P.M and Chen, J.B.L. (1989) *Negotiating Control: A Study of News Sources*, Milton Keynes, Open University Press.

Frame, D. (2001) 'Husband pays high price for kerb crawling', *Manchester Evening News*, 18 October.

Franklin, B. and Murphy, D. (1998) 'Changing times: local newspapers, technology and markets', in B. Franklin and D. Murphy (eds) *Making the Local News*, London, Routledge.

Garland, D. (1997) 'The limits of the sovereign state', *British Journal of Criminology*, 36, 4: 445–71.

Garland, D. (2001) *The Culture of Control*, Oxford, Oxford University Press.

Gandy, O. (1993) *The Panoptic Sort: A Political Economy of Personal Information*, Boulder, CO, San Francisco, CA, and Oxford, Westview Press.

Gill, P. (1998) 'Making sense of police intelligence: the use of a cybernetic model in analysing information and power in police intelligence processes', *Policing and Society*, 8, 3: 289–314.

Glasgow Media Group (1986) *War and Peace News*, London, Routledge.

Glover, M. (1998) 'Looking at the world through the eyes of . . . Reporting the "local" in daily, weekly and Sunday local newspapers', in B. Franklin and D. Murphy (eds) *Making the Local News*, London, Routledge.

Goode, E. and Ben-Yehuda, N. (1994) *Moral Panics: The Social Construction of Deviance*, Oxford, Blackwell.

Gordon, P. (1987) 'Community policing: towards the local police state?' in P. Scraton (ed.) *Law, Order and the Authoritarian State*, Milton Keynes, Open University Press.

Graef, R. (1997) *Talking Blues: The Police in Their Own Words*, London, Collins Harvill.

Grierson, J. (1979) 'First principles of documentary', in F. Hardy (ed.) *Grierson on Documentary*, London, Faber & Faber.

Graham, S., Brooks, J. and Heery, D. (1996) 'Towns on the television: CCTV in British towns and cities', *Local Government Studies*, 22, 3: 1–27.

Hall, P.T. (1998) 'Policing order: assessments of effectiveness', *Policing and Society*, 8, 3: 225–53.

Hoyle, C. and Young, R. (1999) 'Restoring the faith', *Police Review*, 16 July.

Jacobs, L. (1971) *The Documentary Tradition*, London, Hopkinson & Blake.

JICREG (Joint Industrial Committee for Regional Press Research) (2001) 'Newspaper readership report', available online: www.jicreg.co.uk

Johnston, L. (1991) 'Privatization and the police function: from the "new police" to the "new policing"', in R. Reiner and M. Cross (eds) *Beyond Law and Order: Criminal Justice Policy and Politics into the 1990s*, London, Macmillan.

Kilborn, R. (1996) 'The new production context for documentary production in Britain', *Media,Culture and Society*, 18, 1: 141–50.

King, M. (1991) 'The political construction of crime prevention', in K. Stenson and D. Cowells (eds) *The Politics of Crime Control*, London, Sage.

Kinsey, R., Lea, J. and Young, J. (1986) *Losing the Fight Against Crime*, Oxford, Blackwell.

Kritzman, L.D. (1988) *Foucault: Politics, Philosophy, Culture*, London, Routledge.

Lynd, H. (1958) *On Shame and the Search for Identity*, London, Routledge & Kegan Paul.

McCahill, M. (1998) 'Beyond Foucault: towards a contemporary theory of surveillance', in G. Armstrong, J. Moran and C. Norris (eds) *Surveillance, Closed Circuit Television and Social Control*, Aldershot, Ashgate.

Morrison, D. (1995) *Theoretical Criminology: From Modernity to Postmodernism*, London, Cavendish.

Norris, C. and Armstrong, G. (1997) *The Unforgiving Eye: CCTV Surveillance in Public Space*, Hull, Centre for Criminology and Criminal Justice, University of Hull.

O'Malley, P. and Palmer, D. (1996) 'Post-Keynsian policing', *Economy and Society*, 25, 2: 137–55.

Osbourne, D. and Gaebler, T. (1993) *Reinventing Government*, New York, Penguin.

Pilling, R. (1998) 'The changing role of the local journalist: from faithful chronicler of the parish pump to multi-skilled compiler of an electronic database', in B. Franklin and D. Murphy (eds) *Making the Local News*, London, Routledge.

Pasquino, P. (1991) 'Criminology: the birth of a special knowledge', in G. Burchell, C. Gordon and P. Miller (eds) *The Foucault Effect: Studies in Governmentality*, Hemel Hempstead, Harvester Wheatsheaf.

Price, M. (1997) *Television, the Public Sphere and National Identity*, Oxford, Clarendon Press.

Rose, D. (2001) 'Beware Blunkett's law', *Observer*, 'Special', 1 July, available online: www.guardian.co.uk/Archive/Article/0,4273,4213827,00html

Rose, N. (1990) 'Governing the enterprising self', in P. Heelas and P. Morris (eds) *The Values of the Enterprise Culture*, London, Unwin Hyman.

Rose, N. (1993) 'Government, authority, and expertise in advanced liberalism', *Economy and Society*, 22, 3: 283–99.

Schlesinger, P. and Tumber, D. (1994) *Reporting Crime: The Media Politics of Criminal Justice*, Oxford, Oxford University Press.

Shattuc, E. (1997) *The Talking Cure*, London, Routledge.

Sherman, L.W., Strang, H. and Woods, D.J. (2000) *Recidivism Patterns in the Canberra Reintegrative Shaming Experiments (RISE)*, Canberra, Centre for Restorative Justice, Research School of Social Science, Australian National University.

Short, E. and Ditton, J. (1998) 'Seen and now heard: talking to the targets of open street CCTV', *British Journal of Criminology*, 38, 3: 404–29.

Sigler, C. (2000) 'I told my son's killer: "I forgive you"', *Guardian*, 10 January, available online: www.guardian.co.uk/Archive/Article/0,4273,3948775,00html

Skogan, W.G. (1990) *Disorder and Decline: Crime and the Spiral of Decay in American Neighborhoods*, New York, Free Press.

Stanko, E. and Newbury, T. (1994) *Just Boys Doing Business*, London, Routledge.

Stenson, K. (1993) 'Community policing as a governmental technology', *Economy and Society*, 22, 3: 373–89.

Swinden, E. (2001) 'Police discuss tolerance zone for vice girls', *Manchester Evening News*, 18 January.

Taylor, P. (2001) 'Cleaning up the streets of shame', *Manchester Evening News*, 21 January.

Walklate, S. (1989) *Victimology: The Victim, the Criminal and the Criminal Justice Process*, London, Unwin Hyman.

Woodward, S. (1998) Interview with author, 14 December.

Young, A. (1996) *Imagining Crime*, London, Sage.

Young, R. and Goold, B. (1999) 'Restorative police cautioning in Aylesbury: from degrading to reintegrative shaming ceremonies?' *Criminal Law Review*, 126–38.

Websites for restorative justice

Thames Valley Police: www.thamesvalley.police.uk/about/rj/index.htm
Restorative justice knowledge base: www.rjkbase.org.uk

5

Neighbours From Hell: productive incivilities

Thus far I have been concerned principally with programmes about crime. It is because the police officer is the most common image of authority that it has been a relatively straightforward process to relate the police to the operations of governance and to describe television's role in this process. In the remaining chapters of the book I consider various new forms in the expanded field of documentary practice in which the connections with authority are new and sometimes less overt.

This chapter focuses on one such example of the new documentary brand, *Neighbours From Hell*, and considers the extent to which this series, and others like it, keys into and contributes to the emergent discursive formation on the role of the active community.

Productive incivilities

Any generalisations about the incidence and awareness and fear of crime clearly need to be modified by consideration of differences in geographic as well as social space; these along with actual crime rates are pocketed in particular kinds of residential areas. (Herbert and Darwood 1997: 161)

In August 1997, the UK's ITV network screened the first *Neighbours From Hell*. The programme was an hour-long special at prime-time and featured a range of stories concerning the behaviour of people caught up in disputes with their neighbours. There was considerable surprise that the programme attracted 11.5 million viewers, a very healthy figure at any time and an astonishing one for a 'documentary', however loosely defined. The success of the show was such that both ITV and the BBC ordered more of the same, resulting in a scheduling battle in 1998 that was more typical of the inter-channel rivalry occasioned by the launch of a new soap opera than of factual programming.

Neighbours From Hell has inspired quite a debate, with numerous voices claiming that the programme marked a watershed of sorts for the making of serious programmes in the UK (Mulholland 1998).

Since 1997 the brand . . . *From Hell* has become sufficiently established that its range has been extended to take in 'hellish' drivers, holidays, builders, nannies and even facelifts . The brand has been sold to the US television market, with Dick Clark Productions entering a joint-venture with Carlton (www.carltonint.co.uk/press 1htm) in 1999.

The production of a documentary *series* is hardly new. The UK's venerable documentary tradition has depended on them, with examples ranging from *First Tuesday* and *World In Action* (now both cancelled) to *Panorama* and *Dispatches* (both living precariously on the edge of the schedules). What is distinctive about *Neighbours From Hell* is that it is aimed so unambivalently at the 'popular' market. Furthermore, in contrast to traditional documentary, the series does not appear to have any sort of identifiable 'position'. The enlightened liberal space that once determined the documentary perspective has here been replaced by an approach that is usually sensational and always populist in its instincts. What holds together . . . *From Hell* is the 'packaging'. Irrespective of theme or subject matter, all episodes of . . . *From Hell* use the same title music and graphics.

Thus branded, . . . *From Hell* can select from a diversity of potential subjects, as two examples will illustrate. First, *Salesmen From Hell* featured hidden-camera footage of a salesman using underhand techniques to sell a bed to an elderly couple. This might inspire questions concerning the rights of the salesman and whether he was afforded any opportunity of clearance over this footage. But such questions connect to unfashionable civil liberties' issues. The . . . *From Hell* series builds in a level of public relations. For instance, once the 'sting' has been revealed the company is given an opportunity to make amends by sacking the 'rogue' salesman. Thus, in some small way, the programme has helped to right a wrong in the big bad world of sales. The underlying message is that spaces that are not subject to surveillance are ever diminishing and we had better patrol our own behaviour as well remaining vigilant of the behaviour of others. Second, real horrors were revealed in *Facelifts From Hell*, in which a range of trusting individuals were shown to have been permanently disfigured by the work of incompetent surgeons. The public interest here was served by naming the surgeons concerned, while the audience would have been drawn by the much-advertised disastrous consequences.

As the brand's leader, *Neighbours From Hell* merits special attention. From a marketing perspective, 'the neighbours' represents a shrewd choice of subject. The majority of the viewing public live in close proximity in urban areas; those in rural districts may be more remotely situated, but they still have to deal with – and at times depend on the goodwill of – their neighbours. Thus 'the neighbours' is a theme that concerns us all.

A frightened neighbourliness is often front-page news in reports of everyday disputes, over noise, boundaries, etc., escalating into serious confrontations. Local television news programmes are also concerned with monitoring the quality of neighbour relations. We know this because *Neighbours From Hell* uses reports from regional television news programmes. These archived items require little research and may be purchased from the local companies.

This combination of factors helps to make *Neighbours From Hell* a hugely successful programme. Its ratings are comfortably higher than those achieved by many of the documentaries of the golden days of factual programme-making, and that alone makes the series worthy of individual consideration

Neighbours From Hell is ostensibly about the extraordinary disputes that arise between neighbours, but the programme is also necessarily about citizenship and why civility is not a natural condition but one that has to be sought after. As it provides a snapshot of Britain's community life it is important to put the series in its political perspective.

Changing communities

The ideal of the neighbourhood as a space where families can live in relative safety has long been a project central to government. But as we have seen the political climate changed substantially when Mrs Thatcher came to power in 1979 and launched a series of policies which have altered the meaning of neighbourhood. From that point on, the meaning of 'community' has been contested.

Although first given legislative expression by the Labour administration of 1945–50 the welfare state was accepted by the Tory Party and not substantially changed during the next thirty years. The welfare state underpinned a mixed economy in which the operations of the state worked with the market. What developed was a climate in which the State, working more or less hand-in-hand with local government, via experts planned 'ideal' environments for its citizens. Markedly paternalistic, the plan was to create neighbourhoods where communities could develop organically and provide the sort of intimate care impossible to legislate into being. It is only against the backdrop of this welfare consensus that the real impact of the first Thatcher administration can be understood. When Mrs Thatcher famously said, "There is no such thing as society, only individuals and their families", she was keying into an emergent counter-discourse that criticised welfarism.

> But this was precisely what enabled them to interlock into a powerful, mobile and polyvalent counter-discourse that sought to 'restore' the family its 'rights' to autonomy and privacy, to reconstruct its legal status as a domain outside the powers of the law, and to decolonise the intimate environment. (Rose 1989: 207)

The Tory Governments of 1979–97, as I have already noted, had a focus on law and order that stressed the importance of the neighbourhood. The community specifically was addressed in anti-crime campaigns such as 'Together We'll Crack It". Crime was depicted as a destroyer of communities – neighbourhoods comprising families. This depiction of crime as a threat to the family was to feature in various official campaigns as well as the new community-oriented police programmes already discussed.

Perhaps the most high-profile attempt to fashion communities out of families was Neighbourhood Watch (hereafter NW). The scheme, which took its inspiration from an American scheme, stressed the importance of organic communities of home-owning families. In the USA NW is one of a range of schemes, including Radio Watch and Citizen Patrol, all of which have a closer working relationship with the police than does the UK's NW (*Neighborhood Watch Bulletin* 1999). In 1989 there were 74,000 NW schemes in the UK and by 1990 600 new schemes a week were being launched (Bennett 1991: 272).

Fear of crime was the principal motivator of NW. It was hoped that NW would 'improve contact between the police and the public'. The first scheme in the UK arose as a result of the local police's failure to meet the demand for extra policing (Bennett 1990). In both the USA and the UK, NW schemes originate in dialogue between public and police. It is clear that the scheme keys into multi-agency approaches to crime some of which were discussed in earlier chapters. The key to all NW schemes is the notion of *empowerment*.

Here new modes of neighbourhood participation, local empowerment and engagement of residents in decisions over their lives will,
it is thought, reactivate self-motivation, self-responsibility and self-
reliance in the form of active citizenship with a self-governing community. (Rose 1996: 335)

It is revealing that the best responses to NW came from families in the
more affluent high-status areas. Home Office evidence indicates that
support for and participation in the schemes 'is significantly related to
being worried about becoming a victim of burglary and perceiving the
probability of victimisation as high' (Bennett 1991: 278). It is noteworthy that this group also had a more favourable view of the police, as
well as less experience of them. That this anxiety has not abated is signalled by the presence on some of the more affluent suburbs of patrolling private security firms with an undefined relation to the police.
Some working-class districts have become increasingly neglected
remote urban spaces where decay has put new pressures on families.
Here we witness the fragility of public order.

Yet harsh policies of economic adjustment in the 1980s; a widespread
crisis of political legitimacy, and the exclusionary impact of the space
of flows over the space of places . . . took their toll on social life and
organisation in poor local communities. (Castells 1997: 63)

Both the national and the local press have given NW and similar
schemes a great deal of support. In 1996, the *Mail on Sunday* launched
a campaign to give councils powers to deal with perpetually noisy
neighbours. The tone of the following report is typical of that in which
the campaign was conducted. Headlined 'Noise Tragedy Eviction', it
explained:

A woman whose loud late-night parties were blamed for a 57-year-
old neighbour committing suicide has been evicted from her council
flat. Angel James, 21, drove widowed mother-of-two Sylvia Stewart
to take a drugs overdose after constant complaints about music and
parties which went on from 6 pm to 5 am, it was claimed. (Self 1996)

Battling neighbours featured in the *Mail*'s reports are described as
coming 'from Hell', with a nod in the direction of the television series'
title. Disruptive individuals who want nothing to do with their communities help bind together the rest of the readership. Thus the
paper's moral outrage can be legitimately directed at such outsiders.
Headlines such as 'Court Block On Nuisance Family' (20 June 1996) or

'Jail For Hell Families' (25 November 1996) indicate the tone of the coverage: councillors are often called on for comments on 'tearaway teenagers' and the authorities are questioned to determine what efforts are being made to protect the good neighbours; and 'the good of the community' is commonly invoked in such reports. This approach plays well to the audience of elderly conservative home-owners.

Prior to the Thatcher administration it was the job of local government to help effect changes in the community, but as we saw in the last chapter the reforms in that sector in the 1980s and 1990s entailed many local authorities losing their powers. When this loss of power is combined with the aggressive privatisation of many services, it is not hard to understand why gaps began to open up between neighbourhoods. As Hughes (1996: 27) wrote: 'There now exists a profound democratic deficit . . . in the arena of local democracy'. In the State's 'systematic' dismantling of the local authorities, power was either centralised or 'given back' to the communities through the 'responsibilising' strategies that underpinned multi-agency approaches to crime.

Since New Labour took office in 1997 it has built on this use of the community through its revamping of NW schemes. It has a National Strategy for Neighbourhood Renewal, with four key outcomes for those in deprived neighbourhoods: 'better education, better health, lower unemployment and less crime'. In its New Deal for Communities Programme launched in 1999 anti-social behaviour orders (ASBOs) were introduced, whereby 'local authorities and the police can seek an order from the courts to protect the community from the actions of those who cause harassment, alarm or distress through anti-social behaviour' (Home Office 2000: 1). The value of the 'local' area to New Labour is also evident in its efforts, since 1997, to address and galvanise communities via the local press.

The Crime and Public Protection Bill 'will enable the use of new technology to monitor the movements of a wider range of offenders' (Home Office 2000: 1). People are taking up the challenge to feel safe in their homes by using videophones and externally mounted CCTV cameras to monitor their properties. (As we have seen this often produces material for 'reality TV'). Neighbourhood Watch asks that people supplement this electronic recording with organic surveillance, to watch and deter offenders and therefore increase the flow of information to the police.

New Labour's think-tank Demos has conducted research which reveals the complexity of the community question: 'Demos has found that in the late 1990s the communities of old cannot be recreated. Today, people from different backgrounds tolerate living next door to each other but rarely form supportive communities (Jupp 1999: 2). The strong community is a far rarer commodity than New Labour appears to imagine. Furthermore the means of achieving community may not always bring harmony. Writing of social atomisation in the 1980s, Richard Sennett (1971) referred to pseudo-communities with 'counterfeit' feelings: 'Their only sense of relatedness comes from feeling the same, trying to exclude the others who are different (in terms of class, race or moral status). Their intolerance of ambiguity gives an exaggerated sense of threat and disorder' (Sennett 1971 quoted in Cohen 1985).

It is precisely this disharmony that drives *Neighbours From Hell*. The programme offers jagged snapshots of modern day citizenship, with a focus on how different communities police themselves. The series's heroes are those individual families acting autonomously but with an innate sense of decency to restore order to their patch of the neighbourhood. But in this they are creating not *communities* but what Castells (1997: 61) describes as a 'a defensive identity, an identity of retrenchment of the known against the unpredictability of the unknown and uncontrollable'.

The series

Neighbours From Hell is an examplary hybrid, designed to increase the audience by combining a range of attractive features. It offers many: the immediacy of local news reports; aspects of access TV; legal issues so that we may play at being judge and jury; video-vigilantism in the use of grainy camcorder footage capturing dangerous and often illegal acts; the emotional thrills of the docu-soap and new police reality programmes (although few police officers are shown in action). The presenter delivers commentary in an ironic tone which occasionally conflicts with sober documentary purpose. The reports afford voyeuristic glimpses of people who, like us, live in neighbourhoods, but whose world, unlike ours, appears to be out of control. We are bound to ask what sort of citizenship is this?

The series screened during January and February 1999 featured a total of fifteen reports. Two-thirds of the participants could be identified as economically and spatially disadvantaged (working-class families living in rented accommodation or council estates). The problems here were concerned with the infringement of neighbours' aural or spatial borders. The police featured in half of the incidents, though mostly as commentators rather than as active participants. This is important, for the series is not about the forces of law and order but situations in which people discover the limits of the law for themselves. It asks: What happens when the law is not enough? How do people order themselves when the system breaks down? The focus is on specific individuals who seem to be unwilling or unable to make the compromises necessary to harmonious neighbourly relations. How do communities order themselves so that calling in the police is the last resort? In other words can we police ourselves?

Each item begins in the same way – with a general view of the city, town or village in question and then gradually focuses on the actual location of the incident. This is a very traditional approach. But given that the programme is all about a nexus of looks in a new climate of surveillance this opening sequence might be read as that of a spy satellite scouring the country for signs of disorder. The narrator introduces us to the participants, each of whom defines 'the problem' as he, she or they see it. This is then often followed by a reconstruction of the incident that sparked the trouble. Sometimes the subject's own camcorder footage is integrated with the narrative. If a legal decision has already been made against an individual then there is a change in the representation – that person is shown in slow motion or in mug-shot, the signifier of criminal guilt and as such the programmes's duty to impartiality can be abandoned. The validity of the judgement is 'proven' by the suffering of the family. If a case is ongoing then both sides of an argument are displayed so that we might decide for ourselves on guilt or innocence.

It is interesting to note that the criminal has no further recourse to law if he or she has been found guilty of the offence prior to the transmission. Thus what might have been shame at the local level is now turned into a national spectacle. In other words, the offender has lost any claim to anonymity. Once the law has made it clear that the individual can now be branded a criminal it is fair to 'name and shame' him or her. This reflects something of the new policies being adopted in some American states noted in chapter 4. It is also symptomatic of the times that producers of these shows are unashamedly concerned with catching criminals. This represents a paradigm shift away from the traditional documentary codes of objectivity and expert analysis towards a simple faith in the value of authority.

The visual language of *Neighbours From Hell* is literal and sensationalist. When a window is said to have been broken we get a close-up of exactly that. When we hear of shadowy figures this is precisely what we are shown. Those who choose not to speak to the crew are featured in 'grainy long-lens stills that offer a visual shorthand for the presumption of guilt' (Sutcliffe 1997: 17). The show is unashamedly sensationalist in its focus on human-interest stories and the maximising of an emotional response. This is not to suggest that traditional documentary has always shyed from adopting dramatic and emotional appeals. However, when it has resorted to such tactics it usually does so within a more formally structured enquiry into a social problem. In *Neighbours From Hell* the social and political context is stripped away so that the viewer's gaze can focus on the pitiful object of attention.

The segment featuring the Sumners is typical of this emotional approach. The story begins with a slow-motion drive-by tracking shot of a 'dangerous estate' where youths, their faces digitally obscured, lurk on corners. We then cut to an interior where the young couple tell (and we see as reconstructions) of the break-ins and the window smashing. The culminating incident involved their baby who was almost hit by a stone thrown by one of the youths. As a result of this the Sumners decided to inform the authorities, a decision that saw their troubles escalate. The gangs stepped up the level of harassment and the couple was forced to abandon their home, thereby falling from the housing ladder and losing over £6,000. The final shot is of the couple leaving the ransacked home, all their possessions in a van. In a country where home-ownership has become a badge of middle-class status– and a fundamental objective of government policy with obvious ideological connections to the value of the family unit, this scene is sure to have a powerful resonance.

Stark contrasts are drawn between the law-abiding nuclear family, their baby a symbol of innocence, and the literally faceless youths. The family is always filmed in daylight, the parents sitting together on a settee. The youths are seen only at night, via infrared cameras, speaking in the shadows. After the tearful testimony of the victims, we hear the shadowed gangs speaking in street code of the "respect" the couple should have shown them. The traditional forces of law and order have proven ineffectual: in the end, all that the Sumners can do is to sell up and move.

The Sumners' story featured an interview with a gang-member (who may or may not have been party to the harrassment of the Sumners), but offered no context for the gang's behaviour. The gang remained uninvestigated and was all the more sinister because of this. By castigating gangs of youths in this fashion, *Neighbours From Hell* keys into the already negative coverage that young men were receiving in television news and the popular press. Dangerous young men were photographed joy-riding on 'sink estates' or selling drugs in council block hallways. As ever, youth disorder was stratified by class. Drug use by the middle-class was tolerated by those commentators who could not bear to be hypocritical. Those left on the estates were inevitably considered fatherless and suffering the crisis of masculinity. The liberal press debated the youth problem while the right-wing broadsheets described their housing thus:

> More trouble broke out last week on several of those hideous housing estates designed to accommodate society's poorest in that familiar 'Early Ugly' style to which it was assumed they would, in time, become accustomed. Few people who have visited them will be surprised about what is happening, because most would regard having to live on one of them as the nearest thing to a life sentence. (*Sunday Telegraph*, 26 July 1992, quoted in Wykes 2001)

Wykes has noted (2001: 98) how news trends in the 1980s and 1990s painted a grim picture of community life in Britain's inner cities. We soon became familiar with the visual shorthand for the dangerous streets: 'Instead, what began to emerge was the wholesale condemnation of the communities where these young men lived. Poverty, unemployment, lack of facilities, policing, were only addressed as a result of already "dangerous places".' But whereas documentary might have investigated the reasons behind such urban decay, *Neighbours From Hell* unthinkingly condemns such areas. The series helps reinforce a perception of a lawless otherworld characterised by incivility, thus increasing viewers' fear of crime. When faced with such terror and an impotent police force what else is there to do but propagandise on behalf of surveillance technologies? Yet such technology hardly fosters friendly relations, and, as a result, suspicion breeds a frightened neighbourliness which in turn increases the fear of crime that modern policing programmes both create and seek to dispel.

Neighbours From Hell has a vested interest in urban decay. It shares this interest with those in the surveillance and security industries who need the public to feel fearful so that they will buy more of their technology. A self-policed order that arises from the community can be served by these technologies.

Neighbours From Hell does not confine its focus to the shadowy underworld of the working class. It features also reports of problems afflicting the 'respectable' suburbs. In one episode viewers encountered the Smiths who had recently moved into a block of flats, one of which was occupied by a Mr Hope. The latter offered to give his new neighbours free access to satellite television and connected them up to his own system. All participants were happy with this arrangement until one day Mr Smith noticed a tiny lens positioned in a panel at the side of the screen. Mr Hope had been secretly taping the couple and over time had amassed a large number of tapes. The series' voyeuristic interest in the story was justified by the fact that the law could only prosecute Mr Hope with unlawfully *filming* a minor (when she wandered into her parents' bedroom), a misdemeanour for which he was given a three-month sentence. While the viewers see videotaped images of the Smiths' undressing, we hear strong calls for a change in the law to protect such innocents.

This item focuses on a principal theme of the series – the sanctity of the family space. The intruder was an unmarried middle-aged man, already, according to the ideals of the series, an outsider. He was portrayed in slow motion, his guilt declared in the newspaper headlines superimposed on the images. He was given no opportunity to speak. This story underlines our awareness that we are all potential targets of surveillance and that this threat extends even to the private space of the family. Mr Hope had violated the sanctity of the family and tested the limits of the law. Yet without such violations television could not make such profitable programmes. This in turn connects to other CCTV-led stories which indicate how technological systems are at work interrogating the private domestic sphere and seeking to regulate the functions of the family. Such stories encourage us to become more self-aware as we operate what Rose calls the 'unceasing reflexive gaze of our own self-scrutiny' (Rose 1989: 208).

The vast majority of the series' stories show law-abiding family units living alongside others, some of them living alone, whose interests and habits were sources of conflict. The widow trying to get back her land and the old lady living with a large number of dogs were pictured as odd-balls – at once part of Britain's rich tradition of eccentrics and yet also individuals out of step with 'normal' family life. It was made clear that without the intervention of the law, 'war' would break out between neighbours because of the ever-present threat of incivility.

In defending the interests of victimised families the series adopts an authoritarian populism and cultural traditionalism. Such an approach is in keeping with trends in modern criminology, discussed earlier, whereby the public's and, in particular, the victim's view of crime becomes a significant determinant in designing policy objectives. By depicting outsiders as 'other', the series dismisses the idea of dialogue as ridiculous – an approach that is hardly conducive to productive debate.

In some cases, however, the series appears to perform a sort of access function in which people are given an opportunity to tell their stories from the front-line of an uncivil nation. What is of interest here is the presentation of these situations as a problem of governance, that of self-governing families and only secondarily that of the police

The last episode of the 1999 series featured the problems of those who live on the Cranhill Estate in Glasgow, a stereotype of drug-riddled urban squalor. The telling of the story brings together many of the themes featured by the series. We learn from the Cranhill report that the process by which democracy emerges is in part as a defensive identity but principally as a voluntary association developed through, in the words of Jordan and Arnold (1995: 175), 'informal practices that foster the norms of participation, co-operation and civic responsibility'. Despite the signs of neglect and the damage caused by unseen others, it is families coming together voluntarily who do the work of self-governance and, in doing so, aid the police by policing themselves.

The Cranhill Estate is described by one of the police officers whose 'patch' it is, as one of the most dangerous places in Glasgow. The report then moves on to the inhabitants, who tell of how drug-dealers and their clients have made life unbearable. People were dissuaded from carrying money by the fear of being mugged; others were afraid to go out because of the very real possibility of being burgled. The situation climaxed in the death by heroin overdose of a 13-year-old. As Councillor McCall recalls: 'The priest said we were all to blame.' The first half of the programme concludes with footage of the funeral. The second half chronicles the way in which the inhabitants fought back against these conditions. It began with a candle-lit vigil in which twenty people were expected to participate, but to the organisers' surprise 500 joined in. Thus ensured of support, the inhabitants decided to tell the police what they knew, in other words 'grass-ing' for the sake of their families, as had the Sumner family, discussed above; and they set up a residents' association to vet those applying for housing. As a result the number of known dealers is down to two. The report ends with the police praising the bravery of the inhabitants and revealing the increased number of arrests.

Of note in this report is the people's frustration at their inability to undertake family duties such as leaving their homes to attend chris-tenings and at having to keep watch over their children when they were playing outside. What seems remarkable here is their dedication to their community when the reaction of many viewers will have been to leave the area as soon as possible. The programme thus demon-strates what can be done when people are prepared to work together. Community can be restored only by making a hard choice, to side with the forces of law and order rather than giving in to the drug-dealers – 'the participation of the governed in the elaboration of the law constitutes the most effective system of governmental economy' (Dean 1994: 191). The very idea of initiating dialogue when faced with such extraordinary conditions seems laughable. The offenders are beyond the pale: here, as throughout the series, their silence is indic-ative of guilt. The programme underlines the value of adopting a pragmatic response to such a situation. Side-stepping tricky political questions of culpability enables the producers to focus on what is immediately understandable. Other possible reasons for the state of the neighbourhood, such as the neglect of urban planning, misguided policy directives and new socially divisive policing strategies, etc., are literally no longer in the frame. To include them would be to cloud the issue with unnecessary complications that might draw our eyes away from the drama. By empathising with the victimised families, we reject the offenders as alien 'others'. Efficient governmenance should not make them our problem. Our focus is the family.

At least three reactions to such television are possible here: a pleasure at not being there; a fearfulness at the incivility of others; and a concern that the law be updated and the police given more powers to act swiftly and decisively. Such reactions help to foster increased calls for the extension of policing and an emphasis on the need for self-governance. Clearly the law is not always enough, and while waiting for it to catch up we need to police ourselves. In its presenta-tion of victims who fight for their families *Neighbours From Hell* pro-vides a fascinating glimpse of self-governance in action.

> Liberal practices of government might act on *free* subjects, i.e. those
> that exercise some type of choice. It equally might act on free *subjects*,
> those whose subjection operates through the exercise of choice. This
> double sense of a power over free subjects sums up the paradoxical
> quality of neoliberalism quite nicely. (Dean 1994: 193)

Neighbours From Hell's neglect of expertise is justified on the ground
that it speaks to the democratising of knowledge and the rise of populism. But perhaps it also points to a more disturbing trend, that of the
flattening out of the world. The series seems content to let 'the people'
speak for themselves, but it presents their voices in a way which is
emotionally manipulative. It is symptomatic of a time when the documentary-maker's expertise, like that of others, are no longer considered necessary. In the new populism the worth of expertise can be
questioned.

In *Neighbours From Hell* the social is potentially chaotic. Communities are either at Wilson's tipping point on the edge of crisis or are
lost to faceless violent forces. The viewers' main project is to make
themselves secure and electronically remote from all signs of dangerous difference. But what sort of community can be built on such foundations? Perhaps one reason for the acceptance of CCTV is that the
public has acquired its insecurity and fear though such television.

Neighbours From Hell has a complex relationship with the democratic project. After stepping back from the emotional impact of the
series we realise how little we are being offered in terms of analysis.
As documentary, such work contributes to the debate on privacy but
in a way which fuels the call for more surveillance and more disciplinary technology. It cannot have escaped people's attention that those
most in need of help in the community are those most alienated from
the official authorities. But rather than investigate their conditions
and offering some critical perspective, Neighbour from Hell actively
participates in widening the divide that polarises people into categories of good and bad, black and white. It offers a depressing picture of
contemporary life. Sutcliffe refers to the life of Mal Hussain who suf-
fered multiple attacks and lived his life under siege conditions.
Neighbours From Hell made this

> something infinitely more malevolent – a vision of the mob cruelty
> that can emerge when the law retreats and leaves a fertile ground for
> hate to grow. The account of his purgatorial life rounded off easily the
> most depressing film broadcast for months. (Sutcliffe 1997: 26)

When the law retreats or is absent we have little choice but to police ourselves. In picturing this underworld, *Neighbours From Hell* reminds us also about a group of people rarely mentioned but growing in number – the poor. But they are not a problem for society any longer. They are best considered as a sort of nuisance. Depicted in grainy camcorder footage throwing stones or making aggressive threats, they dwell beyond the fringe of respectability. In *Neighbours From Hell* the poor are mostly the deserving poor. Little context or explanation is offered for their status: the poor just *are*, and it is our role to insulate ourselves against them and what they represent.

Conclusion

Some critics were uncomfortable with *Neighbours From Hell* because it failed to do what 'serious' documentary does – contextualise the problem, address the wider issues, interview the government ministers and officials responsible – in short, to enlist levels of expertise. Its apparent willingness to flit from one scene to another makes it frivolous when considered against a documentary tradition of sober and focused enquiry. In place of progressive solutions to people's problems viewers are presented with citizens united only by their want of good neighbours. Citizenship is reduced to something as simple as 'Why can't we just get along?'

Neighbours From Hell connects to the processes of governance by praising those families and communities who seek to defend their way of life. At the end of every episode it offers viewers a free booklet which gives advice on how disputes can be handled, and other help, advice and 'further reading'. This publication is produced with the assistance of the Birmingham Citizens' Advice Bureau (Carlton is based in Birmingham). It is in such subtle ways that we can measure the distance traversed from the documentary traditions of the past. Thus, rather than assembling a tier of professionals offering their views on a real solution, *Neighbours From Hell* focuses on the popular belief that today's viewers are interested in the stories rather than the context. This is television remodelling itself, stepping back from its role as an expert and handing that job over to people who are actively engaged in sorting out neighbourhood disputes.

New Labour has begun to look at ways of tackling the social exclusion *Neighbours From Hell* can only film. The Policing and Crime

Reduction Unit has completed a series of reports designed to aid the community. It recommends local solutions:

> [S]chemes must be tailored to meet the specific needs of the areas in which they operate and must involve all relevant agencies working on the ground, as well as local people . . . partnership is likely to be an aspect of neighbourhood warden schemes which combine security, housing and environmental goals. (Jacobson and Saville 1999: 1)

There are not many signs that stable communities exist any longer. While many people clearly value having good neighbours, programmes such as *Neighbours From Hell* and the new police documentaries discussed earlier help reinforce a security-conscious mentality so that we need rely on the ties of community less and less. What remains uninvestigated are the reasons why neighbourhoods become the 'hellish' places that they are. It would be useful to see television programmes which at least acknowledged the complexities of building communities, rather than our present diet which merely film their collapse.

Bibliography

Burchell, G. (1991) 'Peculiar interests: civil society and governing the system of natural liberty', in G. Burchell, C. Gordon and P. Miller (eds) *The Foucault Effect: Studies in Governmentality*, Hemel Hempstead. Harvester Wheatsheaf.

Bennett, T. (1990), *Evaluating Neighbourhood Watch*, Aldershot, Gower.

Bennett, T. (1991) 'Themes and variations in Neighbourhood Watch', in D.J. Evans, N.R. Fyfe and D.T. Herbert (eds) *Crime, Policing and Place: Changing Perspectives on Crime Prevention*, London, Macmillan.

Carter, M. (1998) 'Time for a reality check', *Broadcast*, 18 September.

Castells, M. (1997) *The Power of Identity*, Oxford. Blackwell.

Cohen, S. (1985) *Visions of Social Control*, London, Polity Press.

Dean, M. (1994) *Critical and Effective Histories: Foucault's Methods and Historical Sociology*, London, Routledge.

Garland, D. (1997) 'Governmentality and the problem of crime', *Theoretical Criminology*, 1, 2: 173–211.

Eyre, R. and Liddiment, D. (1998) 'Let battle commence: is ITV in inexorable decline?' *Guardian*, 12 January, CD ROM, p. 2.

Hardy, F. (1978) *Grierson on Documentary*, London, Faber & Faber.

Herbert, D.T. and Darwood, J. (1997) *Crime Awareness and Urban Neighbourhoods*, London, Sage.

Holden, M. (1996) 'Court block on nuisance family', *South Manchester Reporter*, 20 July.

Home Office (2000) *Government Crime Reduction Strategy*, London, Communications Development Unit.

Hughes, G. (1996) 'Communitarianism and law and order', *Critical Social Policy*, 16, 49: 17–41.

Jacobson, J. and Saville, S. (1991) *Neighbourhood Wardens: An Overview*, Crime Reduction Research Series Paper 2, London, Home Office Policing and Reducing Crime Unit.

Jordan, B. and Arnold, J. (1995) 'Democracy and criminal justice', *Critical Social Policy*, 16, 4: 170–82.

Jupp, B. (1999), 'Love thy neighbour', *Guardian*, 27 October.

Loveday, B. (1998) 'Local authorities and crime prevention' (review article), *Local Government Studies*, 24, 1: 113–18.

Miller, P. and Rose, N. (1993) 'Governing economic life', in M. Gane and T. Johnson (eds) *Foucault's New Domains*, London, Routledge.

Mulholland, J. (1998) 'What's up docs?' *Guardian*, 26 January.

Neighborhood Watch Bulletin (1999) Fountain Valley, CA, Neighborhood Watch.

Rose, N. (1989) *Governing the Soul*, London, Routledge.

Rose, N. (1996) 'The death of the social: re-figuring the territories of government', *Economy and Society*, 25, 3: 327–56.

Self, A. (1996) 'Noise tragedy eviction', *Mail on Sunday*, 18 August.

Sennett, R. (1971) *The Uses of Disorder: Personal Identity and City Life*, London, Allen Lane–Penguin.

Short, E. and Ditton, J. (1998) 'Seen and now heard: talking to the targets of open street CCTV', *British Journal of Criminology*, 38, 3: 404–29.

Sutcliffe, M. (1997) 'Television: last night', *Independent on Sunday*, 15 July.

Walklate, S. (1998) 'Excavating the fear of crime: fear, anxiety or trust?' *Theoretical Criminology*, 2, 4: 403–18.

Wykes, M. (2001) *News, Crime and Culture*, London, Pluto Press.

Young, J. (1998) 'The tasks of a realist criminology', *Contemporary Crises*, 2: 337–56.

Website address

Carlton International's *Neighbours From Hell* brochure:
www.carltonint.co.uk/press1htm

6

Judge TV

> It's amazing how people like judging. Judgment is being passed everywhere, all the time. Perhaps it's one of the simplest things mankind has been given to do. And you know very well that the last man, when radiation has finally reduced his last enemy to ashes, will sit down behind some rickety table and begin the trial of the individual responsible. (Foucault quoted in Kritzman 1990: 326)

In this chapter I pull together some of the themes that featured earlier in the book and point ahead to new programme forms which highlight the individual and the self. 'Judge TV' is a new hybrid form which combines features of the talk-show with the language of new action-oriented police programmes. It offers the symbolic reward of instant judgement as well as keying into the sound-bite policies which have become increasingly important in political discourse. Judge TV evokes the community's moral sense and highlights the role of shame. Accordingly in this chapter the focus of attention shifts from the community to the citizen. Judge TV directs our attention to the individual's moral responsibilities at a time when definitions of 'citizenship' are changing. Its populist authoritarianism attempts to fashion a citizenship in keeping with a conservative ethos which stresses the value of the family. Once again law and order is the terrain on which responsible citizenship is defined.

From talking to judging: what works?

> Therapy is a method of learning how to endure the loneliness of a culture without faith. (Rose 1989: 216)

The concept of the public sphere haunts all discussions of the talk-show genre. Habermas's ideal space wherein citizens come together to debate issues without private interest or financial interest in a rational manner is said by some to have found its modern home in the talk-show, Thus Dahlgren (1995) writes: 'That such programmes should be understood as part of the public sphere is, however, without doubt.' Shattuc (1997: 95) has argued for the significance of Oprah's 'potentially radical public sphere'. These debates reflect a broader concern with 'public space' which these writers hold to be necessary in an increasingly commercialised environment.

When talk-shows first came to prominence, in the 1970s, they were regarded as open spaces in which individuals were encouraged by liberals such as Phil Donahue to disclose their worries and insecurities. The earlier incarnations of *Oprah* also represented a space where minority groups negotiated the terms of their representation. Priest and Dominick (1994) have shown that some of those who appeared on early talk-shows described themselves as self-disclosers with an overt aim to challenge and improve the terms of their representation. Such a strategy fitted the identity politics of the 1970s with its slogan 'The personal is political'.

The talk-show offered a setting in which experts had the role of making respectful assessments of individuals and recommending person-centred forms of treatment such as counselling. The key concept here is, again, *empowerment*. Talk-shows provided a space for people to gain acceptance, to come to terms with their identity, to have others 'speak' about experiences which they believed were their's alone (Carpignano, Anderson, Aronowitz and DiFazio 1990). And while it may be an overstatement to suggest that difference was always respected and acknowledged on talk-shows, for the most part they were representative of a liberal drive towards flexible selves, selves that could be reconstructed in a safe place. Indeed *Oprah* represents one of the last such spaces where the belief in the power of the individual to transform is expressed in therapeutic discourse.

As the talk-show developed in the 1980s all four components of the genre – host, guest(s), expert, audience – were engineered to produce performances which legitimise therapeutic discourse that privileges the self as a transformative project. The apparent openness of the talk-show appears to welcome diversity, although what are applauded most vigorously are very much conventional models of behaviour: 'Audience! Join with me now in barking at Rudy' (*Ricki Lake*, 29 January 1998).

By the late 1980s talk-shows had audiences large enough to

sustain two dedicated cable channels. There were obvious commercial reasons for the talk-show's popularity with producers – it is low-
cost, made according to formula and has an enthusiastic audience
keen and ready to participate. Perhaps even more attractive was the
potential of a very different orientation that challenged the liberal
ethos of the early talk-shows. The *Morton Downey Jr* show, for
example, had a right-wing perspective and a confrontational
approach to its subjects. Where Oprah and Donahue, and some contemporary hosts, Sally Jesse Raphael for one, nurtured identity transformation in a supportive setting, the new talk-show hosts were
aggressive agents of normalisation.

The talk-show gained a tragic notoriety when a guest on *Jenny
Jones*, thinking he was to meet a secret – hetrosexual – admirer, who
turned out to be a gay man from his neighbourhood, subsequently
sought out and killed the man. A debate was sparked in the public
sphere concerning the influence such programmes may have. The
Jenny Jones show received a heavy fine. No significant differences in
the content and tactics of the talk-show have, however, been noticed
as a result, either of the tradgedy or of the fine (Gritten 1999).

By the end of the 1990s *Jerry Springer* had become the most popular
talk-show, garnering higher ratings than even the esteemed *Oprah*.
Springer has been called the 'sultan of salaciousness', and his show
receives up to 4,000 calls a day from incorrigible exhibitionists. *Jerry
Springer* is notorious for its provocative themes – from 'Newlyweds
Headed for Divorce' to 'I Was a Circus Sideshow Freak' – for which it
has been widely criticised (Allen-Mills 1998). One critic wrote of
Springer: 'He doesn't have viewers. He has rubbernecks. His success
is the appeal of the traffic accident' (Carter quoted in Coles 1998: 2).

The show's hallmarks – the mockery of difference, the engineered
fights, the free rein given the audience to abuse the guests – appear to
have an enduring appeal. The discourse is, however, confused.
Having for an hour allowed the audience to chant 'Whore!' or 'Loser!'
at the guests, Springer's closing summary invokes a typically liberal
sensibility, despite the ridiculing of the very discourse which
informed the show's progenitors. Springer has brushed aside such
criticism, declaring that the only thing his guests do not do is talk.
Nevertheless, it is noteworthy that Springer maintains the three-
minute sermonising when that time could be used to show another
irate guest attempting to rip off his or her partner's head.

A recent variant on the more traditional talk-show approach is

Maury Povich's occasional showcasing of 'radical' techniques in teaching wayward young folks a lesson. This usually involves the latter being sent to a bootcamp for 'live, on-air, teen-rebel rehabilitation'. Once they have undergone this experience, Povich gently interviews his visibly traumatised and reformed guests about how they feel. (Husband 2000). This 'treatment' has proven successful enough to be taken up by the *Sally Jesse Raphael* team. Shame is clearly an important part of the process here. But it is also noteworthy that techniques once thought to be the preserve of the disciplinarian right have found their way into a quasi-therapeutic discourse with a focus on the behaviour of the individual. Traditional divides between left and right seem to be unnoticed here.

Some talk-shows retain the earlier approach to their subjects–guests. Oprah remains a very significant figure in the genre and her show is for many the standard by which others are measured. But she has moved noticeably into the emotional–spiritual growth area as she has matured, along with her audience, into early middle-age. Formerly Oprah could be depended upon for an openly personal response. She had a tendency to relate the experiences of those she encounted in her studio show with her own life experiences. Her fluctuating weight was something to which millions of women could relate, and is a sub-plot that still runs. Oprah has not entirely discarded that personal openness, but she is now more clearly linked to the personal development movement. She also has a successful magazine, 'O', and a book club, a recommendation from which is said to be worth to authors many thousands in sales.

Oprah's totemic power as the Queen of Talk was challenged by the popularity of shows like *Jerry Springer*. Her decision to quit the genre, because of 'the circus of fist-fights and betrayals', sent a quiver through the industry. She has yet, at the time of writing, to quit, so her earlier announcement has at least helped her to relocate away from the rowdy newcomers (Hellen 1999: 3).

British audiences have for some time shown an interest in talk-shows, despite early protestations that such emotional displays were unlikely to survive in the more self-contained ethos of the UK. In addition to programmes imported from the USA, home-grown varieties such as *Esther*, *Kilroy*, *Vanessa* and, more recently, *Trisha* were not slow to develop. In 1999 these shows became the subject of press attention and front-page news when one of the guests on *Vanessa* was revealed to be a 'fake', an actor. This was soon followed by revelations of fakes in rival show *Trisha* (Rowe 1999). An investigation was launched and both the BBC and the ITC promised stricter vetting of participants. There was much pontification in the broadsheets concerning the decline of British television, though the problem of 'fakes' had to do with the fact that such guests are booked by researchers on part-time contracts working under a great deal of pressure. Someone who is known to one or two researchers as a reliable performer tends to be passed around between researchers of different shows and so becomes a 'serial guest'. It is only occasionally that people are found out.

What links UK and US versions of the talk-show is the 'guiding' of audiences to make decisions. The talk-show can be seen as an instrument of discipline where the power of the norm is vested in the audience. What differentiates the many varieties is how that norm is activated. Unlike mainstream critics, most of whom are openly dismissive of the form, many academics have celebrated the talk-show as a carnival in which middle-class values are subverted. The audience is celebrated as a fount of wisdom who treat the whole enterprise as a joke beyond tired middle-class moralising. Yet for all the critics' celebrations of the 'honesty' of the audience (Fiske 1989; Shattuc 1997; Taverner 2000), an analysis of what they applaud reveals them at least acting as a reactionary group. What they are encouraged to operate is a normalising judgement. The host gives the crowd licence to punish deviance because that deviance invariably involves the betrayal of an established – predominantly heterosexual – relationship. It is the breaking of a 'relationship' with which audience members can identify, and so the abuse is 'justified'. Promiscuity and sexual experimentation meet with audience chants of 'Whore' and 'Weirdo' on *Springer*. Jerry might make a specious bid for understanding, but his audience want to abuse. 'Normalising society has turned out to be a powerful and insidious form of domination' (Dreyfus and Rabinow 1982: 198).

By 2003 talk-shows had changed. The vast majority have rejected the talking cures associated with liberal attitudes and their tarnished expertise, and have chosen to look for solutions that can be seen to work. The disappearance of the expert is common to nearly all of the current talk-shows. He or she was previously valued for importing a legitimising context from the world beyond the studio. The expert represented a sobering element, necessary to temper the overly enthusiastic, untutored responses of the audience. The omission of the expert may be read as indicating that such legitimation is no longer needed, that the frank and unashamed responses of the public are all that the form requires. In this way the shows can sometimes be rather brutal celebrations of the 'good sense' of the audience, a good sense that is increasingly expressed in judgements that the chastised guests are asked to live by.

In an effort to grab a drifting television audience, the *Springer* 'cam' tracks down the aggrieved to their natural habitat, *Sally* and *Maury* send guests off to bootcamp, while *Ricki*'s people hit the streets and then vote on the ideal solution. We can see what needs to be done. And if the process works – it usually does, if one can go by the subjects' tearful and humiliated responses – justice is seen to have been done.

Judge TV

> There is right, there is wrong, and each of us has choices. The choices we pick determine our future. On this show we will always reward people who make the right choice.
> (Mills Lane: www.tvtalkshows.com)

Judge TV's transparency and the quick decisions it provides can be understood as part of the call for the increased visibility of public institutions and the democratising of the legal process. In this light televising actual court cases is akin to showing real police officers storming a bar – both maximise the visibility of justice by showing the law in action.

When America's Founding Fathers built the first courtrooms they made them large enough to accommodate a wide cross-section of the community. However in the nineteenth and twentieth centuries the architecture of courtrooms have allowed for only small public galleries. The so-called Sunshine in the Courtroom Act of 1972 was couched in democratic terms as promoting the opening up of the legal process to a wider public (NCPPR 1997). Since that time courtrooms have proven to be a regular fixture on television. The exhaustive televising of the O.J. Simpson trial was perhaps the most extensive expression of interest in legal proceedings. Although much of that trial involved legal niceties ratings indicated that there may be an audience for this sort of television.

The commercial viability of televised trials was tested in the launching of Court TV, a cable channel which devotes its daytime schedule to legal proceedings. Established in 1992, by 1998 it had televised 400 trials, the majority of which are little known. The channel is funded by advertising and subscribers, as are the majority of channels.

Two-thirds of the cases covered are criminal, the rest civil. Like any other commercial operation, Court TV is dominated by news values, with journalists looking for stories that will amuse their viewers (Sullivan 1998). Court TV's roving reporters also utilise the internet to offer the public a degree of interactivity to comment on cases aired in real time. But although it is a commercial concern Court TV maintains a high public profile through initiatives such as 'Choices and Consequences' which 'aims to help young adolescents – 10-to-15-year-olds – stay out of court by fostering an understanding of the consequences of violent or reckless behaviour' (www.courttv.com).

Court TV made headlines in September 2000 when it began 'airing a series of real-life criminal confessions under police interrogation' as part of its new *Confessions* series. The innovation attracted a very negative response: '"This type of violent TV programming brings the media to an all-time low", wrote one LA councillor', but *Confessions* represents one more way in which law and order is opened up to the public (Kettle 2000: 17). Critics have questioned the effects that this democratisation may be having.

> Could television be responsible for altering the attitudes, judgments and behaviours of trial participants, creating a radically new relationship between media and courts? In other words, does television result in distortion of courtroom behaviour distinct from other possible distortions? (Boylan 1994: 1)

In Britain the televising of trials has not been an issue because cameras are not permitted in the courtrooms. Indeed even the taking of photographs is not allowed; instead an artist is employed to make sketches in court. However, the considerable public interest aroused over the Lockerbie trial and the case of serial killer Harold Shipman have led lawyers and academics to discuss the possibility of recording trials. Some argue that an educational purpose can be served by recording trials for study; this would also enable a measure of access to victims unable to undertake long journeys to attend trials. Critics of this view respond that televising individuals under trial conditions may further traumatise them. British lawyers of this persuasion echo the fear of their American counterparts that television will simplify affairs:

> People have to understand that trials are not entertainment. They have a very serious purpose. They are not soap operas. Potentially, people lose their liberty and the important thing is that the accused gets a fair trial. (BBC 2000)

We don't want an interactive television system to allow lawyers to tell the jury that 'over two thirds of our viewers think you should find for the plaintiff'. We expect judges and jurors to make decisions that may well be unpopular – antimajoritarian. Televising the events will make it harder to achieve that goal. (Mikva 1998: 3)

While this debate goes on it is certainly the case that cameras are more in evidence in American courtrooms than ever before. The introduction of the internet and other technologies seems to offer a further democratisating of the legal process. In one sense this democratising can be taken to be an uncovering a formerly hidden process, but this needs to be qualified by the fact that the cases we get to see and comment on are hardly representative, being rather cases of unusual and thus newsworthy kinds. Furthermore, the claim that trials will extend the public's understanding is not backed up by the evidence. What little research there has been into Court TV, for example, indicates that it's purported educational effects are minimal. In an experiment conducted by New York University, 'public understanding of the judicial process had not improved during the 18 month courtroom television experiment' (Boylan 1994: 2).

The best-known representatives of televised law in action are, of course, the judges. The first popular television presentation of real legal processes at work was *The People's Court* (1991–93). In these – mostly civil – cases the benign Ed Koch issued judgments on a range of individuals, sometimes adding a nugget of wisdom to illuminate the sentence (Stein 1998). It was not until the 1990s that television judges began to occupy more space in the schedules.

The television judges of the 1990s tended to be more forceful than Ed Koch, and their pronouncements had more in common with sound-bite populism than with the solemnity of the law. In order to function as sites of authority, these judges have to be suitably qualified for the role. Ideally TV judges should have risen from a working-class background or else have in some way distinguished themselves from the rest of the legal profession. They should retain the signifiers of ordinariness – 'straight-talking' and 'commonsensical' – in their speech and style; and they should have experience of the bench, and be recognised for their expertise in relevant areas – Sheindlin was a judge in the Family Court Division of New York, Mablean had been a divorce court lawyer, Ed Koch had been mayor of New York. They should also command an authority beyond the world of the courtroom, either through their continuing practice (Judge Joe Brown) or

their track-record of speaking engagements and tours.In these important ways the television judge demonstrates an authority altogether
different from that of the talk-show host.

Many talk-show hosts have endured some well-publicised personal crisis that is considered to qualify them as facilitators of audiences' judgements of others (Oprah's history of abuse; Lake's weight
problems; Roseanne's complex sexual history, etc.). As the shows run
their hosts develop expertise: they learn to emote and provoke, and,
significantly, to empathise with audience and guests. What television
judges bring, however, is knowledge. They may have acquired celebrity along the way, but their primary qualification for being there is
their ability to formulate a legal judgment which is both duly
informed and likely to resonate with their audience.

While Judge TV appears to be something novel, what it offers is
a very ancient linking of moral and legal judgment. Judge TV derives
part of its authority by legitimising the common sense of the audience
in a forum dedicated to rational expertise which also has popular resonance as a symbolic site of justice. In expressing the common sense
of the people in their judgments the judges key into the prevalent
appetite for punishment which fits the crime.

As a mechanism Judge TV works in a way very different from
that of the talk-show. While there is an 'audience', they have no role
to play in making a judgment and behave just as members of the
public are expected to conduct themselves in court. Indeed they form
a very well-ordered assembly sitting in ranks. The judge does not
address them. In place of talk-show geniality is a swift and brutal
common sense; in place of compromise is judgment which cuts across
the ethical fuzziness of the talk-show. The defendant and the litigant
are selected by producers from courtroom trials covered in the local
papers across the nation. They are then screened to appear on the
show – the producers are very anxious to avoid the labels of sleaze
associated with talk-shows and the all-too-common accusations of
fakery. But an important requirement is that they be 'good' television:
'We vet people so they're passionate and articulate.'

The body and questions of sexual identity are largely missing in
Judge TV. Participants are fixed in position by the architecture of the
courtroom. In place of performance is a return to more formal enquiry
concerning blame and shame. Judge TV helps to narrow the debate
about the responsibilities of the individual by banishing the social
context as irrelevant. The people are there to be taught a lesson. While

the audience may not speak in Judge TV the judge speaks both for them and to them by adopting the *patois* of what is fondly imagined to be 'the street'. Such a commonsensical approach helps us to consider the role of justice in our own lives.

We have seen how the new police documentaries dispense summary justice. Judge TV works in a similar way. It uses the legal apparatus to enframe a narrative in which participants compete to shame one another. This reading is underscored by the fact that participants do not suffer financially for being in the show but are there 'for all the emotion of being wronged and treated unfairly' (cnn.com). This does not always work out. One participant wrote of his 'big mistake' in April of 1999:

> What a joke!! I got shafted even though I had documented evidence (That was edited out of course) and a case that was supposed to be a slam dunk!! My advice to anyone . . . If you have a serious legal case, DON'T GO TO SEE 'JUDGE' JUDY!!! (Lewneytwo 2001)

This use of shame is also co-extensive with the return of shame in the legal context although it is represented in a way almost entirely contrary to the principles of restorative justice. Thus Judge Joe Brown, whose show airs at mid-day, provides a perfect example in a 1999 WB 38 press release:

> I had this case . . . a guy broke into a woman's house and stole some valuables. Now I could've just given him jail time but what would he learn? So I decided to to let the victim go over to his house so she could take something from him. The thief said, 'Judge, why are you letting her do this?' and I said, 'Now you know how it feels.'

The strict authoritarian stance of Judge TV might be connected to the rise of right-wing interests in the USA and those policies which encourage marriage and militate against single mothers, anti-abortionists, etc. This reading becomes more ideologically persuasive when we consider the aims of those involved in Judge TV to propagandise outside the show. Judge TV adopts a strident voice, a voice which can be read as illustrating the desire of the right-wing to seize the political agenda. Discipline is thus central as sign of regulation:

> Disciplinary power is exercised on departures from the rule, on non-observance of imposed norms, and its aim is essentially corrective, to restore or reproduce the norm, to close the gap between the (deviant) actuality of human behaviour and the programmed norm. (Smart 1983: 71)

But, as we have already seen in some of the tactics employed in talk-shows, it is no longer a simple matter of sorting out left from right.

Judge Judy

> I believe if you're a violent criminal and you've established that by your conduct, you have no right to a good time when you go to jail. You're not supposed to be beaten and tortured but jail's not supposed to be pleasant. (Gritten 1999: 3)

Oprah Winfrey had (and still has) a mission to educate and inspire her audience. She keys in to the human potential movement and is unabashed about proclaiming the significance of a spiritual life. Judge Judy Sheindlin also has a mission. She wants to shift the blame for events back on to individuals, not the sociopolitical frameworks in which they live. Her focus is on using television to offer the 'skills' she has developed to 'take my message to more people every day' (www.judgejudy.com).

> Tap-dancing around responsibility has become an art-form in the courtroom and in American society . . . By shifting the emphasis from individual to government responsibility we have infanticized an entire population. (tvtalkshows.com)

Big Ticket produces *Judge Judy*. The producer, Larry Lyttle, has said that he wanted to hire Sheindlin the moment he saw her in court because of her 'star' appeal. Since the series started *Judge Judy* has proved Lyttle right by garnering high ratings and a great deal of publicity. At one point *Judge Judy* was even more popular than *Jerry Springer*. However, the producers are very anxious to dissociate themselves from the talk-show genre, which they feel is discredited. Big Ticket stresses that the contestants are real and their complaints genuine. Being before Sheindlin is as close to the real thing as contestants can get, though, as Sheindlin has pointed out, she has no jurisdiction over those appearing. Instead what contestants sign in a binding agreement. (Myers 1999) The show relieves the participants of any financial burdens and instead uses them as moral illustrations. Contestants get $100 for appearing on the show; and the loser does not have to pay – the show pays. This may represent a good deal for many people. Furthermore, there is some distance between the law and the show, as one disgruntled participant made clear: 'Just before you go on they give you a paper to sign stating that the "Judge" doesn't have to go by any laws and we have to live by the decision' (Lewneytwo 2001).

It is clear, then, that participants are either those who feel they have very little to lose or those who have a great desire to be seen on television. It is also significant to note that *Judge Judy* does not abide by any laws but represents a space for the *performance* of justice rather than the thing itself.

What cannot be easily conveyed here is the aggressive and abusive treatment handed out to those participating. Fans have collected Judy's *bon mots* on a website (tvtalkshows.com), where we can read immortal phrases such as: 'Excuse me, sir – does it say stupid here' (pointing to forehead) and 'You must be penalized for being so dumb'. These are typical of the epigrams collected by devoted fans and made available online (tvtalkshows.com/judgejudy/). As delivered by the lady herself they are funnier than when read on the page.

Sheindlin has written four books on what might be called the socialising influence of the family. In such texts we see how Sheindlin uses the discourse of empowerment in helping individuals to be themselves and to make their own choices. This is not part of any therapeutic discourse. In *Beauty Fades, Dumb Is Forever*, Sheindlin tries to instill in women – with the help of provocative and hilarious examples from her own life – the urgent need for 'building a solid foundation within' (www.angelfire.com/on/judgejudy/). Here is a new sort of feminism, one focused entirely on the self. This is a brand of feminism which focuses on identity at the expense of broader social and political themes. As a result it is instantly accessible and makes no concrete demands on anyone.

Sheindlin's own political position came to prominence in an unfortunate way when she was touring one of her books in Australia. In Brisbane she was reported to have said of heroin addicts – to cheers from the assembled audience – 'Give them all dirty needles and let them die' (Huffington 1999: 1). Such an ill-judged remark was bound to cause controversy. Bob Aldred of the Alcoholic and Drug Foundation of Queensland described her comments as 'callous and deplorable. Even in a democratic society, the arrogance of a TV celebrity using the tragedy of young lives struck down by drugs for her own commercial gain is nothing short of repulsive' (Aldred 1999: 1). Sheindlin's apology was not quite the whole-hearted response for which the Australians were looking. The Australian *Daily Telegraph* ran an editorial headlined 'IS SHE SORRY? JUDGE FOR YOURSELF' in which her standpoint was quoted: 'I feel badly if words that I used hurt them, but am I going to apologise to a [drug advocacy] group that has an agenda? Absolutely not. This group has an agenda, and that's legalising drugs' (Media Awareness Project 2000).

Given her high public profile it is hardly surprising that Sheindlin has come in for criticism. Her crude snap decision-making is considered most unprofessional by her legal peers, because she employs a populist style which simplifies the complexities of criminal justice. Perhaps the best-known of Sheindlin's opponent is Alan Dershovitz, a Harvard law professor who believes that participating in *Judge Judy* would have made even Mussolini or Pinochet feel uncomfortable. As he put it: 'There is no place for such abusive misconduct in our judiciary. That is why we now have judicial misconduct boards to monitor and discipline the kind of bullying that is the daily grist of Judge Judy's mill' (Dershovitz 2000: 1).

It would be easy to bracket Sheindlin and other television judges as simply members of the new right. The conservative strategists appointed by President Bush's administration certainly have a great deal in common with the television judges. At the core of this group are lawyers known as 'the Federalists' who hope to undertake a radical transformation of the American legal system that will place the emphasis back on the family. However no direct links appear to exist between the show's producers and the Government. It might, however, be said that the strident language adopted by television judges echoes that of the sound-bite pronouncements of politicians of both right and left. After all, law and order is a subject where public feeling is most easily roused.

We should also consider the responses that television judges provoke. It may well be that the judges' verbal excesses are such that viewers simply discount their pronouncements. While apparently endeavouring to restore some ideal of family togetherness, however, it may be that the incessant marital breakdowns that have become 'grist to the mill' of Judge TV should be read as indicating the futility of such work. Perhaps the judges need to act in this aggressive fashion given the fact that so few litigants stay within the parameters so passionately recommended.

Connections

> The public spectacles of abuse, inquiry and condemnation are intrin-
> sically bound to this constant necessity to generate images and iden-
> tifications that will reestablish and police – in the subjectivity of each
> of us – the boundaries between the licit and the illicit. (Rose 1989: 202)

The performances of justice in Judge TV may usefully be connected to
a complex of practices which appear to have opened up the law to
public scrutiny. The transmission of confessions, the broadcasting of
robberies, the real-time car chases, even the accountability of the
police are all rendered visible by democratising discourses. Their aim
is to make the work of law and order transparent to the community.
Sometimes this produces spectacle, at other times sober judgments.
That new technologies such as the internet enable us to seemingly
take part in this process is cited as evidence that law and order is
becoming a matter for the people rather than for the professionals
alone. Thus empowered by evidence, we willingly enter into the
governance of ourselves and of others.

Judge TV's appeal may stem from the connections it makes with
instant justice seen elsewhere – in fiction and the expanding field of
documentary practice. It directs our attention to the role of morality
in public life. It puts shame to work in ways which key into the
debates and policies concerning the role of the community in solutions to crime. Just like a prime-time drama Judge TV fleshes out our
conceptions of justice and then provides narrative closure. But Judge
TV is not a 'product' of right-wing thinking, although it is easily
linked to the style and rhetoric of the right, a rhetoric that becomes
more strident the less consensus there is (Mathieson 1997: 231). While
the authorities may like to use television as a site of governance, television producers have a more commercial motivation. We also have
to consider the myriad intentions of those who willingly participate
in these shows. Furthermore the increasing media literacy of the populace represents a point of resistance which blunts the forces of
authority and further complicates governance.

But this is not to dismiss the genre. For governance to work, it
has to feel like an organic process which has arisen naturally from the
community. To participate in 'responsibilising' strategies is to con-
cretise citizenship in what appear to be self-generated terms rather
than simply following authority. Judge TV purports to be a moral
force directed as a populace in need of guidance from patriarchal

figures. But governance goes on in a seemingly democratic space in which we are enabled to autonomously frame judgements. Without this sense of autonomy and the freedom it implies governance becomes instruction:

> Government concerns the shaping of human conduct and acts on the governed as a locus of action and freedom. It therefore entails the possibility that the governed are to some extent capable of thinking and acting otherwise. (Dean 1999: 15)

Governance functions by offering choices. The choices that are made available and how are they legitimised are the crucial factors. Both Judge TV and the talk-show seek to exercise authority. Judge TV differs from the talk-show in concentrating on censure; and it affords the populace no opportunity for debate. It can operate in this way because it offers moral authority and 'experience' as well as expertise in the law as the means by which we can share in the judging of others and of ourselves. In its snappy and aggressive way it links into other dominant elements of the changing discursive formation:

> If morality is understood as the attempt to make oneself accountable for ones actions, or as a practice in which human beings take their own conduct to be subject to self-regulation, then government is an intensely moral activity. (Dean 1999: 11)

Bibliography

Aldred, B. (1999) 'Australia: attack on TV star's drug jibe', *The Age*, 18 November.
Allen-Mills, T. (1998) 'King of trash TV finds gold in that there gutter', *Sunday Times*, 15 February.
BBC (2000) 'Head to head: cameras in court', BBC Online Network, available: http://bbc.co.uk/hi/english/in_depth/2000/lockerbie_trial/newsid
Boylan, J. (1994) 'The watchful eye: American justice in the age of the television trial', *Columbia Journalism Review*, available online: www.cjr.org/year/94/4/books-thaler.asp
Boyne, R. (2000) 'Post-panopticism', *Economy and Society*, 29, 2: 285–307.
Braithwaite, J. (1989) *Crime, Shame and Reintegration*, Cambridge, Cambridge University Press.
Burchell, G., Gordon, C. and Miller, P. (eds) (1991) *The Foucault Effect: Studies on Governmentality*, Hemel Hempstead, Harvester Wheatsheaf.
Carpignano, P., Anderson, R., Aronowitz, S. and DiFazio, W. (1990) 'Chatter in the age of electronic reproduction: talk television and the "public mind"', *Social Text*, 9: 33–55.
Coles, J. (1998) 'Sleazy does it for Jerry', *Guardian*, 19 February.
Dahlgren, P. (1995) *Television and the Public Sphere*, London, Sage.
Dean, M. (1999) *Governmentality*, London, Sage.

Dershovitz, A. (2000) 'The case against Judge Judy', *Daily News*, 26 March, available online: www.nydailynews.com/2000-03-26/News_and_Views/Opinions/a-61244asp

Dreyfus, H.L. and Rabinow, P. (1982) *Michel Foucault: Beyond Structuralism and Hermeneutics*, Hemel Hempstead, Harvester Wheatsheaf.

Fiske, J. (1989) *Television Culture*, London, Routledge.

Garland, D. (1996) 'The limits of the sovereign state', *British Journal of Criminology*, 36, 4: 445–71.

Gritten, D. (1999) '*Judge Judy*'s a hit – now get over it', 16 September, available online: www.cnn.com

Hall, S., Critcher, C., Jefferson, T., Clarke, J. and Roberts, B. (1978) *Policing the Crisis*, London, Macmillan.

Hellen, N. (1999) 'Oprah walks out on "death wish" television', *Sunday Times*, 7 February.

Huffington, A (1999) 'The new callousness' (syndicated column), *Los Angeles Times*, 30 November, available online: www.ariannaonline.com

Husband, S. (2000) Trial by television', *Observer*, 'Magazine', 6 August.

Kellner, D. (1995) *Media Culture*, London, Routledge.

Kendall, G. and Wickham, G. (1999) *Using Foucault's Methods*, London, Sage.

Kettle, M. (2000) 'Anger as US television airs killers' confession', *Guardian*, 11 September.

Kritzman, H. (1990) *Foucault: Politics, Philosophy, Culture*, London, Routledge.

Lewneytwo (2001) Personal correspondence with the author.

Mathieson, T. (1997) 'The viewer society: Michel Foucault's "panopticon" revisited', *Theoretical Criminology*, 1, 2: 215–34.

Media Awareness Project (2000) 'Australia: is she sorry? Judge for yourself', *Daily Telegraph* (Australia), 11 March, available: http://65.54.246.250/cgi-bin/linkrd?_lang=EN&lah=26265bc9a7e292d919d049106c6c0b1d&lat=1044733012&hm_action=http%3a%2f%2fwww%2emapinc%2eorg%2f

Mikva, A. (1998) 'Playing to the crowd: why televising trials will turn our courtrooms into circuses', *The Gavel*, 21, 3: 1–3.

Myers, M. (1999) 'Interview: Judge Judy', *The Gallery*, 21, 9: 46–50.

NCPPR (1997) Press release: 'The public has a right to know: it's time to allow cameras in federal courts', National Centre for Public Policy Research, 5 May.

Palmer, G. (1999)' Governing through crime: surveillance, the community and local crime programming', *Policing and Society*, 10: 321–42.

Pasquino, P. (1991) 'Theatricum politicum: the genealogy of capital–police and the state of prosperity', in G. Burchell, C. Gordon and P. Miller (eds) *The Foucault Effect: Studies in Governmentality*, Hemel Hempstead, Harvester Wheatsheaf.

Priest, P.J. and Dominick, J.R. (1994) 'Pulp pulpits: self-disclosure on *Donahue*', *Journal of Communication*, 44, 4: 74–95.

Rose, N. (1989) *Governing the Soul: The Shaping of the Private Self*, London, Routledge.

Rose, N. (1998) *Governing Ourselves*, Cambridge, Cambridge University Press.

Rowe, M. (1999) 'ITC gets tough on talk-show "trash"', *Independent on Sunday*, 14 February.

Shattuc, E. (1997) *The Talking Cure*, London, Routledge.

Smart, B. (1983) 'Michel Foucault', in D. Garland and J. Young (eds), *The Power to Punish*, Aldershot, Ashgate.

Stein, J. (1998) 'Here come the judges', *Time*, online edition, 24 August, available:

www.time.com/time/magazine/1998/dom/980824/the_arts.television.
here9.html

Sullivan, T. (1998) 'TV jury: have cameras in the courtroom undermined US justice system?', Court TV Online Forum at:
www.pbs.org/newshour/forum/January 1998

Taverner, J. (2000) 'Media, morality and madness: the case against sleaze TV', *Critical Studies in Media Communication*, 17, 1: 63–85.

Walklate, S. (1989) *Victimology: The Victim, the Criminal and the Criminal Justice Process*, London, Unwin Hyman.

Website addresses for Judge and Court TV

www.tvtalkshows.com – see either /judgejudy/bio or /judgemillslane/bio
www.angelfire.com/on/judgejudy/index.htm
www.courttv.com/about/aboutcourttv.html
www.judgejudy.com/home/mein.asp
www.lanceaswell.com.judy

7

Spectacles of shame

> Social control is expected to move extensively and deeply into all domains of society, so that the boundaries between private and public, formal and informal and, metaphorically, between prison and community are progressively broken down. (Deflem 1992: 184)

This chapter continues the focus on surveillance and the use of shame by discussing how the language of video and CCTV has been imported into light entertainment in ways which may well be helping to defuse what might otherwise have seemed like a threatening technology of discipline.

Importing the technology of surveillance into light entertainment helps form the discursive formation which obscures civil rights' issues and puts the emphasis on personal security, increasing common anxiety in the process. By making it a source of amusement surveillance becomes less threatening and easier to accept. To what degree we are monitoring our own behaviour or scrutinising ourselves is hard to judge, but relating such entertainments to discipline seems more credible than ever in a carceral society. My particular focus is on the 'scam' show in which individuals are set up by friends and family. By incorporating an expanded role for a variety of 'scams' in light entertainment a new hybrid is formed which is less of a gamble than an entirely new show as well as being lower in costs.

Light entertainment

> In addition to escape from the affective relation to an exterior world, then, light entertainment like the variety show also reproduces in its sensibility a cognitive interior world of social identity, more inclusive than just class identity, providing pleasure through confirming the personal in the collective. (Lusted 1998: 182)

Of the various categories of television programme, light entertainment is the one at the farthest remove from the sober discourses of documentary and drama. Its distance from the legitimate is further emphasised by its lack of 'roots' for light entertainment is transatlantic in style and content. Light entertainment can encompass many different genres of programme, such as game-shows, quiz-shows and one-off 'specials', but audience research, ratings and scheduling indicate that light entertainment is made for the family, the working-class family in particular. Its appeal 'crosses boundaries of age and gender [and] to some sense of a common and shared experience of social class position rather that a fragmented one' (Lusted 1998: 180). Indeed, at a time when much television seeks a niche audience, light entertainment still aims itself at the family as a whole.

Light entertainment might be thought of as providing the backdrop of a party for which family members are 'dressed for best'. When they answer a question correctly there is cause for a boisterous celebration. The holiday atmosphere is tacitly acknowledged by stars and hosts when they ask family members as a group whether they have enjoyed being VIPs for a day. The family is validated by light entertainment, its ordinariness made magically worthwhile by the celebratory thirty minutes of transmission. The family is central to light entertainment as icon, as a space for ritual role-play and as a machine for patrolling norms.

The sets of light entertainment programmes at the more glitzy end of the market, such as *Blind Date*, *Telly Addicts* and *Play Your Cards Right*, are gaudy and loud, but what is being conjured up here is *glamour*. In such settings, next to the stars, the ordinariness of people is emphasised. In this world even products like irons and mowers take on a sheen of glamour, framed as they are by micro-celebrity hostesses. Here the business of consumption is transformed into something magical. The worlds of capital and labour have been dismissed to be replaced by a magic system in which people advance by a little skill and with a lot of luck before purchasing real items with make-believe money. The never-ending supply of families willing to appear on such programmes only confirms how magical and valuable this form of television is for so many.

The behaviour of the audience is wildly enthusiastic as people are actively encouraged to take part, to declare themselves as hungry and as keen as the contestants. To chant the catch phrase, to scream 'Take the money!' at a contestant while making suitably animated gestures

– all of this is very far removed from staid world of the news where ordinary people feature most often as victims, subjects of a discourse in which they have little power. Here, though, the people are loud, vibrant, defiant. This is television to be enjoyed, where we see participation at its most complete. It is this process of immersion which can be read as a threat.

> [P]opular culture is always a threat; by always occupying the subordinate, illegitimate pole in the field of cultural relations the values embedded in the practices and representations are antithical to, what are by definition, the minority values of elite cultures. (Mills and Rice 1982: 24)

Light entertainment declares itself *as* television. There is no pretence at realism here, no window on the world or the proscenium arch. The audience is not minded to consider whether what they are watching is a documentary fake or if the shop-assistant in the docu-drama is acting up for the camera. This is television as pure entertainment, to be consumed and forgotten. This utopian sensibility which lies in its feelings of abundance, energy, transparency, intensity and community (Dyer 1992: 181) informs all the forms of the light entertainment family.

Light entertainment as carnival

> Carnival does not know footlights, in the sense that it does not acknowledge any distinction between actors and spectators . . . Carnival is not a spectacle seen by the people:they live in it, and everyone participates, because its very idea embraces all the people. (Bahktin quoted in Fiske 1987: 245)

In this reading carnival is a place to escape restriction, to celebrate the body. The vulgarity of the carnival makes it repulsive, beneath consideration, to the bourgeois. Because of its focus on the excesses of the body carnival is seen as a space of resistance to the dominant arbiters of high culture. But there is an important difference to be noted between carnival and light entertainment. For Bahktin (1968) carnival is a site of abandon which is also space for resistance. Can light entertainment be said to have the same function? Given that many of its competitions are about winning consumer goods, staged against sets which are temples to consumerism, it may be difficult to pursue this line of argument. What sort of resistance is taking place here? It may be more profitable to argue that an atmosphere of carnival is generated which permits indulgence but which remains inextricably linked to consumerism. The brutal energy of the carnival is incorporated into the spectacle, its power used to serve the engines of consumerism.

Thus light entertainment is a space where the ordinary is both celebrated and diminished, where the body slips the bounds of respectability, where brittle glamour momentarily transforms the pedestrian. It is a land of brutal innocence at once open to the ordinary and yet also anxious to distance itself from it. The scam-show is the space where fun is to be had from the fact that we are, as never before, under surveillance by a variety of technologies.

The scam

> Modern society may be read as a discourse in which the nominal freedom of action is cancelled by the ubiquitous look of the other. It may be interpreted sociologically as a field of signs on which the metadiscourse of the Panopticon is reimposed everywhere, even in places where it is not installed. (Poster 1992: 91)

Although much of what has been said in this book implies a panoptical environment in which we monitor our behaviour in heavily surveyed public space, television itself functions as a synopticon in that it offers the opportunity for the many to look at the few.

> [S]ynopticism characterises our society, and characterises the transition to modernity. The concept is composed of the Greek word *syn* which stands for together and *opticon* which again has to do with the visual . . . In a two-way and significant double sense of the word we live in a viewer society. (Mathieson 1997: 219)

The panoptic function isolates individuals and subjects them to examination and various other 'micro-penalities'. Here they are made subject to normalisation. What happens between the recording of the scam itself and the moment of transmission is a shift from the panoptic to the synoptic. While the many now see the few we are encouraged to learn the lesson of self-discipline.

The scam-show has a long history in television. *Candid Camera* first emerged in the US in the 1950s and was soon exported to the UK. It is one of television's oldest international brands, with most nations having some version of it (Al-Khatib 1997). In these early *Candid Camera* shows people were scammed by a variety of means and their embarrassment offered up for viewers' amusement. It is worth noting that these images of bemused and embarrassed scammed individuals were first shown in the 1950s, a time when members of the public started to feature on television in a variety of other guises, as subjects of reports in news programmes and documentaries, etc. We soon grew used to seeing people being duped by television pranksters. It was another facet of our inclusion within the shifting understanding of 'public' in which everyday surroundings were turned into spaces for testing human behaviour.

Candid Camera brought us closer to 'real people'. We recognised the scenarios, and we saw some of our own traits in the 'targets'. We might borrow the carnival metaphor to suggest that we see ourselves here distorted in a 'hall of mirrors'. The sheer surprise of the victim conveys the realism necessary in order for the scam-show to work. *Candid Camera* emerged in an age more innocent than the present, one in which there was considerably less surveillance and far less under-standing of television. Our shared innocence made the scam doubly shocking. But in an age where surveillance is the norm and television companies proliferate, it is difficult to set up the scam in ways that will titillate a jaded audience.

In the early 1990s Noel Edmonds was one of UK television's biggest stars and a staple of the light entertainment world. His Saturday-night show *Noel's House Party* was a cornerstone of the BBC's schedule. The *House Party* consisted of a range of games and tests involving families and celebrities. What distinguished the show from others was its use of technology. Transmitted towards the end of the show was a feature called 'NTV'. The feature would begin with a shot of someone in a suburban setting, watching TV, unaware of being filmed. After a few moments of audience laughter at this, Noel would speak *through* the TV set to the victim – to his or her great surprise. Eventually all the crew would emerge with cameras, leads and micro-phones, while the victim, recovering from the shock, would invariably see the funny side of it, before having to complete some test or other for public amusement.

Viewers were surprised by the NTV sequence because it brought them to several realisations: that the family and/or friends of the victim fully approved of the lesson being taught in this way; that the technology was available to do it; and that the producers believed it would make excellent entertainment. At the heart of it was the shock of the subject–victim, startled in the home environment. What had been proposed as a nightmare scenario by some (Terry Gilliam in

Brazil, for example) is presented here as a suitable entertainment for the family.

The NTV feature remained an important part of the show, but by the mid-1990s the idea of using the family to scam those who need to be taught a lesson had spread to other formats

In shows such as *Beadle's About* and *America's Funniest Home Videos* ordinary people are encouraged to send in video-clips of themselves falling down, fumbling a speech or dropping a baby, etc. This is the 'unrestrained ungovernable body, a bringing down of all to the equality of the body principle' (Fiske 1987: 243). In video-clips we witness the body escaping the binds of ritual at weddings, school plays. Our laughter here is an odd mixture of cruelty – because we are laughing *at* rather than along *with* someone – and relief – because it is not us, though it easily could be. The laughter also has to be related to questions of power. We have a certain degree of control in watching the scam, because we know that something is about to happen. We have this sense of power over the individuals shown at the same time as we become aware of our own frailty and potential susceptibility to the scam and the technology behind it.

In the new breed of scam programme individuals actively use the media to explore a friend's character defects. Television offers itself as a means to facilitate the 'lesson' taught to erring friends. The glamour of television is not diminished by such participation. Indeed it may be reinforced by it. The star presenter, the captions, the glitzy sets – all of these work to reinscribe the glamour of light entertainment. The very ordinariness of the individuals shown on scratchy home-video footage in such 'exotic' studio surroundings gives glamour back to television. Here ordinariness is defined by the bodies' gauche quality – an awkwardness, the inelegance of which helps define the professional polish of the host at home in a world of stars.

Again production costs are a significant factor here. A professional crew will carry out a great deal of calculation and planning in creating those moments of spontaneity which are the hallmark of such programmes. A scene has to be set up, sets built, actors hired, directors briefed, etc., all of which costs more than might be inferred from what is seen on the TV screen. On the other hand, video-clip shows are very low-cost productions; for example, *You've Been Framed* pays only £250 for each clip, thus ensuring high profitability with minimal production costs. This may be one of the reasons why it is still running after ten years. Something of a parallel is provided by the mid-nineteenth-century Crystal Palace Exhibition. Bennett (1998: 64) has written of how the entrance to the Exhibition had the sign 'You Are Part of the Show', indicating that exhibits were so arranged that visitors were both viewers and viewed. This same sentiment and warning are expressed in Jeremy Beadle's catch-line in *You've Been Framed*: 'And remember, next time it could be you!' This brand of programme works by creating spectacles which activate a shared sense of what is appropriate behaviour in any given situation. Their close affinity with the programmes already discussed is evident.

Case studies

The scam-show has become an increasingly popular part of British television schedules. Its low cost, the apparent willingness of members of the public to take part and the developing appetite for reality TV make it a relatively safe bet in an insecure marketplace. Both *Lie Detector* and *Red-Handed* began life in 1998 on commercial channels. Both in appearance and in content these programmes display features that identify them as light entertainment: they are amusing, glossy, and aimed at the family; they share a concern to reveal 'the truth' about an individual's character by subjecting them to surveillance technology. What makes them contemporary is that ordinary people are given the opportunity to use surveillance technology to gain insight into friends and family which would otherwise be difficult to acquire. Each programme takes up light entertainment's focus on the body and its celebration of the ordinary but gives this a new twist by bringing modern technology to bear on the subject. They illustrate that surveillance is now part of light entertainment. A brief consideration of each programme reveals links between the giddy amusements of light entertainment and the less amusing uses of surveillance technology.

Lie Detector

You can tell a lie but you will give yourself away. Your heart will race. Your skin will sweat. The polygraph will know. Your body language will change. The way you speak will change. I will know. I am the lie detector.

Lie Detector started on Live TV, a downmarket cable station. When it transferred to the main ITV network it flopped badly. Given that it has a high degree of fit with the other programmes in the schedule, the reason for its failure is unclear, though the programme's awkward attempt to combine the discourses of science with the dictates of common sense is perhaps a contributing factor.

The programme's starting-point is a couple experiencing some form of domestic disagreement. They elect to be tested to establish which of them is telling the truth about a particular situation. The presenter, Dominic Green, introduces the couple and links the reconstructions that illustrate their problem before handing over to psychologist Phillipa Mole – the 'lie detector' who confronts viewers in the opening credits. After a brief studio interview Mole subject each of them to polygraph – and other heart and sweat – tests in order to make a scientific judgement as to their truthfulness.

The reconstruction of the domestic disagreement is shown in black and white. Here we see the couple battling it out in a form of psycho-drama, told in an exaggerated style – almost as if the individuals were moving through a photo-story in a teen magazine. Once the issue has been played out the real business of the show –lie-detection – can begin.

The test is shown in two parts, either side of the commercial break. During the test session the seated subject is shown, in brightly lit close-up, making brief responses to Mole's direct questions. This is very much a cross-examination, its legal and scientific overtones recognisable from other programmes. The clinical air is sharpened by the absence of a studio audience and the foregrounding of the testing machines. At the end of the testing, the couple is confronted with the polygraph and other results: one partner is triumphantly vindicated while the other continues to assert a version of the problem which the technology has undermined.

The visual language of *Lie Detector* is in marked contrast to that of other day-time shows with which its subject matter could claim affinity. Blue searchlights introduce the show and serve to create a break in the proceedings. The cold atmosphere and the imperative to tell the truth reinforce the atmosphere as one of interrogation. A resemblance to *Crimewatch, UK* is evident in the presenter's closing words: 'And remember – don't have nightmares!' The set is in two halves – on one side is Mole behind a desk beneath a large screen on which is data tracking the heart rate of the suspect while the other half is a chair and sofa where the quarrelling partners will soon meet.

Having returned to the sofa, Mole makes her assessment. It need hardly be added here that the performances of participating couples are almost inevitably affected by their awareness of being on television. Furthermore, the revelations of fakery in documentaries and the infiltration of talk-shows by actors and impostors have made viewers a little wary of public demonstrations of authenticity. It is nevertheless the scientific discourses operationalised to establish 'the truth' that are of interest here.

The polygraph first came to the viewing public's attention in courtroom dramas. It is a cold and dramatic device to bring into the glossy world of daytime television. But the quest for realism has been intensified in the light of recent exposés of BBC and ITV talk-shows. The polygraph is used as a means of securing closure. As a result it has been adopted by many talk-shows as a way of resolving disputed accounts of events. It is far harder to act under test conditions and so the camera focuses on the body of the suspect in extreme close-up. Shame is the prize in that one partner will have been found to be wrong – it is science that will decide.

The individuals tested in *Lie Detector* are being judged partly by the discourses of science (machines testing bodies) and partly by the community, whose standards are acknowledged by being brought to bear on the couple. The dynamic at work here differs from that of the talk-show. Whether between host and audience or panel members and the viewers at home, what is set up in the talk-show is a community engaged in debate. Everyone has a part to play – everyone has the opportunity to speak. In *Lie Detector* we have a far smaller and more sober assembly in which obeisance is paid to the dictates of science. This desire to claim truth status brings the programme closer to the certainties of Judge TV.

In a parallel development some talk-shows are now using DNA-testing as the pivotal mechanism in cases of disputed paternity. DNA sampling is considered far more veridical than the findings of polygraph tests. When it is revealed that 'X is the father' the audience has reason to attack the individual who has denied paternity. Science is not something that can be argued with. The full force of the audience's ire is set free while science takes a dignified step back into the wings, having done its job.

Connections with social control policies and objectives are clear. In *Lie Detector* we learn lessons that illustrate how 'the truth' is located in bodily responses and is therefore measurable, quantifiable. The willing submission to testing demonstrates a faith in technology (and in television!) in place of a trust in human relations. The result is a picture of human relations actively being constructed by television.

We should also note the speciously reciprocal relationship television has with the participants of such programmes. The ostensible rationale of those who participate is that they are using television to establish the truth, yet it is the television programme that unquestionably profits from the unhappiness and suffering of those involved. At the conclusion of the show the presenter tells us: 'Next time you're thinking about lying – don't. It could be you next on *Lie Detector*!'

This message is a followed with a phone number which we are to call if we think our problems might be solved by such a public airing. Television is offering itself here as a device, a scientific friend who can offer guidance. Such technology is supplemented by apparently innocuous items like the 'truth machines' sold in mail-order catalogues that test individuals' responses to questions by registering changes in skin tone. Such technologies help intensify a matrix of surveillance in which we all stare and test one another in a parody of civic virtue.

Red-Handed

Red-Handed has a more clearly established provenance in the scam-show of the type already discussed, such as *Candid Camera* and *Beadle's About*. The programme was aimed at a Sunday audience and was aired at 7 p.m. before *Coronation Street* and was an immediate success, garnering ratings of around 6 million per episode (it was recommissioned for 1999 but failed to show).

In *Red-Handed* an individual is set up by friends who consider him or her to be too loud, confident, aggressive or rude and want the scam to demonstrate their view to the victim. The set-up is organised by a professional team with assistance from the victim's friends.

The visual language of *Red-Handed* clearly derives from the world of light entertainment – more precisely, the colourful game-shows such as *The Price Is Right*. The insistent use of primary colours and the flashing graphics constitute a desperate bid to hold the attention of an easily distracted audience. For example, when an individual appears contemplative a 'light-bulb' graphic flashes on-screen; and when the scam is uncovered the victim receives a red hand made of rubber. These bright colours and the continual underlining of the theme of the show via the caption-crawler also bring to mind the frantic style of the second generation of talk-shows such as *Ricki Lake* (Shattuc 1997), though a more obvious point of reference is Channel

4's *The Big Breakfast*. By deploying visual language in this manner the show makes clear its aim to appeal to young people. *Red-Handed* brings to mind also those new teen magazines such as *Sugar* and *Mizz* which speak to their readers in this colourful zappy way when dealing with moral issues. This light-heartedness is characteristic of contemporary television's viewer-friendly approach to 'heavy' traditional issues.

Another code utilised in *Red-Handed* is one already discussed in relation to new police documentaries: at the start of the programme, just after the friends have discussed the rationale for the scam, we see footage of the 'victim' being tailed by the camera. This is shown in black and white, as are certain moments during the scam. This is the code for surveillance. Such switching back and fore from colour to black and white illustrates what happens when we cease to be anonymous and are brought into character, into colour (Hebdige 1987). Yet what is signified is the unblinking gaze of the CCTV cameras in whose vision we are all data waiting to be brought into focus. In *Red-Handed* it is a transgression that brings victims into colour, makes them real subjects.

Red-Handed's use of Neil Morrissey as narrator, an actor perhaps best known as one of the 'lads' in *Men Behaving Badly*, further underscores the show's light-hearted approach. By staking out the ground in an ironic manner we are afforded a distance on these metonyms of ourselves 'caught on camera'. We see individuals light-heartedly observing and seeing themselves as others see them. In such a way can the implications of surveillance be glossed over, if not quite dismissed.

But while the visual grammar of *Red-Handed* is bright and breezy, the moral concerns of the programme have more in common with those of talk-shows and other programmes that use confessional mechanisms to interrogate the speaking subject.

At the start of each of the scams which make up a programme those requesting the scam explain that they are 'very good friends' of the victim in question, but that she or he needs to be taught a lesson. Just like *Lie Detector* television appears to be opening itself up here as a mechanism through which ordinary people are helped to realise some 'truth' either about themselves or about others. This use of the form to stage the self may reflect a new trend in social experimentation, as discussed in chapter 8.

Because *Red-Handed* is rooted in the harmless traditions of light entertainment it avoids parallels with the more serious approaches to the self adopted by other programmes. The 'truth' revealed by such a scam is not unlike that caught by hidden cameras and deployed in current affairs programmes about 'real' deviants (Palmer 1998). *Red-Handed* betrays an awareness of the implications of its processes when the victim is shown, in occasional inserts, analysing his or her performance, and in so doing becoming one of us, looking at a 'public' performance of her or his self. In this way victims are returned to the safe anonymity of the watcher. Their victimhood humanises them, though the disposition of a 'good sport' is necessary, given the social force of shame employed by the scam.

Unlike the talk-show, *Red-Handed* does not set the behaviour of its victims in context or explain it away as a result of spousal abuse, narcotics, trauma, etc. No genuinely therapeutic objective underlies the scam. Victims are there to amuse. Beyond its mildly salutary rationale, the show exists primarily to make fun of people. Shame is operationalised to mould behaviours in much the way it is in the new police documentaries discussed earlier. But while the latter generate fear by fostering a sense of responsible citizenship in a guilty community, the laughter generated by *Red-Handed* gives us a different response to shame. Here it is our moral character rather than our social one which is being questioned in the newly opened arena of public space: 'The new technologies of citizenship formation were to gain their power through the subjective commitments to values and ways of life that were generated by the techniques of choice and consumption' (Rose 1989: 225–6).

It is instructive, however, that many of *Red-Handed*'s scams are staged in public places where a high degree of surveillance already takes place (Coleman and Sim 1998). What is appropriate behaviour? While the consumer's outward behaviour – walking around a shopping centre in an orderly fashion, not straying into inappropriate departments – can be monitored by the store's existing system, *Red-Handed* humorously suggests that the next wave of technology will be able to monitor and use information, such as what is said in casual conversation, to increase the efficiency of our shopping experience.

Red-Handed offers an experience of control of which we know little. This time it is us, the viewers, who are doing the unseen looking. *We* know how the situation will turn out, *we* control the object. Control is also the theme of the show, we realise, as we hear the director instructing his actors playing waiters to 'Lie down' or 'Start shouting', etc.

The industry's final line of defence for the scam is the release form. For the scam to have reached the screen means that the individuals concerned will have signed release forms permitting the broadcast. But one wonders what percentage of scams *are* actually aired. It would also be interesting to know what inducements the researchers offer: cash? a moment of fame? What are the pressures that are brought to bear on the 'good sport'?

Red-Handed offers audiences an experiment on human behaviour, on what happens when the gap between what Goffman (1971) called 'front' and 'back regions' is broken down. In back regions we are afforded an opportunity to relax, to be ourselves, to talk casually. The scams of *Red-Handed* may amuse but they also remind us of the ubiquity of new technology. If people are no longer able to use back regions, to relax away from life's pressures, then an important social space has gone. One can, of course, see the value, from a commercial point of view, of eradicating such spaces; but an awareness of the potential of this new technology can only make us anxious to install our own. In such a way do control mechanisms, both external and internal, become the norm, a gentle guide to governance.

Oblivious

A new series has emerged which perfectly illustrates how quickly television will seize upon a current success and turn it into product. In January 2002, ITV2 started airing a series entitled *Oblivious*. It is hosted by Davina McCall, a presenter already famous for her role as the *Big Brother* hostess who chats to/debriefs evicted contestants as they make their exit. In *Oblivious* McCall introduces a range of individuals who for twenty-four hours have been secretly filmed at the request of friends and family. The target is revealed to be a member of the audience, who is then invited down to the stage where the nominating friend or relative is asked to say how the target behaved in given situations. Each correct answer is worth £500 to the victim.

It is interesting to note what fun the producers of *Oblivious* have with the business of surveillance. The use of the *James Bond* theme music keys into the secretive act and serves as an ironic commentary on a trip to the hairdressers or the purchase of onions. The ordinary is simultaneously celebrated and mocked.

On hearing that they have been secretly filmed, the victims invariably are confused. The moment of disclosure is the occasion for that most common of scam-show emotions – shame:

> Shame as a bodily and/or mental response to the threat of disconnection from the other . . . can occur to threats from the bond from the other but it can also occur in response to actions in the 'inner theatre' in the interior monologue in which we see ourselves from the point of view of others. (Lynd 1958: 61)

Viewers might be minded to reflect on the past twenty-four hours of their own lives and to consider how suitable for transmission their activities would prove. We are likely to wonder whether or not we could cope with the revelations and tests of behaviour the show sets up. How respectable and predictable is our own behaviour?

Oblivious showcases the surveillance capabilities of new technology. This is a low-cost product which taps into the developing appetite for the real best as evidenced by the hugely successful *Big Brother*. Even the set design in stark blue is reminiscent of the blue interiors of *Big Brother* against which McCall's impassioned interviews with departing housemates took place. Furthermore the placing of *Oblivious* on ITV2 allows the programme-makers to test the product before deciding whether to move it to ITV1 at an appropriate slot in the schedule.

It would be wrong to suggest that the programmes discussed here are part of some calculated new plan to persuade the public into a happy acceptance of surveillance. There is no evidence of collusion between programme-makers and manufacturers of security technology. However, such programmes are broadcast in a climate where surveillance is becoming the norm. The shock and good humour of the contestants caught on camera in a breezy light-entertainment setting helps to defuse the threat that secret filming might represent.

It is interesting to reflect on how such entertainments work. The scam-show offers us the opportunity to see ourselves as others see us. This has a profoundly moral sense. Caitlin Moran (2000: 15) writes of the time she found £50 in a greeting card on the street and made desperate efforts to locate the owner.

> I recount all this not to buff my halo on your faces but to show you how television has instilled me with more morality that any god. Sixty years ago, it would have been the fear of God's eye on me that made me flit from shop to shop . . . Now it was a small voice that said 'Seven million viewers will be watching this in a primetime slot. Don't you be the one John Suchet introduces as ". . . and now this cold-hearted character".'

It may be that such scams are increasing the anxiety we feel about our performances in public space. It is certainly the case that, with more cameras trained on public spaces than ever before, the likelihood of any one of us appearing on screen is greater than ever. When this is combined with the fact that our personal information is also available in many thousands of databases, it becomes difficult to retain a sense of personal control. The happy smiling faces of people who seem to be amused by the intrusion of secret cameras may well be helping to defuse the threat they represent to personal liberty. Deflem (1992: 183–4) writes of

> the image of a maximum security society, a society in which not only technological engineering is taking over, but also in which people actively engage in self-monitoring. Everything on everybody is recorded, rendering the whole of the community suspicious (guilty until proven otherwise) and creating 'a nation of whistleblowers'.

The scam-show may be one more way in which we develop our propensity to self-police. This is a perfect example of discipline working as a quiet coercion, shaping the way we operate, how we behave, how we see the world. It is when such programmes utilise the trappings of surveillance that they become ever-more pervasive.

In March 2002 Channel 4 screened the first of a series entitled *Make My Day*. In this thirty-minute programme unsuspecting individuals are filmed while witnessing and participating in a range of unusual experiences. These experiences have all been set up to test a subject's character. If he or she can give the right (amoral) responses to each situation then a prize is won (a car, in the first episode).

Make My Day is typical of our time in that it represents a hybrid of other genres, in fact a borrowing so extensive that Mark Lawson (2002) can link it to at least fifteen other shows. What makes this programme interesting is that it keys into other covert surveillance activities. On the same day as the first episode was screened Home Secretary David Blunkett announced the early release of several thousand prisoners into the home detention curfew scheme where each would be monitored by electronic tags. The other prominent front-page story included the exposé of a television producer who had been masquerading as a schoolboy in order to gain insight into life at school, again for a documentary. Both stories key into surveillance and the extending network of control. Blunkett's scheme was a response to the need to reduce the pressure on prisons, the population of which has increased in five years under New Labour from 60,000 to 70,000. Following trials, electronic tagging was declared a success by the Government; but this scheme involves the release into the community of 3,000 ex-prisoners (Johnston 2002). The exposé of the documentary producer excited comment because the school's head-teacher and the students themselves had felt cheated and deceived by the man. They might properly be cautious about who they trust in future (De Bruxelles 2002). Thus we can see that *Make My Day* fits perfectly in a climate where it becomes difficult to know who to trust, where surveillance is a fact of life. In such senses, then, can a light-hearted format both amuse and deepen our anxieties about modern life.

The discourse on personal liberty is recast by such programmes. On the face of it, legislation prepared by the Home Office to detain individuals suspected of being hooligans and the bland amusements of *Oblivious* may seem a world apart, but they both buy into the premiss that if you have nothing to hide then you shouldn't object when the agencies of the State take a look. 'Government is a general form of management in which the issues of territory and sovereignty are secondary matters in relation to the management of men and things' (McNay 1996: 115).

The use of shame, the deployment of surveillance techniques, the role of the crowd–audience–community are all means of governance which find their way into our lived experience of self and others.

Bibliography

Al-Khatib, M.A. (1997) 'Provoking arguments for provoking laughter. a case study of the *Candid Camera* TV show', *Text*, 17, 3: 263–99.

Ang, I. (1991) *Desperately Seeking the Audience*, London, Routledge.

Aron, R. (1967) *Main Currents in Sociological Thought 2*, Harmondsworth, Pelican.

Bakhtin, M. (1968) *Rabelais and His World*, Cambridge, MA, MIT Press.

Bennett, T. (1998) *The Birth of the Museum*, London, Routledge.

Berko, L. (1992) 'Surveying the surveilled: video space and subjectivity', *Quarterly Review of Film Studies*, 14, 1–2: 61–91.

Blumler, J. and Katz, E. (1974) *The Uses of Mass Communication: Current Perspectives on Gratifications Research*, Beverley Hills, CA, Sage.

Clarke, P.B. (1997) *Deep Citizenship*, London, Pluto Press.

Coleman, R. and Sim, J. (1998) 'From the dockyards to the Disney store: surveillance, risk and security in Liverpool city centre', *International Journal of Law, Computers and Technology*, 12, 1: 27–45.

Collins, J. (1992) 'Television and postmodernism', in R.C. Allen (ed) *Channels of Discourse Reassembled*, London, Routledge.

Danaher, G., Schiarto, T. and Webb, J. (1999) *Understanding Foucault*, London, Sage.

De Bruxelles, S. (2002) 'Teenage TV star is unmasked as producer aged 30', *The Times*, 21 March.

Deflem, M. (1992) 'The invisibilities of social control: uncovering Gary Marx's discovery of undercover', *Crime, Law and Social Change*, 18: 179–82.

Ditton, J. (1998) 'Public support for town-centre CCTV schemes: myth or reality?' in G. Armstrong, J. Moran and C. Norris (eds) *Surveillance, Closed Circuit Television and Social Control*, Aldershot, Ashgate.

Dyer, R. (1992) *Light Entertainment*, Bfi Monograph, London, British Film Institute.

Evans, K., Frakes, P. and Walklate, S. (1996) 'Whom can you trust? The politics of grassing on an inner-city housing estate', *Sociological Review*, 44, 3: 361–80.

Fiske, J. (1987) *Television Culture*, London, Routledge.

Gill, M. and Turbin, V. (1998) 'CCTV and shop theft: towards a realistic evaluation', in G. Armstrong, J. Moran and C. Norris (eds) *Surveillance, Closed Circuit Television and Social Control*, Aldershot, Ashgate.

Goffman, E. (1971) *The Presentation of Self in Everyday Life*, Harmondsworth, Penguin.

Hebdige, D. (1987) *Hiding in the Light*, London, Comedia.

Holloway, W. and Jefferson, T. (1997) 'The risk society in an age of anxiety: situating fear of crime', *British Journal of Sociology*, 48, 2: 255–66.

Johnston, P. (2002) 'Blunkett unveils plan to ease jail crowding', *Daily Telegraph*, 21 March.

Lawson, M. (2002) 'One of those days', *Guardian*, 'Media' (supplement), 18 March.

Lusted, D. (1998) 'The popular culture debate and light entertainment on television', in D. Lusted and C. Gerahty (eds) *The Television Studies Book*, London, Arnold.

Lynd, H. (1958), *On Shame and the Search for Identity*, New York, Harcourt.

Lyon, D. (1992) 'The new surveillance: electronic technologies and the maximum security society', *Crime, Law and Social Change*, 18: 159–75.

Mainprize, S. (1996) 'Elective affinities in the engineering of social control:the evolution of electronic monitoring', *Electronic Journal of Sociology*, available online: www.sociology.org.content/vol 002.002/mainprize.html

Mathieson, T. (1997) 'The viewer society. Michel Foucault's "panopticon" revisited', *Theoretical Criminology*, 1, 2: 215–34.

McNay, L. (1996) *Foucault: A Critical Introduction*, Cambridge, Polity Press.

Mills, C. and Rice, P. (1982) 'Quizzing the popular', *Screen Education*, 41 (winter–spring).

Moran, C. (2000), 'He saw what you did, by Zeus', *The Times*, 12 May.

Morley, D. (1992) *Television, Audiences and Cultural Studies*. London, Routledge

Norris, C. and Armstrong, G. (1997) *The Unforgiving Eye: CCTV Surveillance and Public Space*, Hull, Centre for Criminology and Criminal Justice, University of Hull.

Palmer, G. (1998) 'The new spectacle of crime', *Information, Communication and Society*, 1, 4: 361–81.

Poster, M. (1992) *The Mode of Information*, Cambridge, Polity Press.

Priest, P.J. and Dominick, J.R. (1994) 'Self-disclosure on *Donahue*', *Journal of Communication*, 44, 4: 74–95.

Reeve, R. (1998) 'The panopticism of shopping: CCTV and leisure consumption', in G. Armstrong, J. Moran and C. Norris (eds) *Surveillance, Closed Circuit Television and Social Control*, Aldershot, Ashgate.

Rose, N. (1989) *Governing the Soul: The Shaping of the Private Self*, London, Routledge.

Shattuc, J. (1997) *The Talking Cure*, London, Routledge.

Short, E. and Ditton, J. (1998) 'Seen and now heard: talking to the targets of open street CCTV', *British Journal of Criminology*, 38, 3: 404–29.

Stanko, E. and Newbury, D. (1994) *Just Boys Doing Business*, London, Routledge.

Walklate, S. (1998a) 'Crime and community: fear or trust? *British Journal of Sociology*, 49, 4: 550–69.

Walklate, S. (1998b) 'No more excuses. Young people, victims and making amends', *Policy Studies*, 19, 3–4: 213–22.

Website address

Government of New Zealand, Justice Department: restorative justice report: http:/justice.govt.nz.pubs/reports/1996/restorative/chapter 2/html

8

Video lives

Video Diaries

> Neo-television is about making the lives of urban citizens transparent. It is about the publication of private worlds. (Robins 1996: 143)

In amid the revolution that we have seen sweeping through television in the 1980s and 1990s, *Video Diaries* seemed like a rare moment of transcendence. The series which gives ordinary people the chance to have their say on television was a product of that 'Reithian outpost'– the Community Programming Unit (CPU) at the BBC. The very existence of the CPU was cited as proof that access, that 'intriguing and fugitive element torn between democratic theory and notions of representation', is alive and well (Price 1995: 194). *Video Diaries* has been praised by critics as an innovation that could have been developed only by a public service broadcaster which maintains a special duty towards its viewers. But to what extent was *Video Diaries* innovative, enabling or radical? How was it related to the drive that would have us shape our identities via authoritative expertise?

Today video is used in a range of social experiments to remodel the self in line with imperatives and objectives quite different from that of *Video Diaries*. A simple way of outlining these differences is to say that whereas *Video Diaries* afforded individuals a wide brief and a great deal of time to discover some aspect of their selves, more contemporary uses of video demand results, transformations and spectacle in a far shorter time-frame. Thus while use of the video-journal or video-diary may be more widespread today than previously, the identities thereby produced seem more restricted and delimited by executives' stipulations. Television demands particular kinds of identities.

Roots

The CPU came into being in the wake of the success of the 'open door' policy of the early 1970s by which members of the public were helped to make their own programmes, usually about issues in their locality, by the professional crews of the BBC. The CPU has been described as a 'leftist' interpretation of the Reithian ideal of public service (Dovey 1993). Reith was convinced, however, that he knew what the public needed, and he did not welcome the views of those who thought otherwise. As the very idea of access presupposes that members of the public have something to say, and should be allowed to say it, it might be more accurate to credit former BBC Director-General Hugh Greene as the model and inspiration of the open door policy, for his era, the 1960s, seems to have been more attuned to the access project than anything Reith might have championed. Indeed, the rationale of the CPU could reasonably be related to other access innovations of the 1960s, such as the Open University project. The CPU's programmes, like those of the Open University, are broadcast on BBC2, a channel that started in the 1960s and has a firm commitment to education and the arts. Although Channel 4 has experimented with access in a variety of guises, such as the five-minute diary entries broadcast at 7.55 p.m., the CPU is certainly the most open aspect of mainstream broadcasting left in British television.

The success of *Video Diaries* is no doubt related to the principle of access; but it was the quality of the series that drew audiences. That was the view of Jeremy Gibson, the first head of the CPU: 'I like to think it was the quality which won people over' (quoted in Kilborn 1998: 205). Because *Video Diaries* operates within a historical vacuum and with a brief redolent of the expansive outlook of the 1960s – and therefore remote from the harsh new world of the marketplace – it is important that we trace the series' specific institutional base.

I noted in the Introduction how changes at the BBC had a considerable impact on programme production. Between 1988 and 1993 there was significant structural reorganisation and a considerable diminution of union power. O'Malley (1994) estimates that over that period staff cuts totalled 4,500 a year. With its charter coming up for renewal, the BBC was said by some commentators to be meekly accepting the dictates of the Government in order to retain the licence fee as a source of funding (Franklin 1997).

In 1991 the BBC's management introduced the idea of 'producer

choice' which forced individual producers to investigate the most efficient and cost-effective way of delivering their programmes. An internal market for services put the BBC on a business footing and brought
it closer to the rest of the broadcast industry in terms of cost and co-
operation, though as a publicly funded institution it was still insu-
lated from the full impact of the 'real' market.

It would be naïve to suppose that the CPU was unaffected by
these changes. In common with other departments, the CPU had to
come to terms with the consequences of change, and a case can be
made for saying that *Video Diaries* was an apt BBC-style response to
this new climate.

There were two beginnings to the series, both of which reflect the
demands of the new climate. The first of the *Video Diaries* to be commissioned was born not of inspiration but in response to budgetary
restrictions. A diarist proposed going, with a crew, to film in the
Middle East; Jeremy Gibson, at that time head of the CPU, told him
that the budget was insufficient for such a venture and advised him
to finance it himself (Kilborn 1998: 205). The 'on-your-bike' do-it-
yourself principles that underscored Thatcherite individualism were
now informing access. This low-cost, low maintenance, project could
be read as the work of an early independent film-maker, with the
advantage that the resulting footage could be assisted into the appropriate shape in post-production. In this way, the hallowed principles
of access, on which some of the BBC's claim to public service status
have been based, mesh with the new creed of cost-effectiveness and
independence advocated by the Tory Government.

The first of the *Video Diaries* was screened in 1991 and featured a
recording made by a football fan at the 1990 World Cup. Here was a
subject of wide appeal yet which was 'authored' in a way which gave
it a real authenticity. The rough-and-ready feel of the camcorder
bespoke a non-professional film-maker and football fan in circumstances that were, like those of the majority of the *Video Diaries*, far
from ordinary. The result is an access product perfectly in tune with
the market. We are offered a new taste of 'the real' focusing on a traditionally working-class sport now rapidly gaining popularity with
the middle classes. This happy match of popular subject and gritty-
thus-authentic method was to prove a taste of things to come. The new
mission statement was fulfilled in a way which pleased everyone.

Video Diaries has horizontal connections also. The talk-show keys
into the access idea, and the first generation of shows afforded some

opportunity for groups to use television to raise public awareness and so to self-validate their aims. *Video Diaries* is a product of a decade during which social movements, including feminism and other liberatory factions, were active in promoting varieties of 'identity politics'.

> The term is used to refer to a commitment to one of the new social movements which emphasises one element in the construction of our identity: gender; sexual orientation; race; ethnicity or nation. (Sarup 1996: 52)

The CPU had an interest in minority cultures, but always in the form of individual rather than group experience. The lightweight self-operated camcorder, or hi-8, represented a perfect means to express the view that the 'personal is political' as well as catering to television's taste for individuals with stories to tell rather than movements with agendas. The individual who comes across as quirky or odd can be dealt with as an individual rather than as representative of some troublesome group with a specific social cause.

A less-known precursor to *Video Diaries* was the work of Ed Pincus, who started making video diaries (and named them as such) in the 1980s.

> As Pincus developed his philosophical perspective he saw the potential for a new kind of cinematic self-inscription that could emerge from the interactive documentation of the immediate world of the film-maker. Pincus viewed the new mode of documentary as the cinematic democratizer, in which the power relation would be diminished by the film-maker acknowledging his/her presence in the film. (Lane 1997: 8)

Although couched in the language of film, this reads like a description of the *Video Diaries'* project. Pincus, who taught at Harvard, acknowledged that his films were a response to the political shift engineered by feminist politics in the 1960s and 1970s. He recorded intimate details of his open marriage over a 5–6-year period. Those moments in which the camera is left running while the participants discuss the power of the lens 'speak' the authenticity on which the *Video Diaries'* project depends. Interestingly, Pincus spoke to the 'evolving self' thesis, which I believe to be crucial to *Video Diaries*, when he remarked that in his films 'people are treated more as becomings' (quoted in Lane 1997). This is characteristic of a view of people as 'subjects in process', a way of thinking that *Video Diaries* enthusiastically embraces.

The funding crisis of the Public Broadcasting Service in the USA has meant that Pincus and the other video-diary-makers he inspired have not found openings in television schedules to air their work, and it remains known only to students of independent documentary cinema. Yet, as we will see, some of Pincus's concerns and approaches to the domestic as a site of identity construction are echoed in the *Video Diaries*.

It may also be significant to recall how CCTV footage and the new genre of reality TV have provided an abundance of grainy images of individuals coming to terms with their urban environment. Robins has observed: 'The space between experience and detachment has imploded. The seeing self has collapsed into the self seen; the reflecting self has disappeared into the immersed self' (1996: 141).

It has been noted already that the 1980s and 1990s saw the public coming to terms with the idea and practice of surveillance. People saw images of themselves on monitors looking out from shop windows or on entry-phones. Camcorders were introduced into the working environment in order to teach self-presentation. Domestic camcorders recorded special occasions and were taken on holiday, and so people became familiar with their on-screen appearance. The newness of *Video Diaries* has to be measured against this proliferation of the ordinary. The jagged amateur techniques gave documentary a new degree of authenticity.

Few critics discussing *Video Diaries* focus on the medium itself. Beyond the understanding that it is cheap and easy to operate video is seen merely as a tool enabling the interesting diary aspect. Yet artists and critics of the late 1980s and 1990s shared a determination that video could be used to relinquish the naturalistic aesthetic 'which seems implicit in video limiting the medium to the production of blocks of sound and image locked immutably together' (Armes 1988: 166).

For the early users, video was seen a technology that would not only liberate groups to a new visibility but would do so by utilising some of the specific advantages offered by the new medium.

Channel 4 was founded on a commitment to public service. Its remit was to cater for those minority groups and individuals who had not been represented previously. Furthermore it had a brief to encourage innovation. It acknowledged the potential advantages of video in series such as *Ghost In The Machine* and *Timecode*, which offered the first public airings of a new underground community of artists inspired by video. Talented new videographers formed underground

networks, some of which bore a resemblance to the filmic underground of the 1960s. Video was a liberating technology in which the
boundaries of representation could be tested.

By the late 1980s, however, Channel 4 had realised that such programming, while of course valuable, was not financially viable.
Experimental series were not recommissioned, so that the more
radical uses of the technology were confined to the underground or
else were deployed as part of the stylistic repertoire of the pop music
video-maker.

Originating within an institution that has a long-standing commitment to public access and a determination to innovate, BBC2 might
have been expected to offer a home to the video experimentation abandoned by Channel 4. The early 1990s were, however, a difficult time
for the BBC and radical uses of the new technology constituted something of a gamble. Nevertheless, the CPU had an interest in what video
could do to facilitate access. The emphasis in *Video Diaries* was on
content – the message – and as a result the programmes are of limited
aesthetic interest. Thus by 1991 video's potential for difference was
being erased under the sign of access. In this way the borders of dis-
tinctiveness are measured according to established rules of representation. This decision to emphasise content represented part of the
BBC's strategy for coping with a changing market and a Government
hostile to its 'protected' status.

Video Diaries was aired at an important juncture for the documentary. The innovation video offers at the technical level enables viewers
and users to be closer to the subject, and closer can mean more real in
the rhetoric of the form. The new intimacy afforded by camcorders re-
authenticated documentary as a viable means for interrogating the
real. It certainly helped that *Video Diaries* gained considerable critical
acclaim and good audiences (2 million per episode on average).Video
helped to reconnect documentary to its historical role – making
records of people in their actual environments – and offered new
opportunities to extend access. In rejecting artifice, *Video Diaries*
became another means of cementing the image and the real in precisely the way feared by the videographers mentioned earlier. *Video
Diaries* imported the authorising and legitimising discourses of documentary into the personal, and in doing so it imported also documentary's ordering principle into individual lives. The real reproduced
here by amateurs thus appears natural and the documentary-maker's
method is legitimised anew.

The first *Video Diaries* contained much footage which was crude and raw, with bumpy starts, odd bits left in, the camera lurching before cutting into jagged tilt and pans – all of this betrayed the real, i.e. the non-professional. The truth of the subject was made more real by being self-authored. It is because documentary has long traded on the power of the image and has neglected questions of form that *Video Diaries* could build on a long-developed history of revelation. Thus the documentary project to investigate ordinary lives is re-validated by the new subject-auteurs. The latter represent a new breed of self-starting entrepreneurs striving to prove that they were able to do what previously only professionals could do.

It follows from BBC2's institutional commitment to access and empowerment that discussions about *Video Diaries* are tied to questions of social power – i.e. who gets access and why.

> Video is enabling us to think about the way we define these categories and how broadcasting divides its producers from its consumers. In other words, it enables us to think about television and democracy, to reflect upon the fact that television is a source of (unelected) power for those who work in and control the industry – researchers, directors, programme-makers, producers, schedulers, broadcasters. Video is enabling us to think again about who should have power, what they are doing with it and why. (Keighron 1993: 24)

The debate becomes one about fairness, balance and legality, as well as about the power of representation. *Video Diaries* occupies a site of acceptable tension between discretion and disclosure in terms set by the broadcasters. The focus is on the experience of the subject within the frame. The frame itself is not an issue. It is not video's distinctive capacities that are deployed here: its technology is being utilised merely as an enabler.

What those at the CPU stress is the series' openness, the fact that the diarists have complete control and we have no reason to doubt their commitment to this ethos. It may, however, be worth considering the various ways in which the broadcasters measure access to the institution.

The first consideration is the selection of *appropriate* diarists. It is estimated that the CPU receives as many as 6–8 applications a day while the series is being aired, though less when it is off-air. What determines the selection? The CPU has to balance the access afforded to the public against the need to achieve good ratings and critical acclaim – factors necessary to its continued survival. As some critics have pointed out, this has often meant selecting diarists who are not only already close to the media but whose concerns are some way from the access ideology (Corner 1996). 'The Cuban Nipple Crisis' springs to mind – a sixty-minute diary about the nipple-revelation quotient of models in Cuba. The recent trend for providing camcorders to MPs affords yet another insight into a group who already have plentiful access to the media. It may also be worth noting that the BBC needs to make sure that potential diarists are made of the 'right stuff' before entrusting them with the camcorders. While basic techniques can be quickly learned, the qualities expected in diarists are not: 'Diarists, before they are accepted onto the project, are tested to assess their suitability and to establish whether they are sufficiently motivated to complete the task' (Kilborn 1998: 205).

Contributors are offered weekly contact with the producers. It is written into the contract that either the diarists or the BBC can pull out at any time. Given that many of the diarists display an exhibitionist tendency how might this clause be experienced – as a threat to take away the long-sought-after platform? How might these diarists perceive the requests for results made by this dominating broadcast institution? While these interventions are made in the most tactful manner they probably feel like a nudge from Auntie to get on with the homework.

Gibson has said that the diarists should tell a story. The shooting ratio of 180:1 must mean that a great deal of work is done at the editing stage in order to make a story clear. Stories are to be told in ways that are acceptable to both the BBC and the diarists. The striving here is for *balance*. The BBC is anxious to present the diarists in the best possible light. As a result we are always given a rounded picture – Mr X may reveal himself to be a bad employer and a hopeless father but he is very kind to animals, etc.

> Your ego and your attitude and approach can come across from the rushes in a very off putting way that an outsider wouldn't like. It's our job to identify that and try to turn the diarist to take a less ego-centric approach to something and less pushy aspects of his personality which are difficult or confrontational. (Long quoted in Keighron 1993: 25)

This commitment to a balanced portrait ensures a happy mosaic of individuals, but with very few raw edges. Diarists are persuaded into sameness and are actually helped to present the best of themselves.

The final measure of control is expressed through the invisible *professional polish*, the smooth cuts, the sensitive use of music, the transitions, the establishing shots, the maintenance of a steady narrative pace. Given all of these measures of control and the lingering commitment to balance which is the hallmark of the responsible public service broadcaster, it is no surprise that so many *Video Diaries* look the same.

Diary of self

> The self that is liberated is obliged to live its life tied to the project of its own identity. (Rose 1989: 254)

The diary is an enduring means of self-examination which has a variety of antecedents. The Greeks and Romans used diaries to develop the self. The recollection of the day's activities,it was thought, would develop in the diarist an increasing self-awareness that would make cultivation of the self a life project. Many Eastern faiths encourage diary-keeping for reflecting upon and contemplating one's true nature. Diaries featured in Christian sects as a means of monitoring, examining and testing the individual, and as such they facilitate the split in the Protestant self 'between accuser and accused . . . confessing and examining becomes an entirely internalised dialogue between two facets of self – the observer and observed (Sarup 1996: 87).

The diary is a secret affair and still has considerable cultural force as a revealer of truth which enables us to understand the construction presented for consumption in everyday life. Comparisons might be usefully drawn between the revelatory functions of diary and documentary. Like the diary, the documentary can work to reveal the real life behind the stereotypical surface: once we know the complexities we too can better understand the individual. For both to 'work' as afforders of insight to the true, we must be made aware of a dichotomy, a split between inner and outer, between front and back regions (Goffman 1971). A contemporary example is the docusoap which focuses on the private life of someone who works in the public domain. The private life enriches our understanding of the public performance. Here then is the paradox of *Video Diaries* – they are to reveal something secret but has been prepared for the camera. It is designed specifically to reveal the secret, to make public the private.

The opening sequence of *Video Diaries* captures the sense of interiority. After the introduction in which the BBC's minimal yet enabling role is declared, we see a collection of diary images intercut with shots of the camcorder being operated. In combining the two, amateurism is foregrounded as theme and rationale. The closing shot of the sequence is a close-up of an eye. The eye that looks out to us might be the fabled eye of Big Brother and is emblematic of our increasingly surveilled culture. But it also works as a kind of mirror. The series often features moments in which individuals stare into the lens after giving a speech or commenting on some action. The lens is also us, the viewers. These blank moments are often affecting precisely because they slow down the flow of images within the text, and in television more generally, and force us to confront the individual contemplating whatever he or she has discovered about the self. Furthermore, these *faux*-monologues are often infused with a psychological discourse on the internal dispositions which shape our actions (Rose 1998). But because *Video Diaries* chronicles change the self is both the motor determining the change and the construct being shaped by it. The language used is not merely contemplative – it is enabling – the site, the stake and the result of conflicts, contestations and campaigns.

When diarist Steve Marston, a psychiatric team-leader, records his thoughts on how he is going to cope with the loss of his father and the question of access to his son, he worries what it will mean to him as 'a man' – a construct he thus simultaneously asserts is remote from his speaking everyday self. He rehearses his anxiety and then lets the camera run showing just his worried face. What his diary reveals is not merely the activity of trying to care for his father, his son and his 'clients', but what and where he is in all this. Even a frivolous diary like 'The Cuban Nipple Crisis' finishes with the videographer coming to the realisation that his life may have been 'headed in the wrong direction all this time': 'It's been a waste of a location, a waste of my life. Somehow I've got to get out of this.'

The camera interrogates the self as much as it does the world beyond. The fact that it takes less effort to operate than a pen or pencil only encourages the diarist to say whatever is on his or her mind. The result is a great deal of footage which is also a protracted self-analysis – a triumph of the therapeutic.

'Self-observation' of course points to precisely the process that must follow the fashioning of an interpersonal script out of sometimes incongruous material, often very careful self-observation. And self-observation represents incipient self-control, and self-control becomes synonymous with the staging of the self. The actor ultimately must submit to the authorial I while both nervously anticipating the responses of overlapping but always harmonious panels of internal and external critics. (Simon 1996: 50–1)

In *Video Diaries* the narrator is both anterior and interior to the text: everything has already happened to the individual subject. 'At this point I was very worried, but later on I did X and I shouldn't have', etc. The self is split in two for the purposes of story-telling and to lend the text narrative force. In this way the *Diaries* chronicle the difficulties of managing the self 'in everyday life', an activity which we are all encouraged to engage in by a variety of methods through popular media (Goffman 1971). The awkward documentary techniques and the delicate situation of the self responding to change provide a situation with which we can all engage and identify.

It offers itself to the viewer on the one hand as being deeply personal (as indicated by the amateurish elements), but is rendered acceptable (even trustworthy) in terms of familiar television practice by the professional control of its pace, structure and purpose. (Izod and Kilborn 1997: 107)

Izod and Kilborn (1997) have suggested that *Video Diaries* eschew the 'voice of God' that is the traditional marker of documentary. What has been put in its place (and is all too evident in some *Diaries*), however, is a troubled personal god, the interior self watching ones own conduct in a perfect display of self-discipline. This is self-government by a god armed with psy-words.

Video Diaries is often used for interrogating memory, for going back to a troubled past and assessing it. Video explores those inner and outer states in a bid to make presentable sense of oneself. 'Mad, Sad or Bad' chronicled the exploration of an individual undergoing psychiatric treatment. The diarist began by saying how much she did not want to be making it. She concluded it by leaving to meet (off-screen) her birth-mother. The diarist revealed a conflict between the professional psychiatric help offered by institutions and her felt experience and that of other sufferers. The psychiatric world was represented by medicine bottles and the diarist's boyfriend, also a psychiatric patient, describing how doctors had 'set about him with their expertise'. The diarist herself believed that being abandoned by her mother was the

root cause of her difficulties and that meeting her again would allevi-
ate them. Over the course of her diary-keeping, she gained a degree of
self-understanding that had little to do with drug-led treatments but
which was in keeping with Laing's belief (1967) that the social environment is crucial in shaping the schizophrenic. Her situation illustrated how individuals are caught within discourses written for them
elsewhere.

It is noteworthy that this diarist ended her record by leaving to
meet the mother who abandoned her without the camera capturing
the details of the meeting. This elegantly illustrates the respectful distance the CPU maintained from those feelings and moments most significant to the diarists.

Video Diaries, then, offers itself as a modern way of making sense
of people's experiences, of their pasts. The series helped to fashion
memories that work. It need hardly be added that such a use is of a
piece with other technologies deployed by psy-workers to make
knowable the self for examination, measurement and categorisation.

The enabling discourses of liberalism have made access a space
wherein individuals seem to speak freely, but are nevertheless con-
strained both by the strictures of the broadcasting institution and by
the language and good taste of the BBC. The psy-disciplines taken up
by the individual into his or her life project and sanctioned by broadcasters via transmission help legitimise the construction of a self
which is acceptably, measurably, unique.

Video Nation

Video Nation was the next project of the CPU. Beginning in 1993, the
aim was to show the 'rich diversity of views' held by the public. In a
project inspired by Mass Observation and operated in conjunction
with the British Film Institute's National Film and Television Archive
individuals are given some basic training in the use of video before
chronicling aspects of their lives. What eventually appears on screen
are not so much self-portraits as a series of original and sometimes
unusual views on contemporary issues. Those selected to contribute
were chosen according to vaguely sociological criteria. In an attempt
to be representative of the nation's populace, the rich are given the same
access as the poor and downtrodden. In some programmes the contributions are based around a single theme, and fascinating juxtapo-
sitions can thereby occur, as happened with the contributions on the

theme of money. Unfortunately, most screenings are all but hidden in the schedule – at 10.28 pm on BBC2, for example.

Those who applied to take part in *Video Nation* did so because they felt they were either under-represented on television or not represented at all. The series offered them a space to be themselves, in much the same way as early talk-shows seemed a useful and convivial platform. In *Video Nation*, however, control over the performance within the frame remains with the individual. One contributor expressed the view that video enables people to examine 'the last detail of the way we are now' and that such access was an empowering experience. The series has been criticised for being television-on-the-cheap' and full of losers and wannabees; the producers defend the project on the grounds that it validates the importance of everyday life.

It is instructive to compare the occasional quirky fragment of realism in *Diaries* and *Nation* with the new trend towards the consumer self so dominant in contemporary television.

Televideo, ergo sum

[R]egulatory practices seek to govern individuals in a way more tied to their selfhood than ever before and the ideas of identity and its cognates have acquired an increased salience in so many of the practices in which human beings engage. (Rose 1998: 169)

All you have to do on television is to be yourself, provided, that is, you have a self to be. (James 2001: 310)

Previous chapters have drawn attention to the changing context in which the self is formed. We have seen how new technological developments attempt to measure identity for commercial purposes. The traces we leave of ourselves on CCTV cameras are now mirrored by the tiny bits of data which define us after we pay by credit-card at the supermarket checkout. Whatever freedom of identity we may think we have when using the internet, our addresses and activities are increasingly monitored by 'cookies'. The Regulation of Investigatory Powers Act obliges internet service providers to deliver, at the request of the police, whatever information they have on a given subscriber. Furthermore, as was noted in chapter 1, employers are now authorised, under certain conditions, to read the emails of their personnel. In this new surveillance climate it is little wonder that various debates on the self have been engendered.

When Ruth Picardie and John Diamond with witty and amused detachment chronicled their fatal illnesses, this

> represented the logical extreme of a cultural trend which includes newspaper diaries of divorces, chat-show revelations from 'ordinary' people, docusoaps and the prime minister confiding cuddly family secrets on Des O'Connor's studio sofa . . . people now seem keen to nationalise their private lives, turning them into the new public property. (Aitkenhead 1999: 15)

Television has chosen various responses to this theme, the majority of which have neglected to engage with the social, moral and political contexts in which selves are formed. Indeed the territory occupied by video diaries and their odd, yet somehow poignant, sketches of life has been abandoned for a fascination with consumer culture.

By the mid-1990s the video diary had spread into many different formats. Individuals ranging from footballers to children used the video-diary function to tell their stories – sometime with recognisable documentary purpose, on other occasions merely to amuse. The authenticity that video once claimed was now being diminished by overuse – and by the identification of documentary fakes. There could be no better proof of the diary format's assimilation into the language of television than its adoption by a number of advertisers.

The individual, aided by experts, telling us her or his story has now become a television commonplace. John Langer (1998: 169) has written that

> in a culture where an identity-principle is increasingly 'ratified by publicity' these sites become significantly more important for identity validation and the confirmation of prestige when the more traditional and conventional mechanisms are perceived to have broken down or to have failed completely.

Television that looks at the remodelling of the self can have broad appeal. It makes sound commercial sense to invest in programmes which cross cultural and class divides and promise transformation for everyone regardless of background. This keys into a burgeoning cultural movement which promises empowerment through self-belief and finds expression in talk-shows and other hybrid formats designed to help us 'be all that we can be'.

We have already noted how this personal development movement achieves ideological purity in *Oprah*, where tearful individuals are given specific plans to enable them to fulfil their potential. In the USA programmes such as these are the showcase for a giant industry with many thousands of titles and speakers enabling people to empower themselves. The guides and plans of such programmes are often specifically designed for an audience reared on spectacular television transformations. This belief in a malleable self has a high degree of fit with consumer culture, as well as sidestepping 'tricky' social and political issues. Testimony and transformation can make for very appealing, even uplifting, television.

Another reason that producers may give for shifting the focus towards the self is the belief, widely held in television circles, that the audience's attention span is shrinking. Shows which focus on a 'new you' are what fit the bill – the tangible results, the transformations, prove the thesis that the self can be remade and remodelled.

British television has accommodated a wide range of selves in its new hybrid formats. Subjects and programme-makers enter into agreements, and the selves that emerge are the result of negotiation. After a few episodes docu-soap 'stars' are well-advised to get themselves an agent and to begin arranging 'personal appearances'. This is a long way from the victim of Griersonian documentary, as critiqued by (among others) Brian Winston (1995).

The evidence suggests that an increasingly media-literate audience knows that such manipulations are taking place, and that this awareness does not detract from its enjoyment. Viewers are amused by the spectacle of selves entering the process of transformation. This is television demonstrating its utility – television that works.

The new experts in these programmes have backgrounds in the service industry – nutritionists, dietitians, hair-dressers and other lifestylists, all devoted to the consumer self – the 'new you'. Their project is to transform a self for the audience in the quickest, most accessible and viewer-friendly way. At the centre of these transformation is the body, the body to which we are made more sensitive than ever as a cultural text, trained (or tragically not) to emit certain signs.

Case studies

Rather than speak of 'the body', we need to analyze just how a particular body-regime has been produced, the channelling of processes, organs, flows, connections, the alignment of one aspect with another. (Rose 1998: 184)

Body Spies

Broadcast on weekday afternoons in the summer of 2000, *Body Spies* was produced by Bazal, cited earlier as an exemplar of opportunistic new companies moving into the field of documentary practices which would become well known for its production of *Big Brother* (of which more later).

In *Body Spies* a number of individuals, equipped with personal video cameras, have four weeks in which to lose an amount of weight. Friends and family are given access to the cameras so that they can 'spy' on the subject. To ensure that no drastic weight-loss measures are taken, a regimen is drawn up and the project overseen by one of television's friendly faces, Dr Mark Porter.

It is clear that those taking part in the programme are using it as an inspirational and motivating force. Being televised means that their achievement (or failure) is seen by millions. Whether or not *Body Spies'* scenes are set up is perhaps a matter of less significance than the fact that television is providing a platform for such exercises. As Rose (1998) has observed, fitness is a kind of psychic economy of self-esteem and empowerment.

Body Spies exhibits a high degree of fit with other items from daytime television which also seek to transform the self. Thus make-over programmes help the mums who feature in them to show themselves at their best to cries of approval from the grooming gurus and the studio audience. Those who participate learn that the regimes imposed on them can be fun, and the approbation their efforts receive helps validate a process in which exercise and diet are consciously taken on as a kind of duty to the self.

Experts in exercise, diet and nutrition are the new authorities promoted by consumer magazines and daytime television programmes. They all preach from the same text according to which the keys to happiness and self-fulfilment – duties to the self – lie in such gurus' routines.

Fat Club

Susan Bordo (1999: 167) has remarked on the dangers of a preoccupation with diet and slenderness:

> Indeed, such preoccupation may function as one of the most powerful normalising mechanisms of our century, insuring the production of self-monitoring and self-disciplinary 'docile bodies' sensitive to any departure from social norms and habituated to self-improvement and self-transformation in the service of these norms.

Screened at the prime-time of Tuesdays at 8.30 p.m. on ITV, *Fat Club* focuses on the efforts to lose weight of a sixteen-member group of obese individuals who are sent to a gymnasium–villa where experts in nutrition, diet and exercise aggressively assist them towards their objective.

What distinguishes *Fat Club* from other programmes which feature those gamely trying to lose weight is that it shows the discomfort participants experience at the behest of the new experts. Combatants in the fight against obesity are put under considerable peer pressure. Those who do not meet their weekly weight-loss target are deemed to have let themselves down.

Uniformly clothed in white dressing gowns, participants have the appearance of patients awaiting surgery. It makes for good television, of course, that the larger the individual the greater the potential for transformation – and the greater the satisfaction all round when he or she is seen to have 'made it'. Such a process of transformation is not unlike what goes on in *Pop Idol* and similar shows, where experts are given license to abuse the contestants. In a carefully structured arrangement, the contestants undergo a kind of weekly weigh-in against a background of sombre music, followed by evaluations of their relative improvement and what this means.

There is something novel about the mutual exploitation involved in these programmes. The subjects are using television as a motivator/impetus in reshaping their bodies (or, in the case of *Pop Idol*, even their lives). There can be little possibility of a happy life for an obese person. Indeed, when one participant claimed to be happier obese than when slim, the general response was one of derision. It might also be noted that, in a climate of celebrity worship like ours, those who stay the course of *Fat Club* do have a small chance of fame and fortune as they emerge from the regime with 'the inside story'.

WLTM (Would Like To Meet)

> Between the media images of self-containment and self-mastery and the reality of constant everyday stress and anxiety about one's appearance lies the chasm that produces bodies habituated to self-monitoring and self-normalization. (Bordo 1999: 175)

BBC2's *WLTM* first aired in the latter half of 2001 in the prime-time slot of 8.30 p.m. The premiss is simple: three personal-grooming experts are given the opportunity to remodel and re-fashion an individual who has been single or has not dated for some considerable time. The experts have only a few weeks to transform this individual into a successful operator on the dating 'scene'. The programme begins with the team watching footage of the (*pre*-treatment) individual having a casual encounter. This becomes an occasion for much good-natured abuse from the team. The individual is then confronted with the recorded evidence, and treatment – which all agree is absolutely necessary – begins.

The subject is taught the rudiments of body language, to develop self-awareness. His or her wardrobe is opened to the scrutiny and vilification of a style expert, who brings along the 'right' clothes. A great deal of time is spent on make-up and grooming.

After a lot of friendly bullying – and sometimes the subject's tears – on camcorder, the process is declared complete and the subject can now progress to the final test – a date with the object of desire. With the crew monitoring progress via hidden cameras, the dinner-date goes ahead, with the subject having the option of switching off the camera at any time during the meal, should relations turn sour. The entire process is judged a success if the date goes well. There have been no disasters to date.

WLTM is about ironing out an individual's quirks and moulding the identity into something acceptable and attractive. As such, it represents another triumph for style and polish. As we look at the remodelled self we are steered away from any consideration of the 'inner life' while marvelling at what television can do.

Video Diaries still appears in the schedule. It remains a space for the articulation of a self that is the product of various psy-disciplines whose ordinances come to shape the diarists' self-portraits and yet whose final 'achieved' identity is perfectly consonant with the liberal notion of access. But by the mid-1990s the meaning of 'access' was undergoing change. The selves in which television is now interested are those with the potential to display the signs of transformation. The interior life, and its social and political contexts, which underscored *Video Diaries*, are less visually stimulating and also more demanding of viewers than the straightforward accounts of change delivered by shows which highlight the consumerist self.

Bibliography

Aitkenhead, D. (1999) 'Unprivate lives', *Guardian*, 28 July.

Armes, R. (1988) *On Video*, London, Routledge.

Bordo, S. (1999) 'Reading the slender body', in K. Woodward (ed.) *Identity and Difference*, London, Sage.

Corner, J. (1994) 'Mediating the ordinary: the "access" idea and television form', in M. Aldridge and J. Corner (eds) (1996) *The Art of Record*, Manchester, Manchester University Press.

Dovey, J. (1993) 'Old dogs and new tricks: access television in the UK', in T. Dowmunt (ed.) *Channels of Resistance*, London, British Film Institute.

France, L. (1999) 'Two minutes of fame', *Independent on Sunday*, 7 March.

Franklin, B. (1997) *Newzak and News Media*, London, Edward Arnold.

Freedman, E. (1998) 'Producing (queer) communities: public access cable TV in the USA', in D. Lusted and C. Geraghty (eds) *The Television Studies Book*, London, Edward Arnold.

Goffman, E. (1971) *The Presentation of Self in Everyday Life*, Harmondsworth, Penguin.

Graham, A. (1998) 'Smile, you're on *Candid Camera*', *Radio Times*, 1 August.

Humm, P. (1998) 'Real TV: camcorders, access and authenticity', in D. Lusted and C. Geraghty (eds) *The Television Studies Book*, London, Edward Arnold.

Izod, J. and Kilborn, R. (1997) *An Introduction to Television Documentary*, Manchester, Manchester University Press.

James, C. (2001) *Penguin Dictionary of Modern Humorous Quotations*, ed. F. Metcalf, Harmondsworth, Penguin.

Keighron, P. (1993) 'What's up, Doc?' *Sight and Sound*, 3, 10: 24–5.

Kilborn, R. (1998) 'Shaping the real: democratisation and commodification in UK factual broadcasting', *European Journal of Communication*, 13, 2: 201–18.

Laing, R.D. (1967) *The Politics of Experience*, London, Pelican.

Lane, J. (1997) 'The career and influence of Ed Pincus: shifts in documentary epistemology', *Journal of Film and Video*, 49, 4: 3–17.

Langer, J. (1998) *Tabloid TV*, London, Routledge.

O'Malley, T. (1994) *Closedown?* London, Pluto Press.

Pearson, A. (1994) 'Life is cheap at the BBC', *Independent on Sunday*, 20 March.

Pagram, B. (1999) 'Housekeeping, or how to keep up with the mess next door', *Independent on Sunday*, 7 February.

Price, M. (1995) *Television, the Public Sphere and National Identity*, Oxford, Clarendon Press.

Robins, K. (1996) *Into the Image*, London, Routledge.

Rose, N. (1989) *Governing the Soul: The Shaping of the Private Self*, London, Routledge.

Rose, N. (1997) 'Assembling the modern self', in R. Porter (ed.) *Rewriting the Self: Histories from the Renaissance to the Present*, London, Routledge.

Rose, N. (1998) *Inventing Our Selves*, Cambridge, Cambridge University Press.

Sarup, M. (1996) *Identity, Culture and the Postmodern World*, Edinburgh, Edinburgh University Press.

Simon, W. (1996) *Postmodern Sexualities*, London, Routledge.

Winston, B. (1995) *Claiming the Real*, London, British Film Institute.

Conclusion: *Big Brother*
– an experiment in governance

In the spring of 1999 Jon DeMol produced the original series of *Big Brother* in The Netherlands. The programme involved ten housemates interned together over a ten-week period in a specially designed hermetically sealed environment. The housemates were supplied with food and drink and had access to all amenities, but were isolated from all contact with the media and the outside world; there were no television sets, radios, newspapers. Every week each housemate had to nominate for eviction two fellow-contestants; the two with the highest number of nominations would then be subject to public voting. It was the role of the public to select, by telephone vote, which of the two was to survive. By the final week there would be only two housemates remaining. The winner was decided by the public, and took away a cheque for £70,000. As readers will no doubt be aware, the show was an enormous success and has since been sold and adapted all over the world.

Throughout the book, I have applied Foucault's definition of government as the calculated directing of human conduct, the means by which behaviour is shaped to various ends by the expertise of the many agencies of the state. At this point, I propose that *Big Brother* might fruitfully be thought of as an experiment in governance in that it monitors a micro-population, exposes its members to scrutiny and caters for their needs. 'Big Brother', who may be consulted only in the Diary Room and by one housemate at a time, playfully mimics those various disparate agencies which help citizens to fashion their individual selves, and as such provides a fitting conclusion to this study

Since the original series the *Big Brother* concept has been sold to many countries and is about to enter its fourth series in The Netherlands with its popularity undiminished. It has been described by many critics as a perfect example of reality TV. But *Big Brother* exhibits also a number of the other trends discussed in the preceding chapters. The series is an exemplary hybrid, 'part social experiment, part real life soap, and part competition' (ITV Drama Forum 2000). There is perhaps no better example of the entrepreneurial newcomer in the field of documentary practice than Bazal, the producer of *Big Brother* in the UK and of *Body Spies*, and now part of GMG Endemol. Bazal was Britain's largest producer of factual entertainment and was ideally placed to produce the unashamedly populist *Big Brother*. It did not represent much of a risk. By the time Bazal had produced the first UK series, *Big Brother* had already been tested in The Netherlands, Spain and Germany, successively. Within a year of the UK series, the show became a global brand, launching products such as books, posters and even a boardgame.

Big Brother's deployment of constant surveillance reminds us of the spread of CCTV and television's reluctance to do anything but celebrate the technology. The relentless use of cameras in *Big Brother* calls to mind the performances we are required to make in a surveillance society where we have considerably less control over how our identities are perceived. In discussing reality TV, we saw how 'outside', in the urban complex, CCTV operatives can be led by their prejudices to alert the police to the 'suspicious' movements of those already bearing the weight of official surveillance (Norris and Armstrong 1997). The light-hearted antics of *Big Brother's* housemates help to dismiss such old-fashioned concerns by humanising the technology. As such it is part of documentary's slow paradigm shift away from questions concerning public space, a shift which is occurring despite the proliferation of technologies which are changing the meaning of 'public' and complicating our ability to manage our identities in such spaces.

Surveillance in *Big Brother* is banal and benign. The social and political implications of surveillance for society make for less commercially attractive programmes than those which focus on the emotional lives of proto-celebrities. The citizen whose rights might have been troubled by the implications of multi-camera society is now entertained by personal dramas that expand the definition of 'documentary'. When critiques do arise, such as the Mark Thomas investigation of the Data Protection Act, they shock us because they document the inability of citizens to retain control over their image, despite official rhetoric on freedom of information. It may be that programmes like *The Mark Thomas Comedy Product* (2000, Channel 4, UK) are limited in their impact because they are shunted to the margins of the schedule.

Thus *Big Brother* foregrounds the policing of conduct as well as raising questions concerning the meaning of privacy in a culture where celebrity has become so highly valued. Some German critics believed the series was a prurient exploitation of the participants and which might further degrade privacy. Similar criticisms emerged in other host countries. CBS was accused of 'dumbing down' its good reputation when it paid Endemol $20m for the rights to *Big Brother* but the justification came with modest success in the ratings: 'If it makes money it makes the news' (Wittstock 2000). Negative criticism was always probable.

Big Brother represents an emotionalising of the documentary project and has kinship with the series discussed in chapter 8, such as *WLTM* and *Fat Club*, in which individuals are made more human by exposing their suffering and using television to transform themselves. Thus *Big Brother* asks the contestants to consider depthlessness for profit. And so they indulge themselves, knowing that what are taken to be their personalities are woven into the processes of celebrity. Such indulgence (from both sides) enables us to gain a perspective on documentary history. The early pioneers of documentary have been accused of making victims of their subjects (Swann 1989). Their defence would have been to point to the greater good thereby served in expanding our understanding of citizenship. Citizenship is now defined as being a co-operative consumer. It is now less easy to say identify the victims, so populous is the televised game of celebrity.

Big Brother is a long way removed from documentary's traditional claim to deliver the real. What is revealed under the insistent presence of surveillance is not the real but more a self constructed in response to the demands of the technology, the needs of fellow contestants and, of course, the watching audience. In a sense this mirrors the life we lead for others with our public 'face'. And while we can still at least retain some (shrinking) degree of privacy, and thus comfort ourselves with an illusion of depth, a celebrity-led culture proselytises for transparency, openness.

The psychological discourses circulating in and around *Big Brother* are part of the project of governance in that they raise issues concerning correct behaviour and the divide between a public and a private self. *Big Brother* provided a platform for questions of identity via the malleable self-in-construction negotiated by the contestants within the micro-climate of the house.

A psychological experiment

> What rankles most about the whole seedy exercise is the pretence
> that it is some sort of genuine social investigation and not just a
> cynical drive for ratings and profits. (Dunkley 2000: 17)

We have seen how reality TV depends on recognition for its effect –
the acknowledgement that the individual on the screen *could* be you
or I. Our own psychological involvement is often described as *schadenfraude*. However, the justification given for the US version of *Big
Brother* – 'Americans can't get enough of reality fare' (Wittstock 2000:
8) – could not suffice for a channel with a public service remit. Thus
Big Brother is presented to the UK audience as a legitimate psychological experiment.

Big Brother offered an analytical debate within the 'house' as well
as spawning a psychology-tinged debate beyond its walls. In following these debates we can see two linked discourses – one which
offered pop-psychology for entertainment purposes, the other an
enframing discourse which provided a 'serious' psychological debate
which touched on classic public service issues of responsibility to the
contestants and the public.

Channel 4 demonstrated its own allegiance to the psychological
in its press release on the show (Channel 4 2000). There we were
informed that the contestants had been 'extensively psychologically
screened by a professional psychologist', a process perhaps inspired
by Channel 4's lawyers learning of the suicide of a contestant on a
similar programme in Sweden (Flett 2000). As a result 'psychological testing of contestants has become something of an obsession'
(*Guardian* 2000). The contestants were aware that 'a psychotherapist
is available for all participants for counselling. There will be support
for occupants once they have left, if requested' (Channel 4 2000).
Again, one wonders about the value of a counselling session with a
disembodied voice or sharing one's innermost fears with the technology that may well be responsible for having generated them.
Nevertheless, the press pack gave the assurance that 'a team of
mental health professionals will oversee both the selection process
and the psychological well being of the participants while they are
in the house'.

Big Brother had two resident psychologists, professors Beattie
and Collett, whose involvement underscored the status of *Big Brother*
as a psychological experiment. The results of their labours were

disseminated in the 'quality' press, where the scientific value of the project was discussed.

A rather different approach to the psychological issues was offered on the official *Big Brother* website. There we could access the 'flirting index', with a week-by-week breakdown of relevant incidents. Charts and diagrams indicated who had been touched and where on the body. Thus we were provided with a psychologically validated data for our hunch that Mel was a flirt. Other features were a 'kissing index' and 'hugging' statistics (www.channel4.com/bigbrother/ [hereafter *BB* website]). This combination of pop-psychology and 'academic' reflection was perhaps intended to dissuade us from wondering about the social validity of a scientific study which looks at the activities of ten people, most of whom were seeking careers in the glare of publicity.

Although their respectable credentials were listed, the show's psy-experts offered us viewer-friendly readings on body language. Thus our opinion of Nasty Nick is reinforced by insightful and scientifically validated studies of his body language. When replacement Claire arrived the same psychologists helped us understand the significance of Mel's folded arms. This psychological perspective helps to place the show in a public service tradition as well as offering some intellectual ballast to those who may have felt guilty for enjoying the 'soap-opera' elements of the programme.

Yet the serious point of the experiment was rarely allowed out of our sight. Dr David Miller of Stirling University's Media Institute warned that the show may be harming the participants. Experts Collet and Beattie were partly to blame: 'the participants are themselves placed under enormous stress that could lead to long-term difficulties. These two professors are lending credibility to a crass and exploitative gimmick' (Miller quoted in Wojtas 2000: 48).

This condemnation was matched by The Netherlands Institute of Psychologists which deemed the show 'irresponsible and unethical', even though 'the contestants were chosen with the help of four psychologists' (trshcity.demon.co.uk). This sort of justification cuts no ice with Richard Morrison (2000), who declared that the programme 'no more celebrated ordinary folk than a battery farm celebrates chickens'. Much space was given over to discussing the healthfulness of such an experiment. The *Guardian* enlisted the help of Desmond Morris to debunk the scientific pretensions of the show ('laughable') before offering a theory of his own concerning gossip and the importance of maintaining a stiff upper-lip (Morris 2000). In the *Observer* Philip Hodgson (2000), of the British Association for Counselling, suggested that the programme 'vividly' picks up on 'an almost adolescent need in these situations for conformity . . . It's a terrible fear of whether we're approved of, always worrying does my bum look big in this? So much of it is centred around trust.' Another psy-expert, consultant psychologist Dr Raj Persaud, informed us that 'we seriously want to see a crash'. Professor Cary Cooper concurred in talking of the 'ambulance effect', our desire to see other people suffering: 'You see potential disaster and you want to look' (*Observer*, 13 August 2000).

Other writers chose to describe our fascination with *Big Brother* as symptomatic of national decline. Thus Daniel Johnston (2000) in the *Telegraph* referred to the series as 'this beastly caricature of humanity', while Freedland (2000) offered the judgement that 'if *Big brother* is a one-way mirror on the nation, it is not making us look good'. But even here the thinking is psychologically informed, as television becomes the site of projection, the space in which we see what we cannot acknowledge in ourselves.

The synoptic focus of reality TV (Mathieson 1997) was enriched by the activities of the press in feeding our hunger for knowledge about these ordinary people morphing into celebrities in *Big Brother*'s anteroom of fame. Using tit-bits, old photographs, interviews with spurned lovers and anything else they could find, the press threw together 'portraits' which lent depth to the housemates and enabled us to gain rounded pictures of them. Thus armed with pop-psychology profiles essential to a full appreciation, we were enabled to phone-in our votes with appropriate expertise. One of the pleasures the series offered was our control over the duration of a contestant's stay in the house. *Big Brother* offered something previously restricted to the game-show and talk TV – interactivity. Here we were offered the opportunity of actually deciding the fate of another.

As a contestant left the house, having been evicted by a combination of audience vote and housemate vendetta, the psy-disciplines reconverged in the form of Channel 4's after-show experts and psychotherapists' newspaper columns. The psy-disciplines are there to step in to help contestants to readjust to life as new micro-celebrities. In its adherence to the psychological theme, *Big Brother* helped to reinforce the central role of therapeutic discourse in public life. Much like the more sensitive talk-shows discussed earlier, this approach provides a legitimate rationale for the individual to 'work through' personal issues rather than looking at the material circumstances in which governance takes place: 'It's not you. It's me.'

Confessing a self

> Here was co-ed prison life laid bare for the 24/7 CCTV generation. We saw everything. (Lane 2000: 3)

The *Big Brother* project can be understood as an experiment in governance in that it provided food and shelter; it privileged no one individual; it provided health care; it rewarded effort and penalised indolence; it was comprehensive in its monitoring; it allowed freedom of expression while policing exchanges that were potentially conspiratorial; it listened to housemates' problems and offered appropriate expertise; above all, it set the rules with which the contestants' behaviour was to comply. In this proscribed space the participants were free to make their own worlds. In return, the contestants surrendered all control over their images to the benevolent authority of Channel 4, allowing the media to make of them what they would. The only control they had was in fashioning the selves they offered up for manipulation. Thus the drama we saw played out in this artificial environment was one of an ultimately triumphant evolving self designed to appeal to others and to win.

It is no accident that this experiment focused on specific age-range of 22–38. This demographic was selected to match the upwardly mobile audience desired by advertisers. '*Big Brother* has been particularly popular amongst younger viewers; 75% of 16–34s have tuned in' (ITV Drama Forum 2000). This profile was matched by all versions of the show worldwide. As previous chapters have shown, this age-group belongs to a generation that has matured in a climate in which television has focused on providing arenas for the staging of the self. Like the contestants in makeover programmes, *Big Brother*'s contestants have been ready to use television as part of their project to transform themselves.

Foucault (1984) wrote of the gradual dispersal of the confessional impulse throughout society, with agencies of the state taking on the role of the Church and using their authority to offer salvation in this life via the promise of health and security by confessing their 'individuality'. Sexuality has become the key to our identities, to 'who we really are'. To share one's identity with another can be a risky undertaking should its expression transgress the 'norm' – although we have seen how television is often prepared to exploit such difference for entertainment purposes. Such programming is part of the trend in first-person television which Jon Dovey (2000) has described as symptomatic of the new emotional democracy of feminised public life.

Big Brother's hybrid form marries this desire for the 'real' self to sexual themes characteristic of our age. The confessional moments in the programme focus on sexuality either in discussion or in performance. Thus it was rather predictable that sexual identity should have been one of the first subjects discussed by the contestants. When Anna disclosed, to congratulations from Sada, that she was a lesbian there was a distinct *frisson* among the group. It soon became evident that while the rest of the women were heterosexual they were interested in 'experimenting', thus deploying the word favoured by those who see identity as malleable (Sada has since 'come out' and is now living with fellow-housemate Nicola). But this early confession of sexual identity is also crucial to the dramatic dynamic of the show, and represented its potential for exploiting the viewers. Indeed, the one consistent theme in all versions of the show worldwide and given prominence in press treatments was the potential for sexual relationships to develop between the participants. Thus 'self-proclaimed sexpert Andy' teased housemates that he may have had a homosexual encounter (*BB* website: day 2); Caroline told Nicola that she was 'desperate' to have an orgasm, and Nicola responded that her body gives her one 'automatically' after a few weeks of abstinence (*BB* website: day 14); Craig revealed that he had taken part in several orgies and had 'inadvertedly' had sex with his girlfriend in public (*BB* website: day 13). Even the comparatively reticent Anna confessed that she was looking forward to sex after *Big Brother* (*BB* website: day 60).

The housemates' ability to regulate their sexual appetites while being monitored was their clearest expression of self-control. This was something which remained private where the technology sought transparency. The *Big Brother* format helps to push at the line between public and private. The drama derives from the tension between self-restraint and desire. What we viewers are able to hide the contestants (it is hoped) cannot help but reveal. The expert commentary on the interplay between contestants keys into the themes of self-management which are pertinent to our everyday lives. The project of governance is that we learn to align our sexual choices with the help of authoritative expertise. Ideally we are to become transparent – like the contestants – and thus manageable. As Rose put it: 'Government of the modern soul thus takes effect through the construction of a web of technologies for fabricating and maintaining the self-government of the citizen' (Rose 1998: 79).

The site of sexual interest and the locus of self-government in *Big Brother* was the body. In the first episode there were exuberant displays of nudity, as some of the contestants rubbed their paint-laden bodies on the walls to make murals or took showers together. A number of the men had their heads shaved – an act that at once removed their differences (as in prison) and served to bond them together – as well as being a fashionable choice. As the series developed, sexual interest in the body had to be re-inspired through physical challenges. Furthermore Channel 4 indicated its interest in the sexual angle by providing a hot-tub (at a cost of £9,995). When new arrival Clare used the tub to display her £3,000 boob-job, the focus on the body was reignited; and by kissing the unsuspecting Darren, Craig was unwittingly adding to his growing status as a gay icon.

Compared to the Dutch, German and Italian versions of the show, the sexual content of the Channel 4 edition was understated. The closest the show came to showing a sexual encounter was Mel's dalliances with Andrew, but despite the media's extensive attention this never progressed beyond flirting, a strategy which was said to have divided the public especially when she began to use the same 'techniques' on Tom. The sponsor, Southern Comfort, was known to be interested in a couple developing a sexual relationship and was rumoured to have offered a £20,000 reward – another story which attempted to put sex high on the agenda (Dillon 2000). In this context Anna's lesbianism was a problem for the producers because it obviated any possibility of a relationship with one of the men, and towards the end of the series, when it was hoped that a coupling would provide a fitting conclusion, it threatened to further dissipate the sexual tension. It appeared that control was all too easily assimilated.

In the Continental second versions of the series a great deal was made of the sexual elements. Producers believed that they were likely to draw huge ratings, and strippers and prostitutes were hired to take part. This strategy seems to have worked in the French version which saw a couple getting together on the first night. The producers of *Big Brother 2* in the UK also seem to have acknowledged the audience-drawing power of sex by selecting participants considered to be sexually compatible – two gay men, for example, plus a lap-dancer. The

Welsh woman, Helen, made extremely bold overtures to Paul, but he rejected them. Self-control appeared to be at work again, as well as proving an excellent way of maintaining interest.

By the time *Big Brother* had gone into its second series in most countries, the UK and the USA were the only nations whose contestants had not been seen making love on screen. The reasons for this are complex and are partly inspired by the regulatory controls both countries operate. But it may also be the case that television audiences in the UK and the USA have a preoccupation with celebrity and television. Those taking part may have calculated that their sexual reticence would increase their interest value. This was certainly the case with the much-stalled romance of Helen and Paul in Channel 4's *Big Brother 2*. In the British version playing to perceived national characteristics may have proved a winner with the public. Helen's post-*Big Brother* career as a daytime television beauty consultant has certainly prospered.

The second site of identity construction remained the self 'carved out' of the house environment. Our burgeoning enterprise culture produces myriad forms of advice, the theme of which is to see the self as a project, a life work in which we should be constantly involved. *Big Brother* tests these themes by asking what sort of self can be fashioned under the unceasing gaze of the cameras. On arrival contestants were stripped of items that offered any identity or cultural support, such as mobile phones, radios, walkmans, CDs and CD players, PDAs, calenders, clocks or watches (as well as any item displaying a corporate logo!). In this way, whatever emerged would have to be produced via interactions in the 'pure' environment of the house. But what developed on screen was not so much a real self as a media-self. *Big Brother* is part of the new media design, discussed earlier, in which 'ordinary' folk become *personalities* after being on television. It was hardly a surprise that Craig, Mel, Nick, Clare, Tom and Sada all went on to work in the media, while Caroline and Nicola released records, as also did Craig. The contestants were clear about their ambitions and their willingness to use television to advance them. But this lack of 'depth' was taken to be unseemly, and television's involvement in this drew passionate condemnation from 'high-brow' critics for whom the brazenly presented personalities were shallow and crude, media infatuated and 'focused narrowly on television'. Freedland (2000), writing in the *Guardian*, for instance, declared: 'It is striking that not a single minute of *Big Brother* has shown a discussion of what used to be called public affairs: there is not a word about politics. It is all about relationships – with each other, past loves or themselves.'

It should be clear that these individuals were chosen because they typify an age in which enterprising selves utilise the entirety of their experience to further their ambitions. Being on television validates their media-selves. They see their lives as projects and work consciously on them like dieters or keep-fitters or autodidacts in night-class. The enterprise culture offers us the opportunity to fashion a self which can be endlessly remade and remodelled according to ones resources.

> Become whole, become what you want, become yourself: the individual is to become, as it were, an entrepreneur of itself, seeking to maximise its own powers, its own happiness, its own quality of life,through enhancing its autonomy and then instrumentalizing its autonomous choices in the service of its lifestyle. (Rose 1998: 158)

Big Brother became a public platform integral to the contestant's willed self-creation.Thus the private confession in the nomination process has to be understood as part of the strategic game in which individuals are evicted as well as seeming to 'reveal' other sides to their characters. Indeed, flexibility of identity may have had a central appeal as contestants competed to be likable and genuine at the same time. The real is disguised in the ambivalence of performance. Here the house as a device came into its own, offering opportunities for deceit and duplicity at several levels. In confessing to 'Big Brother' the contestants are also speaking directly to camera (and thus to us). Viewers, particularly those viewing via the internet, enjoy the insights of other drama viewers – the illusion of omnipotence – but we also wonder how real is the 'self' which operates internally to objectify themselves for the camera: 'contestants know very well that the celebrity they crave is directly proportionate to the exhibitionism they display' (Jagasia 2000).

The contestants publicly work through the project of identity construction, using the language of the psy-disciplines. Rose has suggested that such language helps to form bonds between the technologies of domination and those of the self. In their deployment of these terms, they reproduce precisely the subject who can be governed apparently through the free choice of marketable lifestyle options. Thus Sada reflected on herself:

> I know I can be self-obsessed and selfish. But I'm OK about not being a perfect person, and millions of viewers have seen me not being

perfect. At least I was honest. I was myself. And if I can see what's wrong with me and learn from it that will be great. (Quoted in Ritchie 2000: 77)

In most of the post-*Big Brother* interviews the contestants reflected on how their selves have been transformed by the house experience. Each one of them would go through it all again; each one of them has learned something about his or her inner self (Ritchie 2000). It is interesting to note that not all European *Big Brother* contestants responded to the scenario in the same way. The Spanish participants subverted the rules in an act of solidarity and nominated each other with one vote, thus removing any potential target for ejection. Pam Wilson has pointed out (in an unpublished paper) that the American contestants came close to staging a walkout, as one way of grasping their opportunity to 'make history', before being gently dissuaded by CBS and by one another. According to Sella (2000: 4), the Dutch contestants tried to break the rules by 'whispering under the blankets, very very quietly . . . But within five minutes *Big Brother* came on so strict and told us to stop'. If the British participants seemed to enjoy and even celebrate their imprisonment, it may have been because they were aware of how things could (and did) work out for them. Each of them produced a useful self – its commodity status a model within easy reach.

For film-makers of an earlier, more settled, age *Big Brother* is a 'joke' documentary, a dystopian nightmare of what the genre could turn into. The spread of surveillance, the reduction of personhood to commodity status and the separation of the psychological from its political base – all once constituted threats to citizens which documentary-makers investigated. In the new paradigm, these circumstances form the background to amusing experiments in identity. The contrast between these paradigms is best illustrated by the debate on the internet.

Connecting to the *Big Brother* house via the internet is truly a combination of the panoptic and the synoptic in that as we watch the internet unseen others can load multiple amounts of information onto our hard drives. I have noted that ISPs are obliged by law to hand over their files at the demand of the police, thus further eroding the privacy of the individual. The RIP Act which facilitates further unwelcome access to our personal information is the sort of affront to civil liberties on which 'old-style' documentaries thrived. For *Big Brother* the internet issue is reduced to a question of whether or not to censor pictures of contestants on the toilet.

The internet also provides us with far more sexually explicit performances by people using webcams to experiment with their identity. On unmonitored sites we see individuals performing for relational communities whose linear commands can read like the ramblings of the id. The aim here is not celebrity but connection, validation. In this more intimate space people are opening themselves up to dissection in ways that television cannot countenance. They suggest the possibility of spaces beyond governance.

To what extent the relationship between the contestants and *Big Brother* can be seen as analogous to that between ourselves and other disciplinary technology is a matter worthy of public debate. Perhaps the appeal of the show is that modern urban life makes our own everyday experience not unlike that of the contestants:

> We too are filmed constantly, by a CCTV presence that makes us the most watched society in the world with cameras in every bank, every shop, every street corner. Thanks to new technology we too perform for the camera, whether its a home video or a webcam. We are slowly abolishing privacy as we used to understand it, replacing it with an acceptance that what was once hidden will now be on display – what was once on the outside will now be on show. We watch and we are watched. Maybe that was the twist George Orwell never imagined: we are Big Brother (Freedland 2000)

Big Brother deployed psy-experts to enframe a living narrative in which individuals fashioned selves in a house given over to an experiment in governance. But, despite the nay-sayers, it would be wrong to suggest that programmes such as *Big Brother* spell out the end for documentary. One could just as easily argue that the form is more vibrantly alive than ever before as it opens up to new users and becomes the wider field of documentary practice. This openness to new technology has enabled more people to 'speak' to us via television than ever before. Rather than being led solely by tradition, expertise and rationality, documentary is now willing to take flight from the discourses of sobriety to engage in new ways with all sectors of the populace. As I have argued throughout, this can trivialise as much as it may liberate. Before we celebrate too loudly, however, it is worth recalling that what may be passing is a tradition which played a useful role in helping to construct the social consciousness of a generation.

Although such documentaries were part of the administrative deployment of expertise in moulding our choices, they did at least present information for public consumption and discussion. We were capable disagreeing with it, of thinking otherwise. And, of course, we still are. But the new documentaries prefer emotion-centred narratives and personalities. Now there is simply less presented for us to think with and about. But we cannot return to the certainties of the past. Perhaps the next step is to heed Foucault's dictum 'to refuse what we are' and to try resisting the normalising operations of government. And the only way we can do that is by finding the means to speak for ourselves.

Bibliography

Boyne, R. (2000) 'Post-panopticism', *Economy and Society*, 29, 2: 285–307.

Bruzzi, S. (2000) *New Documentary: A Critical Introduction*, London, Routledge.

Burchell, G., Gordon, C. and Miller, P. (eds) (1991) *The Foucault Effect: Studies in Governmentality*, Hemel Hempstead, Harvester Wheatsheaf.

Channel 4 (2000) Press release: 'Channel 4 reveals plans for *Big Brother*', 27 June.

Dillon, D. (2000) '£50,000 reward for TV sex stunt', available online: wysiwyg://245/http://www.lineone...00/07/30/newsn/1220bigbrov.d.html

Dovey, J. (2000) *Freakshow*, London, Polity Press.

Dunkley, C. (2000) 'Diary' item on *Big Brother*, *Financial Times*, 21 August.

Flett, K. (2000) 'TV's theatre of cruelty', *Observer*, 30 August.

Foucault, M. (1984) *A History of Sexuality*, vol. 3 London, Penguin.

Freedland, J. (2000) 'We're watching it. Part docusoap, part gameshow, *Big Brother* was meant to be this summer's hot TV hit and it is', *Guardian*, 'Unlimited', available online:
www.guardianunlimited.co.u...ve/Article/0,4273,4049415,00.html

Gandy Jr, O.H. (1993) *The Panoptic Sort: A Political Economy of Personal Information*, Boulder, CO, Westview Press.

Guardian (2000) 'Unlimited' (supplement), 17 July, guardianunlimited.co.uk.ve/Article/o,4273,4049415,00html

Hardy, F. (1979) *Grierson on Documentary*, London, Faber & Faber.

Hodgson, P. (2000) 'Big Brother? It's just another day in the office', *Observer*, 13 August.

ITV Drama Forum (2000) Online: www.itv-drama.org

Jagasia, M. (2000) 'One step too far in tawrdy voyeurism', *Daily Express*, available online: wysiwyg://282/http://www.lineone...xpress/00/07/20/news/n2920–d.html

Johnston, D. (2000) 'The naked apes', *Daily Telegraph*, 12 August.

Kritzman, H. (ed.) (1990) *Foucault: Politics, Philosophy, Culture*, London, Routledge.

Lane, H. (2000) 'It's good to get out of the house', *Observer*, 24 September.

Lyon, D. (1994) *The Electronic Eye*. London, Polity Press.

Mathieson, T. (1997) 'The viewer society: Michel Foucault's "panopticon" revisited', *Theoretical Criminology*, 1, 2: 215–34.

Morris, D. (2000) 'The day of reckoning', *Guardian*, 15 September.

Morrison, R. (2000) '*Big Brother* no more celebrates ordinary folk than a battery farm celebrates chickens' *The Times*, 24 September.

Nicols, B. (1994) *Blurred Boundaries*, Bloomington, IN, Indiana University Press.

Norris, C. and Armstrong, G. (1997) *The Unforgiving Eye: CCTV Surveillance in Public Space*, Hull, Centre for Criminology and Criminal Justice, University of Hull.

Norris, C. and Armstrong, G. (1999) *Maximum Security Society*, Aldershot, Ashgate.

Palmer, G. (1998) 'New police blues', *Jump Cut*, 42: 12–18.

Palmer, G. (2000) 'The spectacle of crime', in D. Thomas and B. Loader (eds) *Cybercrime*, London, Routledge.

Ritchie, J (2000) *Big Brother: The Official Unseen Story*, London, Channel 4 Books–Routledge.

Robins, K. (1996) *Into the Image*, London, Routledge.

Rose, N. (1989) *Governing the Soul: The Shaping of the Private Self*, London, Routledge.

Rose, N. (1998) *Inventing Our Selves*, Cambridge, Cambridge University Press.

Sella, M. (2000) 'The electronic fishbowl', *New York Times*, 21 May, available online: www.unlv.edu/Faculty/gottschalk/fishbowl.html

Swann, P. (1989) *The British Documentary Movement 1926–1946*, Cambridge, Cambridge University Press.

Walklate, S. (1991) 'Victims, crime and social control', in R. Reiner and M. Cross (eds) *Beyond Law and Order: Criminal Justice Policy and Politics into the 1990s*, London, Macmillan.

Winston, B. (1996) *Claiming the Real*, London, British Film Institute.

Wojtas, O. (2000) '*Big Brother* in public eye on ethics', *Times Higher Education Supplement*, 4 August.

Wittstock, M. (2000) 'News from nowhere', *Guardian*, 7 August.

Website address

Big Brother (official website): www.channel4.com/bigbrother

Index